Intuit

QuickBooks
Fundamentals

QuickBooks registration number _____

Payroll service subscription number _____

Payroll service telephone number* _____

Premier plan membership number _____

Premier plan telephone number* _____

Write your Installation Key Code number here. _____

*For a list of Intuit telephone numbers and other contact information,
  choose Help & Support from the Help menu. Then, under Contact Intuit,
  choose Phone Directory.

Contents

Chapter 17   **Payroll and Employees 235**

GETTING ANSWERS

This guide is designed to show you the best ways to set up and use QuickBooks for your type of business. Other QuickBooks information sources are designed to give you the detail you need while you use the program.

Where to start

If you're new to QuickBooks

1 Read Chapter 2, *Business basics,* beginning on page 5, to learn a few business and accounting basics and to see the two most important reports for any business.

2 Read Chapter 4, "Setting up your company in QuickBooks," in the *QuickBooks Getting Started Guide,* to ensure that you set up QuickBooks properly.

3 Read Chapter 4, *Organizing data effectively,* beginning on page 23, to learn how to fine tune your accounts, items, and other data so that you can track the detail you need.

4 Read other chapters applicable to you.

If you want to use QuickBooks Pro or QuickBooks Premier multi-user capabilities on a network

- Read Chapter 3, "Sharing QuickBooks on a network," in the *QuickBooks Getting Started Guide,* to learn about the networking feature and how to set it up.

Getting answers while using QuickBooks

While you're using QuickBooks to perform daily and weekly tasks, you have a variety of ways to obtain useful information and answers to your questions. To contact Intuit for assistance, choose Help and Support from the Help menu, and then, under Contact Intuit, click Phone Directory.

Finding the step-by-step instructions

How Do I menus

Throughout QuickBooks you'll find windows with a **How Do I** drop-down menu. These menus provide quick access to information and instructions for this window.

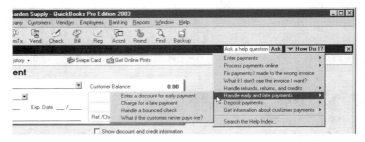

Using the Help Index

The tables in the manual and the **How Do I** menus on the windows are not exhaustive, so we encourage you to search the extensive QuickBooks Help system. (Go to the QuickBooks Help menu and choose Help Index; then enter your subject. You can get back to the index from any Help topic.)

Finding information about fields in a window

If you're unsure of a field or control (such as a button) in a particular window, you can press F1 to get help on the key parts of the window. These "What's important about..." topics provide answers to questions such as:

- What does this button do?
- What kind of information is displayed in this column?
- What happens when I select this option?

Using the Help & Support window

The Help & Support window is your one-stop source for answers to your QuickBooks questions. There you can enter a question in your own words and get immediate answers drawn from both the QuickBooks Help system and our technical support database. For example if your check numbers are out of sequence, you could enter "How do I reset my check numbers?" QuickBooks then finds the answer for you.

In the Help & Support window you can also learn about and sign up for support plans, look up support and product-related phone numbers, submit suggestions for product improvements, report software bugs, learn about training resources, and find a certified QuickBooks ProAdvisor. The Help & Support window brings together a wealth of information about QuickBooks.

To display the Help & Support window, choose Help & Support from the Help menu.

Exploring QuickBooks with a sample company

We've provided sample companies for you to explore QuickBooks to enter data, run reports, and try all the features.

To view a sample company:

1 From the File menu, choose Open Company.

2 In the Open a Company window, choose a sample company file.

To learn about...	Look in the Help Index for...
What's in the sample company files	sample company files

Getting business-specific information

A collection of topics, customized for various types of businesses, provides information about setting up and using QuickBooks for the types of businesses listed.

To view the business-specific information:

1 From the Help menu, choose "Using QuickBooks for Your Type of Business."

2 Select a business type.

QuickBooks lists the topics for that business type (see the following example).

3 Click the topic that interests you. You can also print a topic using the Options menu in the Help window.

Viewing supplemental documentation

Some QuickBooks features and services include supplemental documentation that is provided with your installation in PDF format. To view or print these files, you need a copy of Adobe Acrobat Reader.

You can download a copy of Acrobat Reader from the Adobe website: http://www/adobe/com/.

Congratulations! You're doing what millions of people only dream about doing; taking a skill, a set of knowledge, or a product and building your own business with it. Like any venture—remodeling your house, going back to school, or starting a new business—the more you know about the rules, the goals, and the cost, the better your chance for success.

Business tax issues

With any new business, you have to figure out all the tax requirements: federal (includes income and employment), state, local, and sales. You can find details about these taxes from a variety of sources.

Accountants, tax professionals, small business consultants, and other small business owners can help you understand your tax requirements and wade through the many forms and schedules.

Tax	Resource
Federal taxes include, but are not limited to: income, federal income tax withholding, social security, Medicare, FUTA, and excise.	Request the IRS publication 334, *Tax Guide for Small Businesses* (For Individuals Who Use Schedules C or C-EZ), *Circular E, Employer's Tax Guide*; and *533- Self-Employment Tax*.
You may also need to file information returns like 1099 forms.	Also, request the Small Businesses and Taxes kit, which includes a video about an entrepreneur starting a new business.
	Contact: **www.irs.gov** or 1-800-829-1040.
State taxes could include, but are not limited to, tax on income, sales, and capital gains.	Contact your state tax board. For example, the California Franchise Tax Board.

Tax	Resource
Local	Contact your county officials.
Sales	Contact state officials. For example, the California Board of Equalization or the New York Department of Taxation and Finance.

Tax year definition

You figure your taxable income and file your returns based on an annual accounting period called a tax year. Your tax year can follow the *calendar year* (12 consecutive months beginning January 1 and ending December 31) or follow a *fiscal year* (12 consecutive months ending on the last day of any month except December).

Accounting methods

An accounting method is a set of rules that determines when and how you report your income and expenses for tax purposes.

 The IRS publishes guidelines for your business entity (sole proprietor, partnerships, corporations, and so forth). Check IRS Publication 538, *Accounting Periods and Methods.*

Cash basis

Many small businesses track income at the time they receive the money and expenses when they pay the bills. This method is known as bookkeeping on a **cash basis**. If you've been recording deposits of your customers' payments but have not been including the money customers owe you as part of your income, you've been using cash basis. Similarly, if you've been tracking expenses at the time you pay them, rather than at the time you first receive the bills, you've been using cash basis.

Accrual basis

In bookkeeping on an **accrual basis**, you record income at the time of the sale, not at the time you receive the payment. Similarly, you enter expenses when you receive the bill, not when you pay it. Accountants usually recommend accrual basis because it gives you a better picture of how your business is doing.

The choice is yours

QuickBooks enables you to enter your transactions the same way no matter which method you use for taxes. And, at any time, you can create reports that follow either method. (See page 286.) However, note that the IRS requires that you file your taxes using the "same method from year to year." Changing your tax accounting method requires IRS consent.

QuickBooks comes set up to do your reports on an accrual basis. That is, it shows income on a profit and loss statement for invoices as soon as you record them, even if you haven't yet received payment. It shows expenses as soon as you record bills, even if they are unpaid.

Handling your accounting

Using QuickBooks requires very little accounting knowledge. You need to understand a chart of accounts and the different types of accounts on it. You don't have to know about debits and credits, journal entries, or closing periods.

Your company's chart of accounts

When you keep books for a business or organization, you want to track where your income comes from, where you put it, what your expenses are for, and what you use to pay them. You track this flow of money through a list of accounts called the *chart of accounts*. Your QuickBooks chart of accounts can have:

- Balance sheet accounts
- Income accounts
- Expense accounts
- Cost of goods sold accounts
- Non-posting accounts (includes purchase orders and estimates, which do not appear on your balance sheet)

Some of these accounts are created for you automatically. For example, the first time you create an invoice or statement charge, QuickBooks automatically creates an accounts receivable (A/R) account. You'll add other accounts, such as your checking account, during setup using the EasyStep Interview. You can create and modify your accounts as needed at any time.

Types of accounts

Balance sheet accounts

Your chart of accounts includes *balance sheet accounts*. These accounts track the following:

- What you have (assets)
- What people owe you (accounts receivable)
- What your company owes to other people (accounts payable and other liabilities)
- The net worth of your company (equity)

The following table describes the various types of QuickBooks balance sheet accounts.

Balance sheet account type	QuickBooks account type	Use to track
Asset		What you have and what people owe you
	Bank	Transactions in checking, savings, and money market accounts. You can also use this type of account for petty cash.
	Accounts Receivable (A/R)	Transactions between you and your customers, including invoices, statement charges, payments from customers, deposits of customer payments, refunds, and credit memos. QuickBooks automatically creates an A/R account when you first create an invoice or statement charge.
	Other Current Asset	Assets that are likely to be converted to cash or used up within one year, such as the value of your inventory on hand, notes receivable due within a year, prepaid expenses, and security deposits.
	Fixed Asset	Depreciable assets your business owns that aren't liquid (not likely to be converted into cash within a year), such as equipment, furniture, or a building.
	Other Asset	Any asset that is neither a current asset nor a fixed asset, such as long-term notes receivable.
Liability		What your company owes to other people
	Accounts Payable (A/P)	Outstanding bills. When you first enter a bill, QuickBooks automatically creates an A/P account.
	Credit Card	Credit card transactions for your business expenses. One account per credit card.
	Other Current Liability	Liabilities that are scheduled to be paid within one year, such as sales tax, payroll taxes, accrued or deferred salaries, and short-term loans. Some businesses include the current portion of long-term liabilities in this kind of account.
	Long-Term Liability	Liabilities such as loans or mortgages scheduled to be paid over periods longer than one year.

Balance sheet account type	QuickBooks account type	Use to track
Equity		Net worth of your company
	Equity	A company builds equity from three sources: ■ Investment of capital in the business by the owners ■ Net profit from operating the business during the current accounting period ■ **Retained earnings**, or net profits from earlier periods that are carried forward into the current fiscal year and that have not been distributed to the owners

Balances for balance sheet accounts

The Chart of Accounts window shows a balance for each balance sheet account (except for the special equity account, Retained Earnings).

The IRS recommends opening a business checking account as one of the first things you do when starting a new business.

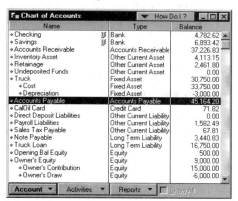

In QuickBooks, each balance sheet account has its own register, just like your check register. The register shows every transaction for that account, as well as the account balance. For example, the A/P register shows every bill from vendors, every payment to vendors, and the total amount you owe vendors.

Note: **Balances are always referred to as the ending balance in the register.**

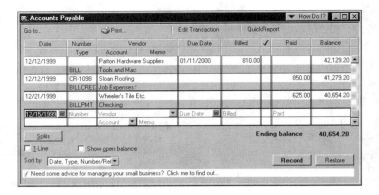

Income and expense accounts

Income and expense accounts (which are the same as Quicken categories) track the sources of your income and the purpose of each expense. When you record transactions in a balance sheet account, you usually assign the amount of the transaction to one or more income or expense accounts. For example, you not only record that you took money out of your checking account, but you keep track of what you spent the money on, such as utilities, advertising, or office supplies.

There are no registers for income and expense accounts, but you can create reports to show totals for these accounts over a period of time.

You may also want to track reimbursed expenses as income. See "Setting up to track reimbursed expenses as income" on page 117 for details.

Cost of goods sold (COGS) account

Many businesses that track inventory have one cost of goods sold account, which is similar to an expense account. A COGS account contains the cost of inventory you have sold.

Powerful accounting reports

The value and performance of your company can be summarized by two reports: the balance sheet and the profit and loss statement. How you set up your accounts will greatly influence the level of detail you can get on these reports. You may also want to create the statement of cash flows report, which details the net change in your cash during a period.

- See Chapter 4, *Organizing data effectively,* beginning on page 23, for more information about how to get the level of detail you need.

- See Chapter 18, *Tracking your progress with reports and graphs*, beginning on page 285, for information about generating and customizing these reports.

Your company's balance sheet

A **balance sheet** is a financial snapshot of your company on one date. This report is useful when applying for a business loan or at year-end to get an accounting of your company's equity, assets, and liabilities.

Assets include what you have and what people owe you. Examples include:

- cash on hand
- money in your checking account
- money you are owed
- furniture
- vehicles

total assets = total liabilities + equity

Liabilities include what your company owes to other people or your company debts. Examples include:

- unpaid bills
- money you owe on credit cards
- loans
- sales tax you owe

Equity is the net worth of your company:

equity = assets - liabilities

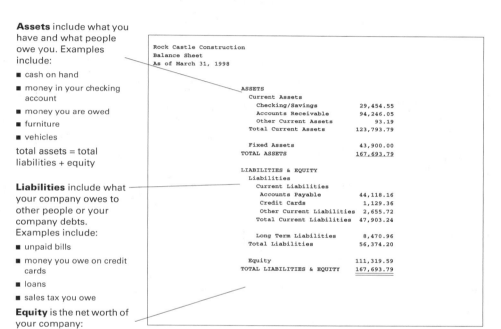

```
Rock Castle Construction
Balance Sheet
As of March 31, 1998


ASSETS
  Current Assets
    Checking/Savings            29,454.55
    Accounts Receivable         94,246.05
    Other Current Assets            93.19
    Total Current Assets       123,793.79

    Fixed Assets                43,900.00
  TOTAL ASSETS                 167,693.79

  LIABILITIES & EQUITY
    Liabilities
      Current Liabilities
        Accounts Payable        44,118.16
        Credit Cards             1,129.36
        Other Current Liabilities 2,655.72
        Total Current Liabilities 47,903.24

        Long Term Liabilities    8,470.96
      Total Liabilities         56,374.20

      Equity                   111,319.59
  TOTAL LIABILITIES & EQUITY   167,693.79
```

Your company's profit and loss statement

Profit and loss statements (also known as *income statements*) show your income and expenses over a period of time.

Profit and Loss Statement

	Oct - Dec '97
Ordinary Income/Expense	
Income	
Construction	
Labor	▶ 29,965.75 ◀
Materials	35,540.21
Miscellaneous	3,002.20
Subcontractors	47,946.63
Total Construction	116,454.79
Total Income	116,454.79
Cost of Goods Sold	
Cost of Goods Sold	5,651.38
Total COGS	5,651.38
Gross Profit	110,803.41
Expense	
Automobile	
Fuel	140.35
Repairs and Maintence	114.75
Total Automobile	255.10
Bad debt	33.99
Bank Service Charges	10.00
Freight & Delivery	70.00
Insurance	
Disability Insurance	150.00
Liability Insurance	1,050.00
Work Comp	825.00
Total Insurance	2,025.00

Your cost of goods sold account always appears after income accounts and before any other expense accounts, so you can see what your net income is before subtracting your business's indirect expenses, such as utilities and office supplies.

Net income = income - expenses

Page 2

	Oct - Dec '97
Interest Expense	
Finance Charge	-5.65
Interest Expense - Other	539.80
Total Interest Expense	534.15
Job Expenses	
Equipment Rental	850.00
Job Materials	18,395.36
Permits and Licenses	700.00
Subcontractors	40,099.00
Total Job Expenses	60,044.36
Payroll Expenses	19,780.38
Professional Fees	
Accounting	250.00
Total Professional Fees	250.00
Rent	2,400.00
Repairs	
Computer Repairs	0.00
Total Repairs	0.00
Tools and Machinery	1,135.00
Utilities	
Gas and Electric	154.40
Telephone	100.71
Water	61.85
Total Utilities	316.96
Total Expense	86,854.94
Net Ordinary Income	23,948.47
Other Income/Expense	
Other Income	
Interest Income	93.42
Other Income	12.50
Total Other Income	105.92
Net Other Income	105.92
Net Income	**24,054.39**

Statement of cash flows report

The statement of cash flows summarizes your sources (inflows) and uses (outflows) of cash. From the report, you can see how your cash position changed over a period of time.

Note: QuickBooks also has the capability to display investing activities, which show you how much was invested in assets such as equipment and furniture.

The report shows how much cash was provided by profit-making activities. ⎯⎯

The report shows how much cash was provided by long-term liabilities and equity. ⎯⎯

Rock Castle Construction	
12/15/99 **Statement of Cash Flows**	
October 1 through December 15, 1999	
	◇ Oct 1 - Dec 15, '99 ◇
OPERATING ACTIVITIES	
Net Income ▶	19,919.42 ◀
Adjustments to reconcile Net Income	
to net cash provided by operations:	
Accounts Receivable	-37,251.83
Inventory Asset	-4,113.15
Retainage	-2,461.80
Accounts Payable	40,779.20
CalOil Card	5.14
Payroll Liabilities	-838.39
Sales Tax Payable	-792.50
Net cash provided by Operating Activities	15,246.09
FINANCING ACTIVITIES	
Note Payable	-17,059.17
Opening Bal Equity	-8,863.39
Owner's Equity:Owner's Draw	-6,000.00
Retained Earnings	8,863.39
Net cash provided by Financing Activities	-23,059.17
Net cash increase for period	-7,813.08
Cash at beginning of period	35,071.57
Cash at end of period	**27,258.49**

WORKING WITH AN ACCOUNTANT OR AN ADVISOR

From time to time, you might need advice that extends beyond the scope of what the QuickBooks documentation or technical support team can supply. In these situations you'll want to contact your accountant or another specialized professional.

After you find the right accountant, review the following table to determine which work situation best fits you and your business.

Situation	What to do in QuickBooks	Comments	See...
Your accountant does not use QuickBooks and/or prefers working with hard copy printouts.	Print out all the reports and lists your accountant requests.	Later you'll need to enter into QuickBooks any adjustments recommended by your accountant.	"Working with an accountant who doesn't use QuickBooks" on page 17
Your accountant uses QuickBooks and would like to review your books "online" and make necessary changes.	■ **Option 1:** You can grant your accountant remote access to your computer.	During remote access, your accountant has control of your QuickBooks software. You can watch what your accountant is doing but you cannot work with QuickBooks yourself.	

Situation	What to do in QuickBooks	Comments	See...
	■ **Option 2:** You can allow your accountant to make changes to a copy of your QuickBooks company file called the Accountant's Copy, and then merge this copy back into your master file. This allows you to continue working in your file while your accountant works in his or her copy.	Restrictions exist on what you and your accountant can change during the period when the Accountant's Review copy is out.	"Working with an accountant who uses QuickBooks" on page 18
	■ **Option 3:** If you have QuickBooks Pro or Premier and have set up multiple users, you can set up your accountant as a user and allow him or her to work onsite in the company file with the rest of your staff.	Your accountant may want to conduct some operations that are allowed in single-user mode only.	"Option 3: Have your accountant work onsite" on page 21
	■ **Option 4:** If your accountant is not local and/or needs complete access to all areas of your company file, you can send him or her a backup copy of your company file.	Proceed with caution! Your accountant's copy will become your master company file when it's returned, so you'll lose any changes you make while it's out. You'll need to reenter them in the new master file.	"Option 4: Give your accountant a backup copy" on page 21

Working with an accountant who doesn't use QuickBooks

Traditionally, accountants and business owners expect that they will exchange paper (books and supporting documents). If this is how you and your accountant will work, you'll need to coordinate the types of information you'll supply. This depends on the type of task your accountant is performing for you.

For example, if your accountant is reviewing your books at year end, you may need to supply the following:

- Profit and loss statement
- Balance sheet
- General ledger report
- Journal report
- Trial balance

Making adjustments

Your accountant's review of your books might require you to make adjustments to various accounts, such as adding the depreciation of a fixed asset. He or she might describe how to make adjustments in terms of debits and credits. To add these adjustments in QuickBooks, use the Make General Journal Entries window.

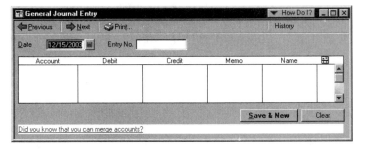

To learn about...	Look in the Help Index for...
Adding or printing journal entries	general journal entries

Working with an accountant who uses QuickBooks

Option 1: Give your accountant permission to access your QuickBooks file remotely

If your accountant has QuickBooks Premier: Accountant Edition, they can use the QuickBooks Remote Access to work with your file directly from their computer. This can save your accountant the time and expense of a visit to your site, and you don't have to worry about preparing a disk for your accountant.

To work this way, set up a time with your accountant to start the session. Your accountant gives you an Internet address and registration number. When you go to the address and enter the number, your accountant can begin the remote access session.

During the session, your accountant controls QuickBooks on your computer. Every action your accountant takes is shown in real time on your screen. Your accountant has access only to your QuickBooks software and programs that integrate with it.

Option 2: Use the Accountant's Review feature

The Accountant's Review™ feature of QuickBooks enables an accountant to make certain kinds of changes in a special copy of the company file. Meanwhile, you can continue to enter daily transactions in the original master file. After the accountant has made the changes, you merge them into the master file.

You...

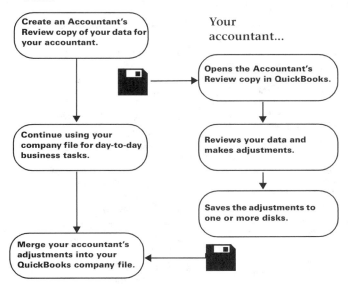

What can and can't be changed

The Accountant's Review feature may not be right for everyone. The accountant can make some kinds of changes but not others.

The advantage of using the Accountant's Review feature is that you can continue to work normally with your master company file (that is, the regular company file from which you make the Accountant's Review copy) and then merge the accountant's changes back into your file.

The following table shows what an accountant can and can't do while using an Accountant's Review copy of your file, and any restrictions you have while this copy is out.

Note: **If you have set up yourself or others as users, tell your accountant the user name and password of the Quick-Books Administrator.** The accountant should enter this name and password when opening the Accountant's Review copy of your file.

Your accountant can...	Your accountant can't...	You can't...
■ View all existing transactions and lists	■ Enter transactions other than general journal transactions	■ Delete any items from lists
■ Add new items to the chart of accounts, Item list, To Do Notes list, Memorized Transaction list (general journal transactions only). To add inventory items, you must have this feature turned on. See page 155.	■ Add new items to the Payroll Items list	■ Reorganize lists (move items or make one item a subitem of another)
■ Create, edit and print 941, 940, and W-2 forms	■ Memorize transactions other than general journal transactions	
■ Edit existing account names and numbers	■ Edit existing payroll items	
■ Edit account and tax information for existing items on Item list	■ Edit or delete existing transactions, including paychecks	
■ Enter general journal transactions	■ Reorganize lists (move items, make one item a subitem of another)	
■ Reconcile new transactions	■ Rename accounts or items	
■ Adjust inventory values or quantities	■ Make items inactive	
■ Create reports	■ Edit names of existing items on the Item list	
■ Change preferences temporarily	■ Adjust payroll liabilities	
■ Print 1099 forms	■ Enter or edit employee YTD payroll setup transactions	
	■ Export changes made to 941, 940, or W-2 forms	
	■ Export changes to preferences	
	■ Memorize reports	
	■ Change a non-inventory part type to an inventory part type.	
	■ Merge new inventory part items with previous, existing inventory part items.	

?

To learn about...	Look in the Help Index for...
Setting up your accountant as a user with all privileges. (Do this only if you have set up yourself or others as users.)	permissions
How to use an Accountant Review copy of your current company file	accountant's review copy

For accountants only: Working with an Accountant's Review copy

The file created from the master company file is a compressed version of a special type of company file. Before working with the file for the first time, you must decompress the file.

Note: If your client has set up users and passwords, you'll need to find out the user name and password assigned to you.

Once you have opened an Accountant's Review copy, it remains the current QuickBooks company unless you open a different company or you close the company. If you try to record a change that is not allowed, QuickBooks displays a message advising that it can't record the change in an Accountant's Review copy.

> **If your computer's system date and time is earlier than the date and time that your client created the Accountant's Review copy, you will not be able to open the copy.**
>
> To correct the problem you'll need to determine which computer has the incorrect date and time, change the date and time, and try to reopen the copy. You may need to have your client cancel the first review copy and create another one.

To learn about...	Look in the Help Index for...
Creating a file to give to your client	accountant's review copy

Option 3: Have your accountant work onsite

If your accountant is local and amenable to working at your office, you can set him or her up as a user and he or she can work while another user inputs invoices and you pay bills.

Pros

- There is no need to make an Accountant's Review copy or a backup copy to give to your accountant.
- Your business continues working as normal.
- Your accountant makes any necessary adjustments to the file.

Cons

- Only five users can simultaneously access QuickBooks Pro or QuickBooks Premier at a time.

- Your accountant may want to conduct some operations that are allowed in single-user mode only.

- Some reports your accountant generates may run slowly in multi-user mode.

To learn about...	Look in the Help Index for...
Setting up your accountant as a user	permissions

Option 4: Give your accountant a backup copy

If your accountant needs to conduct work for you not permitted by the Accountant's Review copy, you may want to give him or her a backup copy of your QuickBooks company file.

> **Consider this carefully.**
> The backup copy that your accountant reviews and changes will become your master company file! We recommend that you do not enter any transactions into QuickBooks while your accountant works on his or her copy.

Pros

- Your accountant will have complete access to all areas of your QuickBooks company.

- Your accountant can make any necessary adjustments to the file.

Cons

- You can't merge transactions between two regular files.

  If you make any changes to your QuickBooks company file during the time your accountant is working on the other version, your changes will be lost when you accept your accountant's version as your new master company.

Creating a backup file for your accountant

Because you're giving your accountant a backup (compressed) version of your file, he or she will need to use the Restore command to access the data.

Note: If you've set up users and passwords, you must also set up your accountant as a user so he or she can access the file.

If you set up and use QuickBooks wisely, you can track enough detail to understand how your business is doing, yet still have a streamlined chart of accounts. You might be used to having a separate account (or subaccount) on your chart of accounts for every detail about your business. With QuickBooks, you can get detailed reports about what you sell, what you buy, your payroll, and so on, without having this detail on your chart of accounts.

The fundamental guidelines for tracking detail in QuickBooks are:

- Track at least as much detail on your chart of accounts as you need for income tax reporting. Any further detail is up to you.

- QuickBooks usually has a particular way of tracking each type of detail that saves you time and gives you meaningful reports. This chapter describes these ways of tracking detail. Unless you also need the detail for income tax reporting, you don't need to duplicate it on your chart of accounts.

Where the detail is

Tracking detail while keeping a simple chart of accounts

A main advantage to using QuickBooks is that as you write invoices, write checks, write purchases orders, and pay employees, QuickBooks is helping you do your bookkeeping.

To make it easy to perform regular tasks, QuickBooks saves information on various lists so you don't have to retype it each time you need it. For example, on the Customer:Job list, you can save addresses, phone numbers, payment terms, and the correct sales tax to charge the customer.

Three of these lists can provide detail for reports while keeping your chart of accounts simplified: the Item list, Payroll Item list, and Class list.

Getting information about your services and products

Will you use QuickBooks to write invoices or statements or track what you sell? If so, you'll use the *Item list,* where you store descriptions of what you sell (or the services you perform).

For example, Stan is a consultant who helps small businesses purchase and set up computers and software. His Item list has separate items for pre-sales consulting, computer systems, installation, accounting software (QuickBooks, of course), word processing software, spreadsheets, and ongoing consulting.

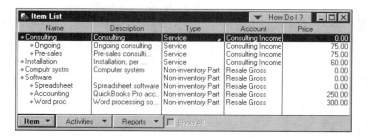

Stan's Item list for his services and products has many different items that he can track on sales reports. For more about using items, see Chapter 8, *Items—your services, products, fixed assets, and more,* beginning on page 75.

You may be accustomed to tracking all your detail by assigning different accounts on your chart of accounts. Stan, on the other hand, can use QuickBooks sales reports to see detailed information about income, hours of consulting, software units, and so on. His chart of accounts has just two income accounts: Consulting Income and Resale Gross. He doesn't need to duplicate the breakdown that is already on his Item list.

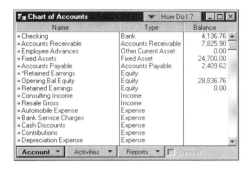

Tracking depreciation

You can set up accounts in QuickBooks to track depreciation. However, it is important to consult your tax advisor or the IRS about taking tax deductions for depreciation of assets.

If you simply want to track depreciation so that your financial statements are more accurate, choose Decision Tools from the Company, Customer, or Vendor Center.

Getting information about your payroll

Rosemary uses QuickBooks for payroll for her three employees. She keeps track of all payroll taxes and insurance deductions.

QuickBooks uses payroll items on its *Payroll Item list* to track all this detail, which Rosemary can see when she runs payroll reports. (For an illustration of a Payroll Item list, see page 257. For examples of payroll reports, see "Getting information about your payroll" on page 277.)

Her chart of accounts has a single expense account for payroll because she doesn't need to duplicate the breakdown that is already on her Payroll Item list.

Getting information for fund accounting

Richard keeps the books for his church. In addition to the general operating fund, the church has a separate building fund and a pastor's discretionary fund. Each fund has its own income and expenses. Instead of trying to subdivide each income and expense account into subaccounts for each fund, Richard has set up a QuickBooks class on the *Class list* for each fund.

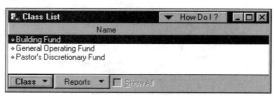

Whenever he records an income or expense transaction, he assigns a fund from his Class list. (See "Entering detail on transactions" on page 38.) He can then create a profit and loss by class report. Because this report has a column for each class, he can tell the board how the income and expenses are broken down by fund.

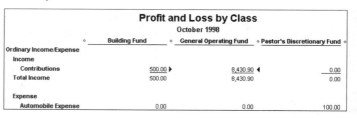

Profit and Loss by Class
October 1998

	Building Fund	General Operating Fund	Pastor's Discretionary Fund
Ordinary Income/Expense			
Income			
Contributions	500.00 ▶	8,430.90 ◀	0.00
Total Income	500.00	8,430.90	0.00
Expense			
Automobile Expense	0.00	0.00	100.00

For more about QuickBooks classes, see "Tracking income and expenses with classes" on page 30.

What are the advantages of using subaccounts?

When you use subaccounts of a *parent* account, reports such as the profit and loss statement and the balance sheet show amounts for each subaccount plus a total for the parent account.

On this chart of accounts, the Automobile expense account has two subaccounts:

- Fuel
- Repairs and Maintenance

Profit and Loss
October through December 1998

	Oct - Dec '98
Expense	
Automobile	
Fuel	140.35
Repairs and Maintenance	114.75
Total Automobile	255.10
Bad debt	33.99
Bank Service Charges	17.50

The expense part of the resulting profit and los statement shows amounts for each subaccoun and a total for the Automobile parent account.

You might want to use subaccounts for two reasons:

- You want a further breakdown of amounts for an existing account. To accomplish this, set up subaccounts for the existing account. From now on, use the subaccounts instead of the parent account. (You may want to edit earlier transactions so the breakdown shows up on reports covering a period before today.)

  For example, suppose you have an Automobile expense account for all automobile expenses. You add subaccounts for Fuel and for Repairs and Maintenance, as in the previous example.

- You already have related accounts that you want to subtotal on reports. (Or you may want to find them more easily.) You set up a new parent account and then make the related accounts subaccounts of the new parent.

  For example, suppose you have separate accounts for Health Insurance, Fire Insurance, and Liability Insurance. You set up a new account called Insurance, and make the three separate accounts subaccounts of it.

What does *Other* refer to on reports?

If you use subaccounts, subitems, or jobs, then sooner or later you will see the word *Other* on a report:

The $18.45 expense for Automobile-Other is for the Automobile main account and not for either of the subaccounts.

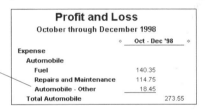

Profit and Loss
October through December 1998

	Oct - Dec '98
Expense	
Automobile	
Fuel	140.35
Repairs and Maintenance	114.75
Automobile - Other	18.45
Total Automobile	273.55

The word *Other* appears when the report has subaccounts (or subitems or jobs) but there is at least one transaction that is for the main account (or item or customer).

To avoid seeing a line or column for *Other*, be sure to use subaccounts (and subitems and jobs) consistently.

To remove the *Other* line or column on a report, double-click its dollar amount to learn why it occurs. When QuickBooks displays a report listing one or more transactions, double-click each transaction in turn. On the transaction itself, replace the problem name with the correct subaccount, subitem, or job.

What's the best way to track my type of detail?

The following table describes situations that require a business to track a particular type of detail. The table suggests the best way to track this detail in QuickBooks.

Situation	How to record in QuickBooks	Comments	See...
You need to track details of services you're providing or products you're selling.	■ Set up items on the Item list for your services and products. ■ Record the sale, using the appropriate items. On sales forms you can edit the item descriptions to add detail you want the customer or client to see.	You can get reports about the items for services and products that you have sold, including quantities and dollar amounts by item.	Chapter 8, *Items—your services, products, fixed assets, and more,* beginning on page 75
You need to track multiple jobs for the same customer.	■ Set up jobs for the customer on your Customer:Job list. ■ When entering any sales for a job, enter both the job and customer name in the Customer:Job field.	Reports by customer or by job give subtotals by job and then a total of jobs for the customer.	Chapter 9, *Customers and jobs,* beginning on page 97
You need to track expenses by customer or job.	■ If you don't have QuickBooks Pro or Premier, turn on the preference for tracking expenses by job. ■ When entering any expenses for a customer or job, enter the customer name or the job and customer name in the Customer:Job field.	You can track expenses by customer alone if you don't use jobs. The profit & loss by job report lists both income and expenses with a separate column for each customer and job.	■ "Setting up customers and jobs" on page 101 ■ "Entering detail on transactions" on page 38
You need to track income and expenses by fund, location, department, or business segment. **Examples:** Religious and arts organizations, retail stores with multiple locations.	■ Turn on class tracking, and set up a class on your Class list for each fund. ■ On every transaction, enter a class as well as an account (where appropriate).	The profit & loss by class statement has a column for each fund (class), so you can see income and expenses by fund.	"Tracking income and expenses with classes" on page 30
You have employees and need to see detail about payroll taxes and other payroll expenses. **Example:** Any company with employees	Use the QuickBooks payroll feature to track your payroll.	The payroll reports show all your payroll information.	Chapter 17, *Payroll and Employees,* beginning on page 235

Situation	How to record in QuickBooks	Comments	See...
You need to track certain details about your customers and vendors. **Example:** Payment terms, customer's sales tax, customer's "ship to" address, vendor's tax ID for 1099 forms, your account number with a vendor	Find and fill in the appropriate field in the New or Edit Customer window or the New or Edit Vendor window. The field you want may be on the Additional Info tab.	If you set up customers and vendors by using the QuickAdd option, go back later, to add missing information.	■ "Setting up customers" on page 101 ■ "Setting up vendors" on page 144 ■ "Editing vendors" on page 146
You want to see reports for a particular group of customers, jobs, or vendors. **Examples:** Residential vs. commercial customers; remodeling jobs vs. new construction; vendors that sell materials vs. subcontractors	When setting up a customer, job, or vendor, assign a type. (Job types are available only in QuickBooks Pro and QuickBooks Premier.)	You can filter a relevant report to limit the transactions to those for customers, job, or vendors of the type (or types) you specify. You can filter a report of your Customer:Job list or Vendor list to limit the names to those for the type (or types) you specify.	■ "Customer types" on page 99 ■ "Job types" on page 100 ■ "Setting up vendors" on page 144 ■ "Customizing the look of the report" on page 288
On your Item list, you want to group similar items together. **Example:** A school store wants to group clothing items and also group book items	■ Set up a main, or parent, item (for example, clothing). Then set up subitems of the parent item (for example, T-shirt, cap). ■ Use the appropriate subitem when entering a sale or purchase of items.	On reports that summarize amounts by item, QuickBooks provides an amount for each subitem, and then a subtotal for all subitems of the same item.	"Using items to subtotal on sales forms" on page 90
You want to track information that QuickBooks doesn't already track for customers, vendors, employees, or the items you sell. **Examples:** Patient's insurance company, item size or color	■ Set up a custom field for tracking the particular kind of information. ■ Fill in the custom field, where relevant, for new and existing customers, vendors, employees, or items. ■ To display and print the custom field on sales forms or purchase orders, customize the form to add the new field.	You can use the same custom field for customers, vendors, and employees if you choose. Custom fields for items are only for items you sell or purchase (services, parts, and other charges). You can filter a relevant report to limit the transactions to forms that have specific text in a custom field.	■ Look in the Help Index for: **custom fields, about** ■ Read "Customizing estimates, sales forms, and purchase orders" on page 40

(continued)

Situation	How to record in QuickBooks	Comments	See...
On your profit and loss statement, you want to see subtotals for accounts that have something in common. **Example:** A construction company wants a subtotal for construction income for labor, materials, and subcontractors	■ Set up a main, or parent, account for the subtotal (for example, construction income). Then set up subaccounts of the parent account (for example, labor, materials, subcontractors). ■ Use the appropriate subaccount when QuickBooks requires you to specify an account.	On reports that summarize amounts by account, QuickBooks provides an amount for each subaccount and then a subtotal for all subaccounts of the same account.	"What are the advantages of using subaccounts?" on page 26

Tracking income and expenses with classes

Do you need to track income and expenses for separate parts of your business or organization? The following table has examples of what you can track by using classes in QuickBooks. (The word *class* has nothing to do with teaching or learning—instead, it is a way of classifying income or expenses *in addition to* assigning an income or expense account.)

Use classes to track the following	Industry examples
Account executives (particularly useful if you plan on using an employee incentive program linked to the employee's business goals and profitability)	■ Advertising ■ PR ■ Consulting
Construction industry standard categories (General, Site Work, Concrete, Masonry, and so on)	■ Construction contractors
Departments	■ Businesses that budget by department ■ Retailers
Funds (General, Building, Outreach, and so on) You could start with two main classes for restricted and unrestricted funds, and then make each fund a subclass of a main class.	■ Nonprofit organizations ■ Religious groups
Locations (if the business has more than one)	■ Restaurants ■ Retailers ■ Service businesses
Manufacturers	■ Distributors ■ Manufacturing reps

Use classes to track the following	Industry examples
Partners	■ Law firms ■ Consulting ■ Any other partnerships
Product lines	■ Distributors ■ Manufacturing reps ■ Sales agents

After you set up classes, you can enter them on any income or expense transaction including payroll transactions. For examples of entering a class on a deposit or a check, see "Entering detail on transactions" on page 38.

You can't assign classes to transactions that involve only balance sheet accounts (for example, transfers from checking to savings, setup of inventory, setup of fixed assets).

You can set up subclasses of existing classes if you need to subtotal information about classes on reports.

To learn about...	Look in the Help Index for...
Turning on the preference for using classes	classes, turning on in QuickBooks
Adding classes and subclasses	classes, adding

Should I use classes, jobs, or types?

Ask yourself: Am I trying to track income or expense activity associated with a particular customer or group of customers or group of jobs?

If your answer is Yes, then you use jobs, customer types, or job types or track expenses by job. The following table shows what you can do with each of these.

To do the following...	Do this in QuickBooks...	Examples of reports to use
Keep track of sales for separate jobs or projects for one customer.	Set up and use jobs for the customer on the Customer:Job list.	Sales by customer summary (which shows each job separately)
See income or expenses for one type of customer, as distinguished from another type. **Example:** A PR writer wants to compare a restaurant with retail clients.	When entering or editing a customer, assign a customer type.	▪ Sales by customer summary, filtered for one customer type ▪ Profit & loss by job, filtered for one customer type
(QuickBooks Pro and Premier only) See income or expenses for one type of job, as distinguished from another type. (Jobs of the same type can be for different customers.) **Example:** A construction contractor wants to compare kitchen remodels with office remodels.	When entering or editing a job, assign a job type.	▪ Sales by customer summary, filtered for one job type ▪ Profit & loss by job, filtered for one job type
Assign expenses to a customer (or to a particular job for a customer).	On every expense transaction for that customer or job, enter the customer name (or the customer and job name) in the Customer:Job field.	The following reports always break down amounts by customer. If you have jobs, they also break down amounts by job. ▪ Profit & loss by job ▪ Job profitability (QuickBooks Pro and Premier only) ▪ Profit & loss budget vs. actual

If you are tracking a segment of your business that is independent of your customers and jobs, set up a class for the particular business segment. Then enter the class name in the Class field of every income or expense transaction for that segment.

You get out only what you put in

If you want to see detail on reports, be sure to track the detail somewhere in QuickBooks.

For example, if Susan needs to know how her yearly travel expenses break down by airfare, lodging, and meals, first she needs to subdivide her expense account for travel expenses into three subaccounts. Then she needs to break down her expenses each time she enters them in QuickBooks.

Similarly, if Richard needs to know what the income and expenses are for each of his church funds, then he must assign at least one fund to every transaction.

What you shouldn't try to track in QuickBooks

Some things should not be tracked in QuickBooks:

- Personal finances

    For tax purposes, it's usually best to keep your business income and expenses completely separate from your personal income and expenses. (If you still want to track personal finances in QuickBooks, set up a separate company file for them.)

- Investments in stock and mutual funds

    If the business owns these investments, you can track the cost basis as an asset. However, QuickBooks doesn't have the investment tracking found in Quicken.

- Details that are not specifically related to your business accounting (even though they may be very important)

    For example, Rachel needs to track when subscriptions expire so she can send reminder notices. Jon sells antiques on consignment and needs to track details about each unique item. Other software, such as a database, spreadsheet, or membership software, can help you track these details.

    QuickBooks has a To Do List, where you can record notes you want to see on the Reminder list on a specific date. You can list personal as well as business notes. See "Making To Do notes" on page 303. To schedule events at specific times, you'll need other software.

Tracking the detail you need

Fine-tuning your chart of accounts

You can fine-tune your chart of accounts at any time by doing the following:

- Add new accounts or subaccounts.

  You can add subaccounts to balance sheet accounts (for example, fixed asset accounts) as well as to income and expense accounts.

- Turn on and use account numbers.

  QuickBooks has an option for specifying account numbers in addition to names. If the account is one that QuickBooks added for you, it already has a number but you can change it.

- Change the name or number of an existing account.

- Enter or edit an opening balance for a balance sheet account if the original opening balance is incorrect.

- Arrange accounts of the same type in alphabetical order (or numerical order if account numbers are turned on).

- Rearrange the order of accounts within the same account type.

- Make one existing account the subaccount of another (or, conversely, move a subaccount to a higher level).

You can drag accounts to a new position on the chart of accounts. When your accounts are not in alphabetical or numerical order, and you add a new account, QuickBooks places the new account above the other accounts of the same type.

Place the mouse pointer over the diamond at the left of the account you want to move.

When the pointer becomes a four-headed arrow, click and drag the account up or down the list.

To make the account a subaccount of the account above, drag it to the right.

If you want to remove accounts from your chart of accounts, see "When you no longer need the detail" on page 41.

To learn about...	Look in the Help Index for...
Adding new accounts or subaccounts	accounts (managing), adding
Turning on account numbers	accounts (managing), numbering
Changing account names or numbers	accounts (managing), editing
Changing or entering an opening balance for a balance sheet account	■ opening balances, changing for existing accounts ■ opening balances, entering for existing accounts
Arranging accounts (and other lists) in alphabetical or numerical order	lists, sorting entries
Reorganizing accounts within the same account type; also, reorganizing other lists that allow subentries (for example, customer:Job list)	lists, reorganizing entries

Setting up accounts to track equity details

equity

The net worth of a company, equal to the total assets minus the total liabilities. All the equity belongs to the owners.

Your company's equity comes from two sources:

■ Money invested in your company (capital investments)

■ Profits of your company

Of course, the owner can also take money out of the company. Such withdrawals, called owner's draws, reduce the company equity.

QuickBooks sets up two equity accounts automatically:

■ Opening Bal Equity

For every balance sheet account you set up with an opening balance, QuickBooks records the amount of the opening balance in the Opening Bal Equity account. (Asset account opening balances increase the equity; liability account opening balances decrease the equity.)

■ Retained Earnings

If you have data for more than one fiscal year, the Quick-Books balance sheet has a balance for the Retained Earnings account equal to the net profit from prior fiscal years. The balance for the Retained Earnings account does not display on the chart of accounts.

Some people like to track owner investments, owner's draws, and retained earnings prior to the QuickBooks start date by putting them in separate equity accounts. If you decide to add additional equity accounts, QuickBooks still adds the Retained Earnings and Net Income lines on your balance sheet.

Equity accounts for sole proprietorships

sole proprietorship

An unincorporated company owned by one person.

Because all equity of a sole proprietorship company belongs to one person, tracking equity can be very simple.

As of your QuickBooks start date, all equity is in the Opening Bal Equity account. You have several options:

- Keep the equity in this account and perhaps rename the account to something such as *Owner's Equity*.

- Transfer all the equity out of Opening Bal Equity into Retained Earnings.

  This action is appropriate for companies that have built up assets as a result of earnings prior to the QuickBooks start date. From now on, you can take owner's draws out of the Retained Earnings account.

- Set up additional accounts (or subaccounts) to track owner's investments, owner's draws, and earnings before your QuickBooks start date.

In this example, a sole proprietor has changed the name of Opening Bal Equity to Owner's Equity and set up three subaccounts with opening balances.

The balance for Owner's Equity equals the total for the three subaccounts.

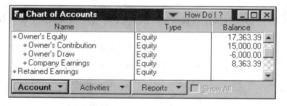

 When setting up a new account for owner's draws, enter a negative opening balance to show the total draws prior to the QuickBooks start date. The negative opening balance indicates that the draws have reduced the company's equity. (Or, enter a zero opening balance and simply record draws from now on.)

Partnerships

partnership

An unincorporated company owned by two or more persons.

In a partnership, each partner owns a share of all assets and liabilities. Each partner may have invested in the partnership, and each receives a specified share of profits. Because partners are not employees, they don't receive salaries or wages, but they may withdraw money against their share of profits.

As of your QuickBooks start date, all the equity is in the Opening Bal Equity account.

- Set up separate equity accounts for each partner.

  If you don't want to see further detail, the opening balance for each partner's equity account should equal the partner's equity as of your QuickBooks start date. Because the company's equity belongs to the partners, setting up the new accounts should reduce the balance of the Opening Bal Equity account to zero.

  From now on, record each partner's capital investment, draws, and share of profits in the partner's single equity account.

  If you want to see further detail by adding subaccounts, the opening balance for each partner's *parent* equity account should equal zero.

- (Optional) Add subaccounts to provide the level of detail you'd like to see on the chart of accounts and on the balance sheet. For example, add subaccounts for each partner's investments, share of profits, and draws.

In this partnership, the balance for Marilyn's Equity equals the total of her subaccounts. Similarly, the balance for Peggy's Equity equals the total of her subaccounts.

The balance for Opening Bal Equity is zero after the partners' equity accounts have been set up.

Name	Type	Balance
◆ Marilyn's Equity	Equity	10,579.76
◆ Marilyn's Draw	Equity	-6,000.00
◆ Marilyn's Investment	Equity	10,000.00
◆ Marilyn's Profits	Equity	6,579.76
◆ Opening Bal Equity	Equity	0.00
◆ Peggy's Equity	Equity	7,783.63
◆ Peggy's Draw	Equity	-6,000.00
◆ Peggy's Investment	Equity	9,000.00
◆ Peggy's Profits	Equity	4,783.63
◆ Retained Earnings	Equity	

Corporations

corporation

A business organization that has been incorporated. A corporation is owned by its stockholders.

In a corporation, you'll usually want to separate stockholders' investment of capital from the stockholders' share of earnings.

To track paid-in capital or investments of stockholders, add an equity account with a name such as *Capital Stock*. Although you do need to have records of the names and investments of each stockholder, you probably won't want to show this detail on your chart of accounts. For the opening balance, enter the total paid-in capital as of your QuickBooks start date.

After you have set up all your accounts, the amount remaining in Opening Bal Equity represents retained earnings prior to the start date. You can rename this account with a name such as *Prior Earnings* or *Pre-1995 Earnings*.

QuickBooks automatically tracks the corporation's retained earnings for completed fiscal years in the Retained Earnings equity account. After the end of the year, you may distribute some or all of the Corporations retained earnings to stockholders as dividends.

To learn about...	Look in the Help Index for...
Renaming Opening Bal Equity	accounts (managing), editing
Adding equity accounts or subaccounts	accounts (managing), adding
Transferring equity out of Opening Bal Equity	equity, transferring from Opening Bal Equity

Entering detail on transactions

Once you have set up to track a particular kind of detail, you should track the detail where appropriate on transactions you record.

- For information about recording checks, bills, and credit cards, see Chapter 13, *Tracking and paying expenses,* beginning on page 167.

- For information about recording deposits, see "Receiving payments and making deposits" on page 66.

For example, Stefan has subaccounts for his expense accounts, so he chooses the correct subaccount when recording a check or bill.

When Stefan chooses the subaccount Equipment Rental from the drop-down list in the **Account** field, QuickBooks enters the account name (Job Expenses) followed by a colon (:) and the subaccount name.

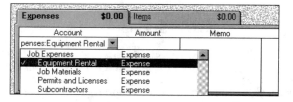

To get reports to show the breakdown you want, use subaccounts or subitems consistently. That is, if you record expenses for a subaccount of a main account, do not sometimes record expenses directly for the main account. Similarly, if you record sales of a subitem of a main item, do not sometimes record sales directly for the main item. To choose a subaccount or subitem in a field, display the drop-down list for that field.

Deborah needs to track the costs as well as the income for each customer's job. Whenever she records an expense or purchases an item for the job, she assigns the job to the expense or item. She can even indicate that the expense or item is billable to the job so she can invoice the customer for it later. (See "Charging for actual time and costs" on page 130.)

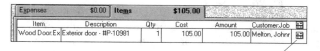

In the **Customer:Job** field of checks, bills, or credit card charges, Deborah enters the name of the customer (and job) for the expense or purchase.

If you track customers but not jobs, you can enter the customer name alone.

The invoice symbol indicates the expense or purchase is billable to the customer or job.

 You can assign customers and jobs to purchases of items as well as expenses only in QuickBooks Pro or Premier. If you don't have QuickBooks Pro or Premier, you can assign customers and jobs to expenses but not purchases of items.

Richard is using classes to keep track of each fund his church has set up. When Richard records income for a fund, he assigns both an income account and the class for that fund.

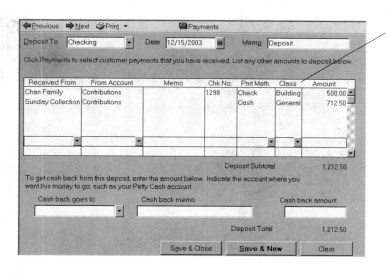

In the **Class** field for the deposit, Richard indicates the fund each contribution is for.

Similarly, when he writes a check, he assigns both an expense account and a class for the appropriate fund.

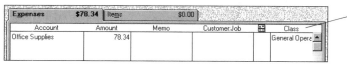

In the **Class** field for the check detail, Richard indicates the fund each expense is for.

Customizing estimates, sales forms, and purchase orders

You can customize your estimates (available only in QuickBooks Pro and QuickBooks Premier), sales forms, and purchase orders to show standard fields (such as service date and customer:job) or custom fields you've set up.

For example, Justine has a custom field for the color of her items. She can add a column for color to all of her forms by customizing the template for each form.

Ralph wants his invoices to display the customer's contract number. He sets up a custom field for contract number for customers. Then he adds this field to the top of his invoices by customizing his invoice template.

Note: **You can't add custom fields to statements.** However, you can customize statements by adding or deleting some standard fields (such as quantity and rate). You can add custom fields to all other sales forms.

For more information, see Chapter 6, *Creating a professional image,* beginning on page 49.

To learn about...	Look in the Help Index for...
Setting up custom fields to track additional information about customers, vendors, employees, or items	■ custom fields, for customers, vendors, or employees ■ custom fields, for the items you purchase or sell
Customizing estimates, sales forms, and purchase orders to add standard and custom fields for customers, vendors, or items	■ customizing forms, fields ■ customers, special orders for

When you no longer need the detail

In some situations, you may want to remove detail from lists or reports:

- The detail is for something you needed at one time but no longer need.

- You realize you don't need all the detail you set up and would like to consolidate some of it.

If the detail is on a particular list (for example, old, completed jobs on the Customer:Job list), the easiest solution is to simply hide the unwanted name on the list. You do this by making the name *inactive*. It remains on the old transactions, but you won't see it on drop-down lists.

If you never used the name at all and don't plan to, you can delete it altogether. However, if you did use it, QuickBooks doesn't allow you to delete it.

If you want to consolidate all transactions for one name with those of another name, QuickBooks allows you to merge the names. This is a good solution if you inadvertently set up and used two different names for the same thing.

Finally, if your data file grows large and you want to remove old transactions as well as unused list items, you can use the Archive & Condense Data wizard.

To learn about...	Look in the Help Index for...
Hiding unwanted names on lists	hiding, list entries
Deleting unused names from lists	deleting, entries from lists
Merging transactions for one name with transactions for a second name	merging, list entries
Removing old transactions along with old names	condensing data

Keeping your data safe can include limiting access to the data through passwords, making regular backup copies of your data, and maintaining an audit trail to track changes to transactions.

 To prevent other people from accessing your QuickBooks company file, always close it when you're finished using it or if you plan to be away from your workstation for an extended period of time.

Using passwords

Intuit strongly recommends that you use both Windows system and QuickBooks passwords, which are designed to limit access to your desktop and to certain areas of your QuickBooks company file—and thereby help to safeguard sensitive company information.

Use a password that you can remember, but that's not someone's name, or something else that other people can guess. It's also good advice to use passwords that include both numbers and letters. Configuring QuickBooks with a password for each account (even in single-user versions) is an important security measure. With password protection set, access to your company file can only be granted with the password you set.

Each QuickBooks user in your company can be set up with a unique password and given designated areas of the program that he or she can work in. Areas include sales and accounts receivable, purchases and accounts payable, checking and credit cards, inventory, time tracking, payroll, sensitive accounting activities, and sensitive financial reports.

Until you set up users (and passwords) in your QuickBooks company file, any person who accesses the file through QuickBooks will have full access.

The QuickBooks password feature provides a basic degree of protection for your data, but it's not a complete security system.

For example, it will not prevent someone from using Windows Explorer to delete a company file. If you need stronger protection, keep your computer and backup disks in a secure area and ensure any network connections to your computer are password-protected.

To learn about...	Look in the Help Index for...
Keeping your company data secure	security

Do you need to use passwords?

Situation	Action	Comments
If you are the only person in your office who uses QuickBooks	Set up system and QuickBooks passwords for yourself to help prevent others from accessing your QuickBooks data. Intuit highly recommends that you use passwords as safety precautions in helping protect your data.	If you used passwords in your previous version of QuickBooks, QuickBooks remembers the owner password you used in that version. When you first open your company file in QuickBooks 2004, you'll be prompted to enter this password.
If you allow others to access your QuickBooks data	Set up users with passwords and specific access areas.	For example, you can allow your business partner to write payroll checks but limit a data-entry person to entering invoices.
If you want to have two or more people working in the QuickBooks file at the same time	Set up users with passwords and specific access areas.	You must have two or more copies of the same edition: QuickBooks Pro or Premier 2004.

Setting up users

When you create a new QuickBooks company file, QuickBooks creates a user called *Admin*. This is the QuickBooks Administrator for that company file.

 When you choose a password for the Administrator, make sure you write it down and store it in a safe place. If you forget this password and need assistance, choose Help & Support from the Help menu, and then, under Contact Intuit, click Phone Directory.

The Administrator has unlimited access to all data in the company file and is the only person who can add additional users and access privileges. For each user being set up, the Administrator designates:

- A password which the user can change later. (The password can contain up to 16 alphanumeric characters and is not case sensitive.)
- Full access, selective access, or no access for each QuickBooks area.

After setup, a summary screen displays the access selections for that user.

Once you have set up more than one user, QuickBooks prompts you for a login when you open the company file.

 Only the QuickBooks Administrator can set up new users and their levels of access.

Once set up, each individual user can change or delete his or her own password. However, the QuickBooks Administrator will still be the only user able to make changes to a user's access.

To learn about...	Look in the Help Index for...
The different access areas of QuickBooks	passwords, access areas
The role of the QuickBooks Administrator	admin
Setting up users with passwords and access	users, adding
Changing passwords	passwords, changing
Deleting passwords	passwords, deleting

Using a password to close an accounting period

Unlike most other accounting systems, QuickBooks does not require you to "close the books" at the end of a period. Closing books is often a complicated process that involves transferring information from one ledger to another and summarizing it. You can ask QuickBooks for reports at any time, not just at the end of a period.

However, you may want to restrict access to the transactions of prior accounting periods to help ensure that the transactions are not changed without your knowledge. By requiring a password to delete, add, or edit any transaction before a chosen date, you can discourage accidental or casual changes made in or with QuickBooks to closed periods, but still make corrections when necessary.

To learn about...	Look in the Help Index for...
Setting a closing date password	closing books

Recording who changed what

You can have QuickBooks keep a record of all changes made to transactions, including the name of the user who made the changes, and then review the changes in the audit trail report.

This transaction has been edited. Current Transaction shows what the transaction is like now; Previous Transaction shows what the transaction was like before the change.

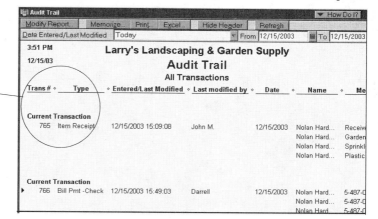

Any transactions labeled *Previous Transaction* have been modified. You can compare the previous transaction to the current transaction to see which part or parts of the transaction have changed. The report shows the user who entered modifications and the date and time of the modification.

To keep a record of changed transactions, you must have the audit trail preference turned on.

If the preference is turned off, QuickBooks no longer keeps a record of the changes to transactions. If the audit trail was turned off during part of the period covered by the report, QuickBooks may not show the modification date of some transactions, but it retains old audit trail information.

If you turn the audit trail preference on, you may find that QuickBooks works more slowly, and your data takes up more disk space and may require more memory. These drawbacks occur because QuickBooks records not only the changed transaction, but also its previous versions. In contrast, QuickBooks overwrites the previous version of a transaction when the audit-trail preference is turned off.

To learn about...	Look in the Help Index for...
Using the audit trail feature and creating the report	audit trail

CREATING A PROFESSIONAL
IMAGE

Creating custom business forms

Creating a custom invoice or other business form is made up of two basic concepts: *customizing* and *designing*. You customize the forms by specifying the fields and columns you want on the form in the Customize window. Design the layout of forms with the Layout Designer window in which you can move and resize objects using the mouse.

Here are just a few examples of how you can customize and design your business forms with QuickBooks:

- Create different versions of a form for use in specific situations. For example, if you ship goods with a packing slip, you can create an invoice form with the title *Packing Slip* instead of *Invoice*.

- Change fonts, add fill color to fields, change border styles, or add images. (Not available in QuickBooks Basic)

- Add new columns and fields and delete ones you don't need. For example, if you've created custom fields for your inventory, you can have the fields appear on the form.

- Decide which fields you want to see for your own use onscreen, and which fields you want your customer to see on the printed form.

- Change the names of fields to make them appropriate for your business.

- Move a field to give it greater visibility.

- Add your company logo.

- Add a field containing up to 1,000 characters to print on forms. For example, you can print a tax ID number for customers, product warranty information, or legal text.

Customizing and designing your QuickBooks business forms

Using the Templates list

When you first set up your QuickBooks company, the Templates list displays only the Standard Intuit forms. As you use certain features, additional templates will be added to the list automatically. For example, as you enter your first cash sale, QuickBooks puts *Custom Cash Sale* on your Templates list. You can choose to customize this form or leave it as is. At any time, you can create customized templates of QuickBooks business forms (invoices, credit memos, sales receipts, purchase orders, statements, and estimates) to suit your business needs.

If you have QuickBooks Pro or Premier Editions, you can also download predesigned templates that span a wide range of business types and layout styles. You can find these templates by clicking Download Templates in the Templates button menu. Downloaded templates are added to your company files's template list where you can use them as is, or customize them even more.

To view the Templates list:

- From the Lists menu, choose Templates.

Use the Templates menu button to do the following:

- Create a new template.
- Edit an existing template.
- Delete a template.
- Make a copy (duplicate) of a template to edit.
- Make a template inactive.
- Use a template for a form.
- Import and export templates.

Note that some of templates will appears on the list only after you have used the feature. For example, after you create a credit memo, the Custom Credit Memo template appears on the list.

The Templates list shows all the templates and the type of form each template is used for.

To preview what the templates look like:

1 From the Lists menu, choose Templates.

2 From the Templates list, select a template and click Open Form.

The onscreen version of the form displays.

3 To see what the printed version of the template will look like, click the down arrow next to Print and then choose Preview. In some cases, you'll only need to click Preview.

Customizing a form's content

You can customize any template form and create any number of versions.

If you plan to print your invoices or statements on preprinted forms from Intuit, you should make only minor adjustments to the Intuit templates. For example, adding a logo, adding your company name and address, or changing fonts still allows you to use preprinted forms and double-window envelopes you purchase from Intuit. You can't, however, add, change, delete, or move columns.

For each form you customize, you decide which fields (including custom fields) and columns to include, what they are labeled, and where to place them.

Enter a unique name for the template in the **Template Name** field.

You can specify if a field or column should appear on the screen version and/or on the printed version you send to your customers.

The last four fields are custom fields that you may want to add to your forms.

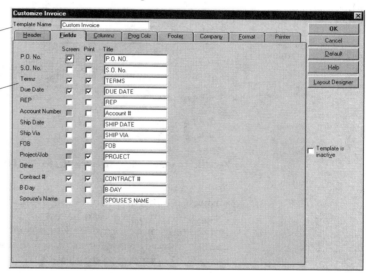

Once you've created your forms, you can save them to use whenever you wish and modify them whenever you want.

The following diagram shows the areas of the form that you can change using various tabs of the Customize window.

Header

Use the Header tab to change the title of a form or other information in this part of the form.

Fields

Use the Fields tab to change the information shown on this part of the form.

Footer

You can enter up to 1,000 characters in the **Long text** area on the Footer tab to print on your custom form.

This information could include legal disclaimers or warranty information.

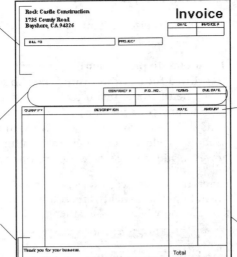

Format

Use the Format tab to add your logo and to change fonts, including font style (italic, bold, etc.) and size.

Columns

Use the Columns tab to change the order in which columns display. The Amount column always displays furthest to the right.

You can also rename, add, or delete columns.

Printer

Use the Printer tab to change the page orientation.

To learn about...	Look in the Help Index for...
Creating custom business forms	customizing forms, about

Adding your company logo to forms

Adding a logo to your forms helps you to create a unique business identity with your customers. If you use preprinted forms from Intuit, you can have your logo professionally printed onto those forms. Or, you can add your own image to be used as a logo on your forms. When you specify a logo file, QuickBooks prints it to the default location, left of your company name and address on forms. If you like, you can move your logo to a different part of the form by using the Layout Designer.

To learn about...	Look in the Help Index for...
Adding a logo to a business form	logos, adding to sales and purchase forms

What happens if I remove a field or column that I've previously used?

If you remove a field or column from a form after you have used it in a transaction, QuickBooks retains all the data that you entered. You can still create reports based on the data.

For example, suppose you have been using a custom field labeled *Color* on your sales forms, and you decide to remove the Color field. When you display invoices that you created before you removed the Color field, the field no longer appears, but you can still create reports based on the color of items you sold. If you decide to restore the Color field at a later time, the field reappears on all the invoices where it originally appeared.

If you delete or add columns, QuickBooks automatically resizes the remaining columns, but you can adjust the widths with the Layout Designer window.

Designing the layout of a form

Another aspect of creating customized business forms can include changing the form's layout. Once you've specified in the Customize window which fields, columns, header and footer elements you want to print, and how you want them labeled, you can use the Layout Designer to move and resize these objects. Using the Layout Designer, you can also add and move fields and images.

Objects are the elements that make up the layout of a business form, including:

- A field
- A column
- The title of a field or column
- The title of the form
- Your company name and address
- Your company logo

Form setup issues

Before you begin moving and resizing objects on your form:

1   Check your printer setup orientation and paper size.

    For example, if you need to lay out a form to fit legal-size paper, you'll need to check that your printer setup is set for legal-size paper.

2   Within the Layout Designer, specify your margins.

When you know the size and margins of your form, it's easier to adjust the fields and columns on the form to get the appearance you want.

How you can create a custom layout

- You can give your company name, address, and logo special treatment on the form. For example, you can center the logo at the top, and put your company name and address in a special font immediately below the logo.

- You can add text boxes to place static text on forms or change the border styles of fields.

- You can enlarge a custom field so that it can hold up to 30 characters. For example, if you're using a custom field to enter e-mail addresses, you can lengthen the field so that it can hold a long e-mail address.

- You can position the customer's billing address so that it coincides with the address window in the envelopes you use. (You can also remove the box around the address so that just the address shows through.)

Note: **Only sample text appears in the fields and columns when you're in the Layout Designer window.** To see what the finished form will look like, you need to print the form, or access a form window and click Print Preview.

To learn about...	Look in the Help Index for...
Using the Layout Designer	Layout Designer, how to use

What if I use double-window envelopes?

You can adjust the fields in the header area of your form so that when you fold the form and place it in one of Intuit's specially designed double-window envelopes, the appropriate fields show through.

QuickBooks displays shadowed areas to show you which part of the form will show through the envelope windows. You can then adjust your fields accordingly.

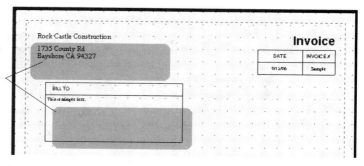

Aligning your fields to match the shadowed areas will enable you to use a double-window envelope with a mailing name and address and your return name and address.

?	**To learn about...**	**Look in the Help Index for...**
	Adjusting forms to fit window envelopes	windowed envelopes

Printing and sending your forms and checks

QuickBooks can print any of your business forms (including statements and invoices) and checks, or you can e-mail them from QuickBooks. Before you print or transmit your forms or checks, make sure you've specified any customizations you want.

If you mail a large number of invoices every month, you can send them through QuickBooks to a third-party service that will print and mail them for you automatically.

Paper options for business forms

When you print your business forms you have three paper options:

- **Preprinted forms**

  These may include your logo, company name, and address. (You can purchase preprinted forms through Intuit. Choose Help & Support from the Help menu. Under Contact Intuit, choose Phone Directory, and then Checks and Supplies.)

  QuickBooks does not print the title of the form on preprinted paper; however, it will print your company name and address unless you deselect "Print Company Name" and "Print Company Address" on the Company tab of the Customize window.

- **Blank paper**

    QuickBooks prints the title of the form (shown onscreen) in large letters at the top of the paper. You can specify whether to print lines around each field. Select this option when printing forms that you've customized with the Layout Designer window.

- **Letterhead**

    QuickBooks does not print in the upper 1.9 inches of your letterhead. You can specify whether to print lines around each field.

You might want to consult your Intuit Checks, Forms and Supplies Catalog for examples of available forms.

Note: **You can't print customized invoices on Intuit forms if your customization includes changes to columns or fields.** However, you can use Intuit's multi-purpose forms preprinted with your company name and address.

Printer setup

Checks

From the Printer setup window for checks, you'll choose your printer from a list of your installed printers and the check type you'll be printing on (voucher, standard, or wallet). You can also print partial pages of checks when necessary.

Before you print checks, you may want to set different preferences for how they print. For example, you can replace the preset date with the date that you print the checks, or control whether certain information prints on the voucher portion of the checks.

To learn about...	Look in the Help Index for...
Setting up your printer to print checks	printer setup, general

Forms

You can set up your printer to print any QuickBooks form, including invoices, sales receipts, credit memos, estimates, statements, and purchase orders. From the Printer setup window for invoices (and other forms), you'll choose your printer from a list of installed printers and the paper type you'll be printing on (see "Paper options for business forms" on page 55 for details).

To learn about...	Look in the Help Index for...
Setting up your printer to print your business forms	printer setup, general

Printing issues

You can print any business form or check directly from the window where you created it, or use the Print Forms command (found on the File menu) to print, in a single operation, a group of forms or checks.

Alignment

You can print samples of your QuickBooks forms and checks to see if the forms line up correctly, and you can make alignment adjustments. If you have trouble getting forms to print correctly at first, print sample forms on blank paper. After printing a sample, place it on top of the real form and hold them both up to the light to see if the text printed correctly.

When you change a form's alignment, QuickBooks shifts all text by the same amount. You can't change the alignment of individual columns.

If you're printing on preprinted forms with a continuous-feed printer, you usually need to make coarse alignment adjustments first, and then make fine alignment adjustments. If you are using a page-oriented printer, you need to make only fine alignment adjustments.

To learn about...	Look in the Help Index for...
Printing your business forms	printing, sales forms
Printing and reprinting checks	printing checks
Sending invoices, statements, or estimates by e-mail	e-mail business forms to customers
Alignment	aligning forms in printer
Printing batches of forms	printing, batches of forms

If the data won't fit on one form

If an invoice or receipt is too long to fit on one page, QuickBooks automatically adds additional pages as needed. Each page of a multiple-page form is numbered, although you can choose whether or not to print those page numbers. The transaction total appears only on the last page.

Setting up banking information

Note: You might have already added your various bank accounts in the EasyStep Interview. These accounts include checking, savings, and credit card accounts.

What to set up	Comments	Look in the Help Index for...
Bank accounts that haven't been added to QuickBooks yet	Enter an opening balance for these accounts or create the opening balance by adding all the necessary historical transactions.	■ accounts (managing), adding ■ opening balances ■ historical transactions
Credit card accounts that haven't been added to QuickBooks yet	None	■ accounts (managing), adding ■ opening balances
Reconcile each bank account (and credit card account) with your bank statements, from the first statement after your start date to your last statement.	Then you'll know that QuickBooks and your bank are in agreement. See "Reconciling bank and credit card accounts" on page 69.	reconciling, bank statements

Setting up online banking (account access and payment)

QuickBooks online banking encompasses both account access and payment features. The Online Banking Setup Interview will answer your questions and walk you through the account setup process.

To access the Online Banking Setup Interview:

1 From the Banking menu, choose Set Up Online Financial Services.

2 Choose Set Up Account for Online Access.

3 Complete the interview for Online Banking Setup.

The following table gives you a brief overview of the online banking setup process. These steps are completed over a period of days or weeks, depending on how quickly your application for online banking is processed at the financial institution.

Also, if you are planning on using online payment, you'll need to set up your payees. See "Setting up online payees" on page 175.

What to set up	Comments	Look in the Help Index for...
Internet access through an ISP if you haven't already set this up for another QuickBooks feature	Choose Internet Connection Setup from the Help menu.	Internet connections
If you don't already have an account (checking, savings, money market, credit card) at a financial institution that provides online banking through QuickBooks, you'll need to open one.	**Note:** You can use the QuickBooks Bill Pay service with any U.S. account with check-writing privileges.	online banking, financial institutions
Submit an application for online banking to your financial institution.	You can access application information over the Internet or contact your institution directly. There will be a period of days or weeks until you receive confirmation.	online banking, setting up
Select an online service for setup, by completing the "Apply Now" section of the Online Banking Setup interview	Enables you to submit an application for online banking at your financial institution.	online banking, setting up
When you receive your confirmation and a PIN/password from your financial institution, complete the "Enable Accounts" section of the Online Banking Setup interview.	Verify that the information sent to you by the financial institution is correct.	online banking, enabling a QuickBooks account

Going online for the first time

You should use online banking within the first month of enrolling for online services. The first time you go online, we recommend that you download the most recent transactions that have cleared at your financial institution.

Note: Financial institutions offer two different types of online banking connections: DirectConnect or WebConnect. DirectConnect offers seamless integration with QuickBooks. WebConnect offers online integration through the financial institution's web site (accessible from QuickBooks or any browser). Contact your bank to learn which type of connection type they provide. If your bank offers WebConnect, you can go to their website for online banking services.

From the Banking menu, choose Online Banking Center.

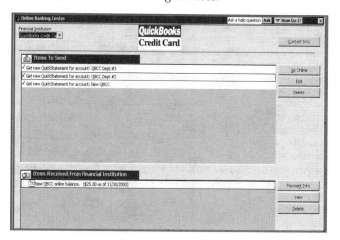

To learn about...	Look in the Help Index for...
Going online for banking	online banking, sending
Direct connection vs. webconnect	online banking, downloading Web transactions

Handling banking transactions

Day-to-day activities

Managing your checkbook

Whether you handwrite checks, print them from QuickBooks, or use online payment, you'll need to enter all the information into QuickBooks to keep your checking account accurate and up to date.

Information is entered into your check register from various QuickBooks sources: the Write Checks window; windows where you pay bills, sales tax and payroll liabilities; windows that record deposits; the monthly reconciliation process (fees, interest, and adjustments); and online banking downloads. You can add and modify transactions directly in the register.

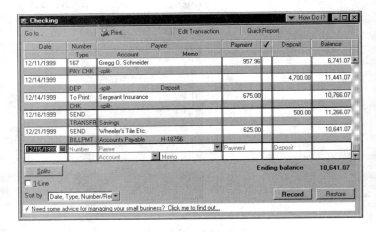

To manage your checkbook most effectively, enter your transactions on a regular basis and reconcile the account when you receive your bank statement.

Some daily checking-related tasks might include the following:

Task	Comments	Look in the Help index for...
Writing a check for expenses	Review the Accounts Payable information before you start writing checks. See "Ways to track and pay expenses in QuickBooks" on page 167. See also "Using checks" on page 183 and "Using online payment" on page 172.	■ checks, writing for expenses and items ■ online payments, writing checks for
Printing checks	You can print checks singly or in batches. You may need to experiment with alignment features the first time you print checks. You can also change the look of your printed checks by changing the fonts or adding a logo.	■ printing checks ■ logos, adding to checks and paychecks
Sorting your check register	The preset sort is by Date, Type, and Document #.	registers, sort by different criteria
Finding a particular check	Use the Find feature on the Edit menu.	finding transactions
Voiding or deleting a check	Choose to void (rather than delete) a check if you want to keep its history in QuickBooks. See also "Voiding or deleting checks" on page 184.	checks, voiding or deleting
Canceling an online payment	You can only cancel payments that the payment processor has scheduled but not yet sent or mailed.	online payments, canceling a payment
Editing information on a check	You can edit check information in the Write Checks window or in the checking account register.	checks, editing
Making a deposit	See page 66.	deposits, bank or checking account
Making an ATM withdrawal	Watch out for ATM surcharges. They can add up!	ATM withdrawals
Reconciling your accounts	See "Reconciling bank and credit card accounts" on page 69. See "Reconciling online accounts" on page 70.	■ reconciling, bank statements ■ reconciling, clearing an online transaction

Handling business credit card accounts

Your business might use a credit card for various purchases.

Task	Comments	See...
Making purchases with a credit card	Enter the charge with all appropriate information. For example, was this item purchased for a customer?	"Using credit cards" on page 185
Handling credit card fees	Enter the fee in the credit card register as *Annual Fee* or *Interest Owed*, as appropriate. Alternatively, you can enter these fees when you reconcile the account with the statement.	"Handling fees and interest earned on accounts" on page 68
Reconciling your credit card accounts	At the end of the reconcile process, you are prompted to write the check to pay for the credit card bill or enter a bill.	"Reconciling bank and credit card accounts" on page 69

Offering more ways for your customers to pay you

QuickBooks offers two services that let you receive customer payments and process them online.

By signing up for one or both services, you can offer your customers more choices for submitting payments. And, because both services are integrated into QuickBooks, you save time in recording and processing payments.

QuickBooks service	What you can do with the service
QuickBooks Merchant Account Service	■ Process credit card payments from your customers, right from QuickBooks, or on the Web using Virtual Terminal Plus. ■ Enter a customer's credit card information manually or purchase an optional card reader from Intuit. The card reader attaches to your computer, so you can swipe credit cards and qualify for lower "card swiped" transaction rates. ■ Record and process a payment in QuickBooks from the Receive Payments or Enter Sales Receipts window. Select "Process credit card payment when saving" in this window to send the charge to the QuickBooks Merchant Account Service for processing. You'll receive prompt notification when the payment has been approved. ■ Receive a statement of the payments that have been deposited to your bank account. ■ To learn more about applying for the QuickBooks Merchant Account Service, from the Customers menu, choose Accept Credit Card Payments, and then Process Credit Card Payments.
QuickBook Billing Solutions	■ E-mail invoices, statements, and estimates directly from QuickBooks. Your forms are sent as PDF attachments, so they look just like what you would print in QuickBooks. ■ Receive payments online from your customers. Your customer can click a link in the e-mail message to pay the invoice or statement online. You decide which payment methods you will accept. You can be paid by credit card through the QuickBooks Merchant Account Service. ■ Receive notification in QuickBooks and by e-mail whenever online payments have been made, and download the payments with a single click. ■ Track when your e-mailed forms are viewed by customers. ■ Send automatic payment reminders for outstanding invoices. ■ Provide customers with an online Customer Account Center for viewing their account information on the Web. To sign up for QuickBooks Billing Solutions, from the Customers menu, choose Billing Solutions - Set Options Online.

To learn about...	Look in the Help Index for...
QuickBooks Merchant Account Service	merchant account service
QuickBooks BIlling Solutions	online billing of customers

Receiving payments and making deposits

Depending on your type of business or organization, your deposits might include payments from customers, gifts from donors, loans from family members, investment money from partners, down payments, tax refunds, or other income. Before you enter any income in QuickBooks, review a recent bank statement.

For ease of reconciliation, you'll want to *imitate* your bank statement in terms of how you receive payments and make deposits in QuickBooks. For example, if your bank statement shows a lump sum for a deposit, you should enter your payments (in the Receive Payments or Enter Sales Receipts windows) and choose to "Group with other undeposited funds" for later deposit; if the statement shows each individual check and merchant charge deposited, you should choose to deposit directly to the account.

Note: To take advantage of QuickBooks' reconciliation features, Merchant Account Service users must select the "Group with other undeposited funds" option in the Receive Payments window or the Enter Sales Receipts window.

Additionally, if your bank separates credit card and check deposits on your bank statement, you can mirror this process using the "View payment method type" filter on the Payments to Deposit window.

Note: Always list all merchant credit card payments that have been processed in one deposit transaction and your checks and cash in another.

?

To learn about...	Look in the Help Index for...
Receiving payments	receiving payments, about
Separating deposits by payment method	deposits, separating by payment method
Making deposits	deposits, bank or checking account
Finding a particular deposit	deposits, viewing a list of
Editing or deleting a deposited payment	deposits, editing
Reminders to make deposits	deposits, reminding yourself to make

Dealing with nonpayment income

For income you receive that is not a customer payment, you can enter the deposit in the Make Deposits window.

In this example, a nonprofit organization is depositing a day's donations.

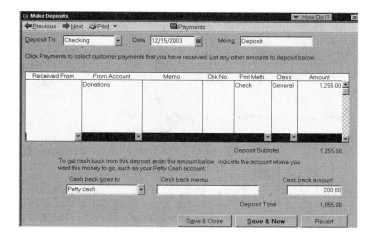

Cash back from your deposit

If you need cash back from your deposit, you can specify the necessary account and amount using the Make Deposits window.

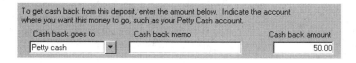

To learn about...	Look in the Help Index for...
Getting cash back from a deposit	deposits, cash back

Printing deposit slips and summaries

Before you take your deposit to the bank, you can print a deposit slip and/or deposit summary that lists customer payments made by cash or check, other income received by cash or check, and any cash back that you will receive.

Note: You do not need to print deposit slips for merchant credit card payments you enter in the Payments to Deposit window.

Printable deposit slips, along with a complete selection of printable checks, are available through Intuit. To order printable deposit slips, choose Help & Support from the Help menu. Under Contact Intuit, choose Phone Directory, and then Checks and Supplies.

To learn about...	Look in the Help Index for...
Printing deposit slips and summaries	deposit slips

Once-a-month activities

Handling fees and interest earned on accounts

Generally, you'll enter these fees, surcharges, and interest earned on an account when you receive the account's monthly bank statement or when you reconcile the account.

- Bank accounts (checking, savings, money market)

  Enter **bank service charges** and **interest earned** when you reconcile your bank accounts (using the Reconcile window), or you can enter them directly into the account's register.

  Be sure to add any **ATM surcharges** you incur during the course of the month to your checking account register.

- Credit card accounts

  You must enter any **finance charges** if you carry a balance forward. The charge can be added to the account's register or in the **Finance Charges** field when you reconcile the account.

  If the card has an **annual fee**, enter this fee directly in the account register.

- Merchant account fees

  Enter any monthly fees for your merchant account service in your expense account.

To learn about...	Look in the Help Index for...
Entering a fee or interest in a register	registers, entering transactions in

Reconciling bank and credit card accounts

You should plan to reconcile your bank (checking, savings, and money market accounts) and credit card statements on a regular basis to make sure your records and the bank's agree.

Situation	What to do in QuickBooks
You haven't reconciled these accounts for a month or more.	Reconcile each month you skipped. Balance each month separately, starting with your earliest statement since you've been using QuickBooks, through your most recent statement.
You added earlier transactions in QuickBooks.	After you add earlier transactions, and you want to reconcile past months, you should reconcile month by month only if you've never used the QuickBooks reconcile feature.
	However, if you've already reconciled one or more months, you should reconcile forward only, that is, reconcile months after your start date. Use the previous months' data for reporting only. You need to mark all older transactions as cleared to reconcile future months.
You are reconciling for the first time.	Enter all uncleared transactions in your account.
	Update the Opening Balance transaction to reflect the amount actually in your account when you began using QuickBooks.
You cancel in the middle of reconciling.	QuickBooks keeps track of the items you've marked as cleared with an asterisk (*) in the cleared column of the account's register. This indicates that the items are still pending and reconciliation wasn't complete.
	When you start reconciling again, you'll need to re-enter your ending balance and your service charges and interest earned. You'll also need to check off additional payments and deposits.

When you reconcile, be sure to add any bank service charges, interest earned, and finance charges.

To learn about...	Look in the Help Index for...
Reconciling a bank account	reconciling, bank statements
Reconciling a credit card account	reconciling, credit card statements
Adjusting for differences	reconciling, adjusting for differences

Matching bank deposits and credit card deposits (Merchant Account Service users)

As a Merchant Account Service user, you can use QuickBooks to help match your customers' credit card payments with the lump sum deposit on your bank statement, as well as account for banking fees.

To do this, in the Receive Payments or Enter Sales Receipts window, select the "Group with other undeposited funds" option.

In the Make Deposits window, you can display credit card payments views grouped by credit card type, which lets you see the individual credit card transactions that make up each lump sum deposit.

Often, the bank deposit total is less than the payments you received from individual customers due to credit card transaction fees. QuickBooks calculates the difference for you automatically and lets you assign the transaction fee to an expense account.

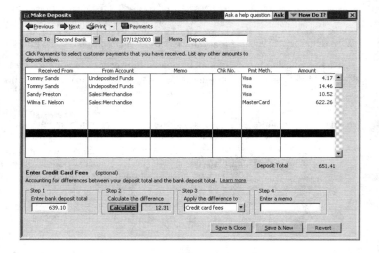

Reconciling online accounts

Reconciling your online accounts is a three-phase process.

1 To download your transactions, go to the Online Banking Center, select your financial institution from the drop-down list, and Click "Go Online."

2 Match transactions.

   View a QuickStatement for the account. The QuickStatement includes all transactions that have cleared your financial institution since the last time you downloaded, including deposits, checks, transfers, and ATM withdrawals, as well as any transactions that were downloaded previously but not been matched.

   When you click View, QuickBooks automatically matches downloaded transactions to those in your account register. For the unmatched transactions, select one of the transactions from the downloaded statement, click Add to Register, and follow the onscreen prompts until the transaction appears in the register. Assign an account from the Account Drop Down list and click Record to enter the transaction in the register.

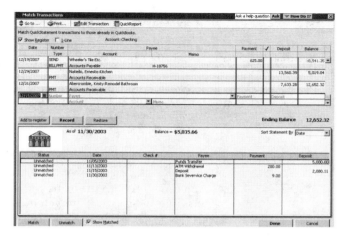

3 When you receive your bank statement for the account, use the Reconcile window.

Note: With QuickBooks, you can reconcile only to the paper statement you receive from your financial institution. With Quicken, you can reconcile to either the online or paper statement.

To learn about...	Look in the Help Index for...
Downloading and matching online transactions	transactions, online
Account reconciliation	■ reconciling, bank statements ■ reconciling, credit card statements

As-needed activities

Obtaining up-to-date account information

Through online account access, you can obtain up-to-date account balance or activity information. You can find out which checks have cleared and verify that deposits have been posted.

To learn about...	Look in the Help Index for...
Getting up-to-date account information	online banking, balances

Transferring funds

From time to time, you may need to transfer money from one account to another.

Task	Comments	Search Help index for...
Making transfers between online accounts at the same bank	■ Enter the transfer in QuickBooks. ■ Send the transfer.	transferring funds, between online accounts
Making transfers between accounts (not online)	■ Complete the transfer at the bank; usually this can be handled with a phone call. ■ Enter the transfer in QuickBooks.	transferring funds, between balance sheet accounts

Tracking loans

You can track both the loans you receive from lending institutions and the loans you make to customers.

■ For loans your business receives, use a liability account.

> Note: If you take out a loan to pay for a new asset, such as a new vehicle for your business, the asset account (for the vehicle) and the liability account (for the loan) are not connected in QuickBooks in any way.

■ For loans you make to customers, use another asset account.

To learn about...	Look in the Help Index for...
Adding a loan account	loans, setting up
Tracking a loan for an asset	loans, paying for assets
Tracking loan payments (reporting on the principal and interest paid)	loans, recording a payment on
Depositing loan money	loans, depositing money
Loans to customers	loans, customer

Handling a customer's bounced check, bad debt, and chargeback

When a customer's check bounces, you need a way to record both the adjustment to your bank account (including any bank charges) and that the customer owes you the amount of the check (plus any penalties or fees you want to impose). If the amount becomes uncollectable, you'll need to write it off as bad debt.

You can record a chargeback from a customer's credit card in two ways. You can process the transaction as a return/refund or you can record it as a business expense, such as a bad debt or return expense. Either way, a chargeback transaction shows up on your bank statement as a separate item.

To learn about...	Look in the Help Index for...
Handling a customer's bounced check	bounced checks
Writing off bad debt	bad debts
Recording chargebacks	merchant account service, chargebacks

Depositing employment taxes

You can deposit your employment taxes with your coupon (Form 8109) to an authorized financial institution or Federal Reserve Bank. These coupons can also be mailed.

Contact the IRS (**www.irs.gov**) for more information. Their Web site has downloadable publications, forms, and small business information.

Sending and viewing online messages

With QuickBooks, you can send messages to any financial institution at which you have accounts enabled for online banking. For example, you might want to send a message to:

- Inquire about account activity
- Inquire about a payment
- Obtain interest rate or fee information
- Request a loan application

To learn about...	Look in the Help Index for...
Sending and viewing online messages	online payments, inquiring about

Modifying online account information

Your QuickBooks account information must be identical to the information on record with your financial institution.

You might need to change the account information in one or both places:

- In the Enable Accounts portion of the Online Banking Setup Interview
- In the Online Info tab of the Edit Account window (go to the Chart of Accounts, click the Account menu button, choose Edit, then click the Online Info tab)

To learn about...	Look in the Help Index for...
Modifying an online account	online banking, editing online account information

ITEMS—YOUR SERVICES,
PRODUCTS, FIXED ASSETS,
AND MORE

QuickBooks uses *items* to keep track of the services and products that are your source of income and the fixed assets that make up your business. It also has special items to make it easy to do calculations on your sales forms (for example, discounts or sales tax). When you use items, you save time typing, allow QuickBooks to do the calculations and keep track of your business assets and income.

Why you probably need to set up items

Items for what you sell

If your business provides a service—writing, haircutting, consulting, legal advice, house painting, or any other service—you may charge by the hour and list the number of hours and your rate on your sales forms. Or, you may simply charge a flat rate for the service.

If your business sells products or parts, you probably list them on sales forms that you give your customers.

In QuickBooks, both kinds of businesses—service and product—can benefit by setting up items to track the services they provide or the products they sell to customers.

Note: **In QuickBooks, "sales" is a broad term.** It refers to any business action that generates income in exchange for services or products, even if you don't think of what you do as selling. For example, a psychologist with patients, a graphic designer with clients, and a roofing contractor with customers all would set up items in QuickBooks for what they sell.

Benefits of setting up items

Here are some specific benefits of setting up items:

- You can use sales forms in QuickBooks to track the details of how your business earns its income. Estimates and all sales forms—invoices, sales receipts, credit memos—require items. So do QuickBooks statement charges, which print on statements.

  (If you're a professional, you may not think of your statements as sales forms, but they are.)

- You can fill out sales forms or enter statement charges quickly. QuickBooks automatically enters the description and rate or price you entered in the item's setup window. When you enter a quantity, QuickBooks calculates the amount.

- When you record a sale (remember, it can be for a service), QuickBooks automatically tracks the income in the appropriate income account. You can fill out a sales form (or enter a statement charge), keep track of your sales, and keep track of income—all in one step.

- You can create reports that show total units of each service or product sold as well as dollar amount totals.

If you're still not sure you need items

Here are some examples of businesses or organizations that use items:

- Rebecca is the bookkeeper for a country club where members sign for meals, drinks, and fees and receive a statement at the end of the month. Rebecca uses items in QuickBooks for each of these. She uses the items to enter statement charges for each member and create monthly statements.

- Mario is a dentist. He has items set up for the various services he provides to his patients: cleaning, x-rays, filling cavities, and so on.

In contrast, some businesses or organizations probably don't need items. Here are some examples:

- John is keeping the books for his church. The church has members who pledge and contribute money, but the church doesn't sell anything or charge for specific services, so John doesn't need to create any sales forms.

- Marina does facials in her home evenings and weekends. Her clients pay at the time of their visit. Marina simply wants to track the income received. She doesn't care to track in QuickBooks how many facials she gives or to whom.

- Rick is a commissioned sales representative. He takes orders for a manufacturer that then invoices the customers directly. Rick tracks the orders in a spreadsheet, not QuickBooks, because the sales are income for the manufacturer, not Rick. When Rick receives a commission check, he enters it in QuickBooks as a deposit.

Items for services or products you purchase

Once you've decided to set up items for the services or products you sell, you might want to use items for the services and products you purchase.

If you purchase products or parts for resale, keep them in inventory, and then sell them, be sure to read Chapter 12, *Inventory,* beginning on page 149. It will help you decide whether to track inventory in QuickBooks.

If you purchase services or products for a specific customer or job, QuickBooks Pro and Premier allow you to set up items that you can use for both purchases and sales. See "Items for reimbursable costs in QuickBooks Pro and Premier Editions" on page 86.

On the other hand, if you don't have QuickBooks Pro or Premier and you don't track inventory, you should not use the same items for both purchases and sales. Instead, use items for entering sales only.

If you purchase property such as buildings, vehicles, computers, or heavy machinery that will contribute to the operating capacity of your company for several years, QuickBooks Pro and Premier enable you to set up items that can help you track their *depreciation.* You need to track the depreciation of such fixed assets both for tax purposes and to get an accurate accounting of the worth of your business. Your accountant can give you more information about using fixed asset items to record purchases and subsequent sales of fixed assets.

Deciding how items should affect accounts

When you set up most items, you must specify which account it should affect when you use the item on a sale or purchase. Then, when you record the sale or purchase, each item on it affects the appropriate account.

In other words, while you are recording the items on a sale or purchase, QuickBooks is adjusting all the right accounts behind the scenes.

Which are the right accounts? If you sell an item, you normally associate an income account with it. If you purchase the same item, QuickBooks Pro or Premier provides a way to associate a second account, usually an expense account, to be used on purchases. See "Items for reimbursable costs in QuickBooks Pro and Premier Editions" on page 86. (Inventory items each have three different accounts, as explained in "Accounts for tracking inventory" on page 154.) If you purchase a fixed asset, you normally associate a fixed asset account with it. When you sell a fixed asset, you normally associate a fixed asset account with the asset.

Before you set up your items, you have to decide how much detail from your sales and purchases needs to show up in reports about your accounts. (The profit and loss statement, for example, is a report on your income and expense accounts.)

You can see details of your sales (such as number of units and dollar amount of each item sold) on the QuickBooks sales reports. You don't need to have the same level of detail on your profit and loss statement. For example:

- Cynthia has a single income account for all sales income. She doesn't want to see any further breakdown on her profit and loss statement, and she doesn't need it for her tax returns.

- Derek, on the other hand, wants to split up income from services and income from materials he buys for a job and then puts on the customer's invoice. Thus, he uses one income account for all his service items and a second income account for all his non-inventory part items (for his materials). Like Cynthia, he has far more items than income accounts.

How many different items do you need?

Every business is different, but knowing how QuickBooks works can help you decide how specific your items should be.

First, once you use an item in a transaction, you can never delete the item unless you delete the transaction or condense your file to remove old transactions and old items. Fixed asset items are not condensed. Thus, if you sell unique items or a rapidly changing assortment of items, you probably want to use more general items. If the prices vary, you can enter prices on the sales form.

For example, Tomas has a men's clothing store. Because his inventory of styles changes so much, he doesn't use QuickBooks to track inventory. To track his sales, he has more general items such as Suit, Sports Jacket, Dress Shirt.

On the other hand, if you have two standard services or products that are similar except for their rate or price, you can save time recording sales by having a separate item for each. Then QuickBooks can fill in the correct rate or price on the sales form.

For example, Mali employs three stylists in her beauty salon. When she cuts a client's hair, she charges more than the rate for a haircut by one of the employees. So she has two separate items for haircuts.

You can change the rate or price of any item at any time. You don't have to create a new item in order to raise your prices.

In QuickBooks Pro and Premier, you can create price levels to increase or decrease inventory, noninventory, and service item prices. Use them on sales forms to automatically adjust the price of an item. Price levels can be created for any customer with whom you have a special relationship.

Finally, if there are items you purchase but never sell but that are **not** fixed assets (supplies for your office, for example), you probably shouldn't bother to put them on your Item lists. They will lengthen your list, and you'll find it harder to pick out the items that you do sell. However, if you plan on using QuickBooks purchase orders, you'll need to set up the items you purchase, even though they are only for your office use.

Setting up items

This section is about adding items to QuickBooks. You can add items at any time—as part of setting up QuickBooks or whenever you think of an item you need to use.

Remember, items are for the services or items you buy and sell. You also may need special calculating items that calculate subtotals and discounts, and that apply specific sales tax rates.

The EasyStep Interview helps you set up a few items, so you may already have some items. Fixed asset items are not set up in the EasyStep Interview.

Where to find information about your items

When you set up an item, you enter information you can use over and over again without retyping, such as the following:

- Name or code
- Description
- Price per unit or rate per hour, if applicable
- For items you sell, the income account to assign income from the sale; for items you purchase, the expense account for purchases of the item

QuickBooks stores information about your items on the Item list.

On the Item list, items are in order of item type.

Within the same item type, they are usually in alphabetical (or numerical) order, but you can change this order.

Subitems are indented under the parent item.

Use the menu buttons to add, edit, sort, or perform other activities on items.

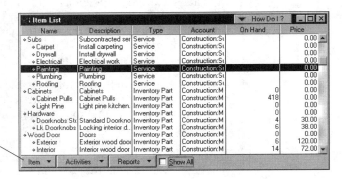

Information about fixed assets is available in the Fixed Asset Item List.

When assets are exchanged using Fixed Asset Manager (FAM), QuickBooks displays a value in the FAM Number column. If FAM has not exchanged data with the Fixed Asset Item List, the FAM Number column will be blank, as shown in the 2007 deliver van entry.

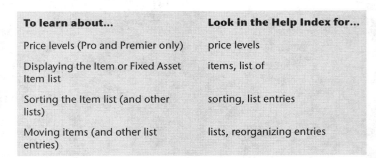

To learn about...	Look in the Help Index for...
Price levels (Pro and Premier only)	price levels
Displaying the Item or Fixed Asset Item list	items, list of
Sorting the Item list (and other lists)	sorting, list entries
Moving items (and other list entries)	lists, reorganizing entries

Types of QuickBooks items

In addition to items for services or products, QuickBooks has several other types of items. This section explains what each type of QuickBooks item is designed to do.

 Use one of the Part item types for any product, not just a part of another product. If you decide to use QuickBooks inventory to track your products, set up inventory parts for them. Otherwise, set up non-inventory parts for your products.

Item type	Use for...	Usual effect on accounts	Comments
Service	Services you charge for or services you purchase **Examples:** professional fees, labor	▪ On sale: Increases income. ▪ On purchase: Increases expenses.	In QuickBooks Pro and Premier, you can set up a service item so that it can affect either income or expenses, depending on where you use it. Price levels can be used on service items
Inventory Part	Products you purchase, track as inventory, and then resell **Examples:** Electrical outlets, T-shirts	▪ On sale: Increases income, increases cost of goods sold, and decreases inventory assets. ▪ On purchase: Increases inventory assets.	Available only if the inventory feature is turned on. Read "Is QuickBooks inventory right for my business?" on page 149 before deciding whether to track inventory in QuickBooks. Price levels can be used with inventory parts.
Inventory Assembly	Assembled products you purchase or create and build, track as inventory, and then resell **Examples:** Gift baskets, Soaker hose starter kits	▪ On sale: Increases income, increases cost of goods sold, and decreases inventory assets. ▪ On purchase: increases inventory assets.	QuickBooks Premier Edition(s) required to create and build inventory assemblies. Available only if the inventory feature is turned on. Appropriate for "light" assembled items; QuickBooks does not track inventory through the manufacturing process. Price levels can be used with inventory assemblies.
Non-inventory Part	Products you sell but do not purchase; items you purchase and resell but do not track as inventory; items you enter on purchase orders **Examples:** Custom-made slipcovers	▪ On sale: Increases income. ▪ On purchase: Increases expenses.	In QuickBooks Pro and Premier you can set up a non-inventory part item so that it can affect either income or expenses, depending on where you use it. Price levels can be used with non-inventory parts.

Item type	Use for...	Usual effect on accounts	Comments
Fixed Asset	Property that will contribute to the operating capacity of your company for several years **Examples:** Vehicles, Computers, Heavy machinery	■ On sale: Decreases assets. ■ On purchase: Increases assets.	In QuickBooks Pro and Premier you can create fixed asset items; in QuickBooks Basic you can view fixed asset items in the Item list and edit or delete transactions in which they're found, but you cannot create them.
Other Charge	Other charges on a sale or a purchase **Examples:** Shipping charge, delivery charge, finance charge	■ On sale: Increases income. ■ On purchase: Increases expenses.	In QuickBooks Pro and Premier you can set up an other charge item so that it can affect either income or expenses, depending on where you use it. Can be either a percentage or a flat amount.
Subtotal	Calculating and printing a subtotal on sales forms	Subtotal items have no effect on accounts.	On sales forms, if you want to apply a discount or add a percentage charge to several items at once, subtotal first.
Group	Fast entry of a group of individual items already on the list **Example:** A group of services and food items provided by a caterer.	Each item in the group affects the same account it affects when used by itself.	Available for either sales or purchases.
Discount	Calculating an amount to be subtracted from a total or subtotal **Example:** A 10% discount given to nonprofit organizations.	Either decreases income or increases expenses (depending on item setup).	Available for sales forms only; not available for statement charges or purchase forms.
Payment	■ On invoices: Payment received at the time of invoicing, so that amount owed on invoice is reduced ■ On sales receipts summaries: To show totals for each type of payment (cash, checks, credit card charges)	Increases the balance of either a specific checking account or the account for undeposited funds (depending on item setup).	Available for sales forms only; not available for statement charges or purchase forms.
Sales Tax	Calculating a single tax or tracking special sales like out-of-state sales Available only if the sales tax feature is turned on (see "Setting up sales tax" on page 195)	Increases the balance in the Sales Tax Liability account.	Available for sales forms only; not available for statement charges or purchase forms.

Item type	Use for...	Usual effect on accounts	Comments
Sales Tax Group	Calculating two or more sales taxes grouped together and applied to the same sale Available only if the sales tax feature is turned on (see "Setting up sales tax" on page 195)	Increases the balance in the Sales Tax Liability account.	Available for sales forms only; not available for statement charges or purchase forms.

Items that calculate

The table of items includes some items used to perform a calculation on one or more lines above it on a sales form.

For example, if you need to subtotal on sales forms, then you need a subtotal item. A subtotal item adds the amounts of the items above it on the sales form and enters the subtotal on the form.

If you have to add sales tax to your sales forms, then you need at least one sales tax item. (You need one for each separate district you collect tax for.)

Finally, there are some items that can be set up either as percentages or with flat amounts, depending on what you need. For example, Carol adds a 10 percent service charge to her invoices. She has set up an other charge item with a rate of 10 percent. She uses a subtotal item before the service charge, so that the 10 percent will be based on the subtotal amount.

Steve gives a 15 percent discount to certain customers. He has set up a discount item with a rate of 15 percent. He also uses a subtotal item, so that the discount will be based on the subtotal amount.

For examples of how to use items that calculate, see page 90 for subtotals, page 92 for discounts, and page 200 for sales tax.

Subitems vs. group and inventory assembly items

Just as you can set up an account with related subaccounts under it on your chart of accounts, you can have an item with related subitems. For example, Cherril keeps the books for her symphony association's gift shop, which sells T-shirts and other items. She has an item called T-shirts and subitems called Adult and Child, each with its own price.

Subitems enable you to put similar items together on your Item list, so you can locate them easily on the drop-down list in any **Item** field. Each subitem can have its own rate or price and its own description. Each subitem can even have its own account, although you would probably assign the same account to all subitems of the same parent item.

In this example, Hardware is a parent item with two subitems under it.

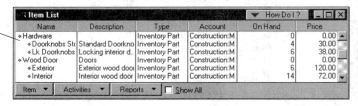

On sales forms, you use subitems the same way you use other items. On reports based on items, QuickBooks subtotals each group of subitems.

Group and inventory assembly items have a completely different purpose from subitems. Group and assembly items allow you to enter a group of items—that is, several different items—at once on a sale or purchase. Group items are appropriate for combining several types of items, such as catering services and food items, on one line in a sales receipt. For an example of entering a group of items, see page 90. Assembly items, available in QuickBooks Premier Edition(s), are appropriate for indicating products you combine and sell as a unit, such as a gift basket containing one wicker basket and three jars of homemade jam.

You cannot group fixed assets or make them subitems of other items.

Adding items to your Item or Fixed Asset Item list

As the table starting on page 81 shows, QuickBooks has 12 different item types. Here is some general information about what to enter for most types of items when adding a new item to your Item or Fixed Asset Item list.

Information to enter	How QuickBooks uses this information
Type of item	After you choose the item type, QuickBooks requests only the information it requires for that particular item type.**(Note**: You cannot create fixed asset items from the Item list. Use the Fixed Asset Item list to do so.)
	After you set up an item, depending on the type, you may not be able to change it to a different type.
Item name or code	Displays this name or number on reports of items and in the drop-down list in the **Item** field (for example, on sales forms).
Item description (optional on all but fixed assets)	Prefills the entire description in the **Description** field of sales or purchase forms.
	Displays the beginning of the description in the drop-down list in the **Item** field.
	You can set up some types of items to have separate descriptions for sales and for purchases.
Rate or price (optional)	Prefills the rate or price in the **Rate** or **Price** fields of sales or purchase forms.
	Some types of items can have a rate that is a percentage.
	You can set up some types of items to have separate rates or prices for sales and for purchases.
Account or accounts	Profit and loss statements report on the income or expense account associated with items used in transactions.
	You can set up some types of items to have separate accounts for sales and for purchases.
	Some types of items (for example, payment items) require a balance sheet account instead of an income or expense account. Inventory items require three separate accounts.
Taxability (required only if you collect sales tax)	If a taxable item is on a sales form and the customer is taxable, QuickBooks includes the item when calculating the sales tax.
Subitem status	If this field appears, you can make an item a subitem of an existing item. QuickBooks displays subitems of the same item together.
Custom fields (optional)	You can set up custom fields that fill your company's needs (for example, size or unit of measure). You can also customize sales and purchase forms to display a column for a custom field. Then QuickBooks prefills the column with the custom field information for the item.

To learn about...	Look in the Help index for...
Adding a new item for one of the following:	
■ A service	■ items, services
■ An assembled product that you purchase or build yourself	■ items, inventory assembly
■ A product or part that is not held in inventory	■ items, non-inventory parts
■ A fixed asset	■ items, fixed assets
■ A miscellaneous charge	■ items, miscellaneous charges

To learn about...	Look in the Help index for...
Adding a new item for a product or part held in inventory	items, inventory
Adding a new item that puts a group of several items on a sales or purchase form	items, grouped together
Adding a new item that calculates a subtotal	items, subtotal types
Adding a new item that calculates a discount on a sales form	items, discount types
Adding a new item that records a customer payment or deposit received at the time of sale	items, payment types
Adding a new item that calculates a sales tax for a single sales tax rate and single sales tax district	items, sales tax
Adding a new item that calculates the total sales tax for a combination of sales tax rates	items, sales tax
Creating subitems of another item	items, subitems
Creating custom fields for items	items, custom fields on
Turning sales tax on	sales tax, setting up

Items for reimbursable costs in QuickBooks Pro and Premier Editions

Perhaps your business purchases services or products for specific customers or jobs and then invoices the customer for the items (with or without markup). For example, Frank is a general contractor who uses subcontractors and invoices for their costs at a higher rate than what they charge him. Tina is an interior designer who buys furniture at wholesale and sells it to the client at retail.

In QuickBooks Pro and Premier Editions only, service items, non-inventory parts, and other charge items each have a checkbox that allows you to pass through their costs at a markup and track costs and revenues in separate accounts. Then you can track both the expenses and the income for these items for a particular job. (For example, the checkbox for a non-inventory part is "This item is purchased for and sold to a specific customer:job.")

Note: **If you don't have QuickBooks Pro or Premier, use expense accounts, not items, for reimbursable costs.** See "Reimbursable expenses in QuickBooks" on page 131.

There are several advantages to using items for reimbursable costs in QuickBooks Pro or Premier Editions:

- It is easy to associate the cost of an item with an expense account and the income with a separate income account when you set up the item.

- You can track the number of units or hours purchased or sold.

- You can use items on estimates and purchase orders.

- If you write a purchase order for an item, you can create a bill from the purchase order and assign a job. Then you can invoice the customer for the item.

- When you enter a bill, check, or credit card charge, QuickBooks Pro and Premier Editions fill in the description of the item and the unit cost after you choose the item from the drop-down list on the Items tab.

- When you invoice the customer for the cost of the item, QuickBooks Pro and Premier Editions fill in the sales description of the item and the sales price.

- You can create reports that compare costs to revenues for each item.

For more information on invoicing for reimbursable time and costs, see "Reimbursable time and costs in QuickBooks Pro and QuickBooks Premier" on page 132.

Services performed by subcontractors or owners

If you charge for services performed by outside subcontractors or you pay owners (or partners) for time worked, set up a service item for each type of service. Be sure to select the checkbox "This service is performed by a subcontractor, owner, or partner." Then you can designate separate income and expense (or equity) accounts, and separate descriptions for sales and purchases.

You can enter different hourly rates for your cost and the sales price to your customer. If you write checks based on time tracked or enter the item on a purchase order, purchase, or estimate, QuickBooks fills in the rate from the Cost field. If you enter the item on a sales form, QuickBooks fills in the rate from the Sales Price field. However, if the subcontracted service is usually billed as a flat fee, and the fee varies, leave the Cost and Sales Price fields 0.00 when you set up the item.

If you pay owners (or partners) and vendors for the same service, you need separate service items because the accounts for the costs must be different. See "Service items for the time data" on page 230.

Products and materials purchased for a job

If you invoice for actual costs of products and materials purchased for a specific customer or job, set up a non-inventory part item for each type of product or service. Be sure to select the checkbox for "This item is purchased for and sold to a specific customer:job." Then you can designate separate income and expense accounts, and separate descriptions for sales and purchases.

You can enter different rates for your cost and the sales price to your customer. However, if the cost of the product or material varies, leave the **Cost** and **Sales Price** fields 0.00 when you set up the non-inventory part item.

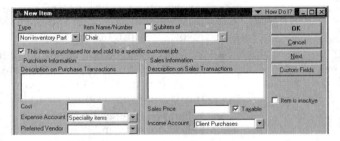

To further aid in tracking the item, you can also specify the customer and job on the purchase order. When you receive the item, this information will prefill on the item receipt or bill. You can use the open purchase orders by job report to find out which items are still on order for your customers.

Miscellaneous charges you pass on

If you invoice for miscellaneous charges incurred on a job, you can set up an other charge item for each type of miscellaneous charge. For example, Frank has an other charge item called Equipment Rental. Be sure to select the checkbox for "This is a reimbursable charge." Then you can designate separate income and expense accounts, and separate descriptions for sales and purchases.

As with products and materials, you can enter different cost and sales prices or leave the fields 0.00 when you set up the other charge item.

Working with items

After you have set up items, use them to enter estimates, sales, purchase orders, actual purchases, and disposition of fixed assets. Remember, QuickBooks uses the term *sales* broadly; it can mean the performance of services or the assessment of fees as well as the sale of products.

You can enter all 12 item types listed in the table on page 81 on any sales form. You can enter all but payment items on estimates. However, you can't enter the following item types on purchase orders or purchases (on the Items tab of bills, checks, and credit card charges):

- Other charge items set up as a percentage
- Discount items
- Payment items
- Sales tax items
- Sales tax groups

(To learn how to record discounts from vendors, enter payments to vendors, and enter sales tax for purchases, see Chapter 13, *Tracking and paying expenses,* beginning on page 167.)

Using items, saving time

When you fill out a sales form, you list each service, product, or fixed asset you're selling on its own line of the invoice or sales receipt, along with the amount the customer owes for that item. Similarly, when you write a purchase order or receive a bill, each service, product, or fixed asset is listed on its own line.

Because information about individual items is listed on separate lines, the items are called *line items.* In QuickBooks, you enter line items by choosing from the drop-down list in the **Item** field of a sales or purchase form. You can also type in the **Item** field and let QuickBooks fill in the rest of the item's name.

Enter an item in the **Item** field by typing or by choosing from the drop-down list.

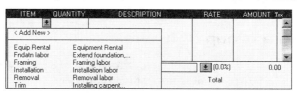

Each item on the Item list can contain all the information you need to fill in one line. You can always change the information, such as the description and rate, as you're filling in a form.

When you enter a quantity, QuickBooks automatically calculates the amount for you.

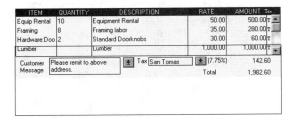

You'll have separate items not only for each service rendered and each product sold, but also for discounts, markups, sales taxes, and subtotals. If the customer makes a partial payment at the time of the sale, you can add an item for the payment.

Using items to subtotal on sales forms

The subtotal item adds up the amounts of the items above it, up to the last subtotal.

You'll need a subtotal item if you ever want to apply a percentage discount or surcharge to several items. Because QuickBooks calculates percentages on the line above, you'll need to subtotal the items before entering the percentage line item.

If you use two subtotals in a row, the last subtotal will add up all the previous subtotals on the form.

The first subtotal line shows a total for all materials.

The second subtotal shows a total for all labor.

This second subtotal also makes the third subtotal include all amounts on the invoice, so a percentage markup can apply to the total sale.

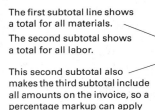

The third subtotal line adds up the two previous subtotals, so that a markup can be applied to the entire sale.

Entering a group of items

The group item allows you to enter several items all at once on a sales form, estimate, purchase order, check, or bill. If you often sell the same group of items together, using a group item saves you the trouble of entering the same set of line items again and again.

When you use a group item, you can enter a quantity for the group that affects the quantity and amount of each item in the group. You can also edit the individual quantity of each item in the group, and edit descriptions and rates.

Using a group item to hide details on a sales form

The more detailed you are in tracking items, the more information you can get from reports. The QuickBooks group item allows you to be very detailed in tracking the items you sell without showing all that detail to your customers. When you set up a group item, you specify whether to print each item or just the group item. (Of course, if you use a group item on a purchase order, you must show the detail to the vendor so the vendor will know what you want.)

For example, Frank has a construction company that sends invoices for full jobs, such as complete remodels. If he used one general service item called *Remodel*, a sales report would show his income from remodels.

If you use very general items, like this one, your reports won't be as useful as if you used detailed items grouped together.

However, Frank uses more detailed items, so he can learn more from his sales reports. Frank breaks down the remodel cost and uses items such as Lumber, Hardware, Markup, Carpentry Hours, and Laborer Hours.

He groups these items under one item called *Remodel*. Even though he chooses not to print the items in the group on the invoice for his customers to see, he still has those details on his sales reports.

QuickBooks shows you the items in the group onscreen, whether you choose to print them or not.

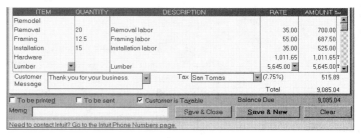

Applying a discount to one or more items

To apply a discount, you have to enter a discount item. If the discount item's rate is a percentage, the item reduces the amount due by a percentage of the line above it.

To take a percentage off several items at once, you must first subtotal the items. On the other hand, if you want to discount one particular item you've sold and not the entire sale, add a discount item directly beneath the one discounted item.

The first discount line follows a subtotal line, so that the discount percentage is calculated for all labor.

The second discount line applies only to one item, so a subtotal is not needed.

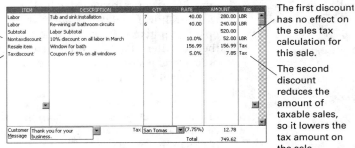

The first discount has no effect on the sales tax calculation for this sale.

The second discount reduces the amount of taxable sales, so it lowers the tax amount on the sale.

If you give discounts of different percentages, you can either set up a separate discount item for each percentage or edit the amount right on the sales form.

Don't use a discount item for discounts that you give for early payment.

Enter discounts for early payment through the Receive Payments window. See "Receiving and depositing payments" on page 126.

Showing partial payments received at the time of sale

If you receive a partial payment toward the amount of an invoice at the time you create the invoice, you'll need to enter a payment item.

The payment item tells QuickBooks to subtract the amount of the payment from the total invoice amount. To record the payment on the invoice, enter a payment item for the amount you've received after you've entered all the items sold.

Use a payment item when you receive a partial payment at or before the time you create the invoice.

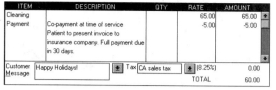

QuickBooks subtracts a payment item amount from the invoice total.

You can set up a payment item so that it automatically deposits the payment directly to a checking or other account. Alternatively, you can set it up so that QuickBooks automatically puts the payment amount into your Undeposited Funds account so you can deposit it with other funds. (See "Receiving and depositing payments" on page 126.)

If you need to track the payment method (check, cash, credit card charge), you can have different payment items for different methods of payment.

Using a payment item is not the only way to record a payment. For some types of payment, you should use a different method:

Type of payment	How to record in QuickBooks
Partial payment received at time of sale	Enter payment item on invoice.
Full payment received at time of sale	Use sales receipt, not invoice. No payment item is necessary, because QuickBooks assumes sale is fully paid.
Summary of payments, by method, for daily sales summary	Use sales receipt to summarize the daily sales. Enter a different payment item for the summary of each payment method.
Payment from customer to pay outstanding invoice or statement	Enter payment in Receive Payments window. Indicate which invoices or statement charges have been paid by the payment.
Advance payment from customer before work is done or sale is made.	Use *one* of the following options: ■ Enter payment in Receive Payments window. ■ Enter payment item on a credit memo. ■ Record a retainer. See the QuickBooks and Your Industry help for law firms, or Look in the Help Index for **retainers**.

Avoid entering double payments.

If you receive payment before the sale and record a deposit before you record the invoice, do not also enter a payment item on the invoice or you will record a double payment.

Adding sales tax to a sale

Sales tax varies greatly from region to region. Read Chapter 14, *Tracking and paying sales tax,* beginning on page 199, for a complete picture of how QuickBooks handles sales tax.

To have QuickBooks calculate the sales tax on your sales forms, do the following:

- Create the sales tax items or sales tax groups you need.
- Specify the sales tax item or group for each customer or job subject to sales tax.
- Identify whether each saleable item (service, non-inventory part, inventory part, other charge) or discount item is taxable by assigning a sales tax code.

Even though you use a sales tax item or sales tax group to specify a sales tax, you don't need to enter sales tax as a line item. Instead, sales tax has its own field at the bottom of the sales form.

On invoices, sales receipts, and credit memos, QuickBooks automatically displays the sales tax you have set up for the customer or job named on the sales form. QuickBooks calculates the correct tax and prints it on the sales form after all the other line items.

To learn about...	Look in the Help Index for...
Assigning a sales tax rate to a customer or job	sales tax, tax assignments
Identifying an item as taxable	sales tax, identifying which items are taxable
Applying a different tax from the one displayed on the sales form	invoices, sales tax on

Changing prices or rates

You can change the prices or rates of many items at one time through the Change Item Prices window. In this window you can tell QuickBooks to raise (or lower) prices or rates by a specified amount or percentage. You can change prices or rates for items individually, or have QuickBooks calculate new prices or rates on several or all items of the same type at once.

If you want to automatically apply an increase or decrease to inventory, non-inventory, and service items, you can use price levels. Price levels allow you to automatically adjust, up or down, the amount charged to customers with whom you have a special relationship. When you apply a price level to an item, QuickBooks calculates the rate to reflect the increase or decrease.

To learn about...	Look in the Help Index for...
Changing prices or rates of items	items, prices
Price levels	price levels

Editing item information

After you've created an item, you can edit information about it at any time, subject to certain restrictions.

Changing item type

In QuickBooks Basic, Pro, and Premier, you can change a non-inventory part or other charge item to a service, non-inventory part, inventory part, or other charge item. However, you cannot change the item type of any other type of item.

Hiding and redisplaying items on lists

You can hide an item on the Item or Fixed Asset Item list without deleting it by making the item inactive. For example, you may have an inventory item on your Item list that you have not stocked in the last six months, but which you may want to stock in the future.

When you make an item inactive, QuickBooks keeps the information associated with that item, but hides the item on the Item list and removes it from any drop-down lists that use items. You do not need to change or delete any transaction that uses the item. If you start to use the item again, you can make it active at any time.

You can display all your items, including the inactive ones, on the Item list by selecting Show All. (Inactive items still appear on reports, but never display on drop-down lists.)

Deleting items

You can delete an item only if it is not used in any transaction or group item. To locate all transactions that use a given item, create a QuickReport for the item for all dates.

If you condense your QuickBooks data through a specified date (to reduce the file size and remove detail), you can also remove items that are not used after that date. Fixed asset items are not condensed.

To learn about...	Look in the Help Index for...
Changing item type	items, changing type of
Changing information about an item	items, editing information
Hiding and showing items on the Item list and drop-down lists in **Item** fields	items, hiding and showing
Making hidden items visible on the Item list as well as on drop-down lists	lists, hiding and showing
Deleting items	items, deleting

QuickBooks uses the word *customer* to mean any person, business, or group that buys or pays for the services or products that your business or organization sells or provides. By entering information about customers, you save time entering customer transactions later—and you can get reports about them.

Should I track customers and jobs?

What does QuickBooks mean by a customer?

customer

Any person, business, or group that buys or pays for the services or products that your business or organization sells or provides.

In QuickBooks, a customer can be any of the following:

- A person or company that buys products from your retail business

- A company that buys products from your wholesale business

- A client of your consultant business or law firm

- A patient of your medical or dental practice

- A homeowner who buys your home repair or remodeling services

- A condominium owner who pays fees to your condo association

- A renter who pays rent to your real-estate management firm

Some businesses don't need to keep track of the names of customers. An example is a retail store or service business that always receives payment with the sale or service.

However, here are some situations in which you would want to keep track of customer names:

- Customers receive your goods or services and then pay you later.
- Customers are supposed to pay a regular monthly fee, and you want to track who has paid and who hasn't.
- You want to track income (and perhaps expenses as well) by customer.

If you are using QuickBooks for an organization that receives money but doesn't really sell anything, you probably don't need to set up customers. For example, a nonprofit or religious organization with members making contributions or paying dues can simply track the deposits without making the members customers. Specialized membership software can keep track of membership details such as pledges, contribution history, and names of family members.

What does QuickBooks mean by a job?

job

A project done for a particular customer.

In QuickBooks, a job is a project done for a particular customer. You must always associate a job with a customer. Use jobs if you do (or expect to do) more than one job for the same customer. For example, Jan does freelance writing for a large company that supplies a separate purchase order for each job. Hank's plumbing business has to keep track of the separate jobs it does for a general contractor.

On the other hand, if your company never does more than one job per customer, or you do not want to track individual jobs, you don't have to enter job names. For example, Doug's printing company refers to each customer order as a "job." However, even though Doug gets repeat business from customers, all he cares about is whether the customer has paid, so he doesn't need to set up jobs for his customers.

Besides using projects for jobs, you can be creative. For example:

- If you manage several apartment buildings, set up the building addresses as customers and the individual apartments as jobs.
- If you invoice against purchase orders, set up each purchase order number as a job.
- If you have a practice or organization that sends one statement to a family to cover individual members of the family, set up the family members as jobs.
- If you have multiple estimates per customer, see the tip in "Estimates and proposals" on page 121.

QuickBooks reports about jobs apply to customers as well. You don't have to set up jobs in order to use these reports. For example, the profit and loss by job report actually applies to both customers and jobs. If you have customers but not jobs, you will still see information about your customers.

If you set up customers and jobs in QuickBooks

When you set up a customer or job in QuickBooks, you enter information you can use over and over again, without retyping, for the following tasks:

- Fast entry of name, address, payment terms, and tax status on invoices and other sales forms
- Tracking payments received and amounts owed
- Contacting customers with overdue balances, including merging names, addresses, and balance information with Microsoft® Word letters
- Reporting of sales or income by customer, profit and loss by job, and profit and loss budget vs. actual by job
- Tracking reimbursable expenses by customer and job
- Printing mailing labels

Note: If you use ACT! or Microsoft Outlook® contact management software to store customer data, you can transfer basic customer information (such as name, address, phone, and so on) from your contact manager to QuickBooks Pro or Premier and vice versa. See "Sharing QuickBooks Pro and Premier information with your contact manager" on page 298.

If you charge your customers sales tax

QuickBooks allows you to assign the appropriate sales tax (such as for a particular county) to each customer. When you enter the customer name on a QuickBooks sales form, the correct sales tax shows up on the form.

Classifying customers and jobs

Both customer types and job types are completely optional. They allow you to get additional information on reports.

Customer types

If your business wants to be able to report on types of customers, you have the option of assigning a customer type to your customers. Then you can filter (restrict) reports to customers of a particular type or group of types, create mailing labels for customers of one type or of certain types, or choose to print statements for all customers of one type. For example:

- Laura wants to know whether her interior design business is earning more money from its residential clients or its corporate clients. She assigns her customers to one of these types: Residential or Corporate. Then she can filter her profit and loss report for one customer type at a time and compare the profits for the two customer types.

- Hugh is a portrait photographer. Every October he mails a brochure to previous customers who have come in for family portraits to remind them to get updated portraits for holiday greeting cards or gifts.

Job types

Job types (available only in QuickBooks Pro or QuickBooks Premier) are useful as an additional way of filtering information on reports. Use job types to classify your jobs differently from customer types. For example:

- Tony, a construction contractor, uses customer types such as Residential and Commercial. In addition, he wants to compare profits for job types such as:
  - Kitchen Remodels
  - Bath Remodels
  - Decks
  - New Houses
  - New Commercial Buildings
  - Restaurant Remodels

- Connie, a freelance writer, classifies customers with customer types such as Corporate, Startup, Retail, or Nonprofit. In addition, she wants to compare income from job types such as:
  - Writing Business Plans
  - Writing Brochures

 Do you want to learn more about using customer and job types in your business? Choose Optimizing QuickBooks for Your Industry from the Help menu. Then select the industry type closest to your own.

Defining custom fields for customers

To track additional information about your customers, you can define up to seven custom fields. For example, you might want to define fields for:

- Web site address
- Spouse's name
- Birthday

After you add custom fields, you can customize your sales forms to include these fields. You can also display and filter for customized field data in your reports. See "Customizing a form's content" on page 51.

Setting up customers and jobs

You may have already used the EasyStep Interview to set up customers and jobs that had open balances as of your QuickBooks start date. You should also set up any customers who owed you money between your QuickBooks start date and today. As your business gains new customers, you should add them as well.

If you want to transfer customer information from ACT! or Microsoft Outlook contact management software to get you started, see "Sharing QuickBooks Pro and Premier information with your contact manager" on page 298.

Setting up customers

You'll use the New Customer window when you set up a customer. Enter as much or as little information as you need to get started. If you don't have all the information now, you can add it later.

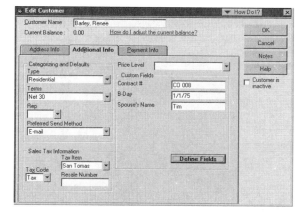

What to set up	Comments	See...
Sales tax (if you collect it from customers)	Before you can assign a sales tax to a customer, you must first set up your sales tax rates.	■ "Setting up sales tax" on page 195 for information about setting up sales tax ■ In the Help Index: sales tax, setting up
Customer types (optional)	Customer types provide you with another way of categorizing your customer base.	In the Help Index: customers, types
Customers	Refer to the following table"Customer information and how it's used in QuickBooks" to help you decide what information to add.	In the Help Index: customers, adding new
Custom fields for customers	Use these fields to record additional information about the customer, like a spouse's name. Once you've set up the custom fields for one customer, the fields will appear for all customers.	In the Help Index: custom fields, for customers, vendors, or employees
Preference to track expenses by customer and job (QuickBooks Pro and Premier only)	In QuickBooks, when you first install the program, you are set up to track expenses by customer and job. However, there is a preference that allows you to turn this feature on and off. If your Write Checks and Enter Bills windows do not have a Customer:Job column, the feature is off. QuickBooks Pro and Premier are automatically set up to track expenses by customer and job.	In the Help Index: preferences, accounting

Customer information and how it's used in QuickBooks

Information needed	How QuickBooks uses this information
Customer name (short) or number	■ Displays on Customer:Job list; sorted alphabetically (or numerically) ■ Displays on all drop-down lists where you choose the customer (for example, on sales forms) ■ Displays on all reports that are by customer or that show the customer name on a transaction
Company name, title, first and last name (optional)	■ Exports to mail merge file for use with word processor ■ Prefills the name in the **Bill To** field
Bill To name and address (optional)	Displays and prints on sales forms and checks
Ship To name and address (optional)	Displays and prints on sales forms that have this field
Contact information (name, phone, fax—optional)	Name and phone display and print on the A/R collections report
Account number (optional)	Required only if you make online payments to this customer; otherwise, QuickBooks does not use this number.
Customer type (optional)	Available as a filter for reports
Payment terms if payment has a due date (optional)	Determines due date on invoices and on statements that include statement charges
Rep associated with sales to this customer (optional)	Determines sales by rep on sales by rep reports
Credit limit (optional)	Warns you if you try to record an invoice that would put the customer balance above this limit
Sales tax information (recommended if you collect sales tax)	Calculates correct sales tax for taxable items on sales forms
Price level (Pro only)	Determines price level associated with this customer.
Custom field information (optional)	After you set up any custom fields relevant to your business, you can customize sales forms to display and print this information. Also, you can filter reports for customers that share the same information
Job information (QuickBooks Pro and Premier only, optional)	Use only if you do NOT plan to set up separate jobs for the customer. Job status displays on Customer:Job list. You can display and filter by job information on any customer list report.

Setting up jobs

You can add your current jobs all at once or as you need them on transactions. As you start new jobs, you can add them as well.

What to set up	Comments	See...
Job types (optional)	You can filter for job types on reports.	In the Help Index: job types
Job status	Five preset descriptions include: ■ Pending ■ Awarded ■ In progress ■ Closed ■ Not awarded	"Setting descriptions for job status" below for information on where job status information displays and how to change the preset descriptions.
Jobs	You can add as much or as little information as you need. Refer to the following table "Job information and how it's used in QuickBooks" on page 105 to help you decide what information to add.	In the Help Index: jobs, adding new

Setting descriptions for job status

In QuickBooks Pro and Premier (but not in QuickBooks Basic) you can note the status of a job when you set up or edit the job. QuickBooks Pro and Premier use the descriptions for the choices in the following places:

- Drop-down list in the **Job Status** field on the Job Info tab of the New Job, Edit Job, New Customer, and Edit Customer windows

- Job Status column of the Customer:Job List window (page 106)

- Job progress invoices vs. estimates report (and when a job status column is added to the customer phone list report or customer contact list report)

- The job status filter on the customer phone list report, customer contact list report, and job progress invoices vs. estimates report

Five preset descriptions are:

- Pending
- Awarded
- In progress
- Closed
- Not awarded

You can change any or all of the descriptions that are meaningful to your company. The only one that QuickBooks Pro and Premier treat in a special way is the Closed description. If you use the Condense feature to reduce the size of your file, QuickBooks deletes estimates only for jobs with the job status of Closed. If you change this description, be sure it still applies to a job that has been completed.

To learn about...	Look in the Help Index for...
Changing the descriptions for job status	job status
Assigning a price level to a customer	price levels

Job information and how it's used in QuickBooks

In QuickBooks, a job is associated with a particular customer. You can also have a subjob of another job.

To set up a job for a customer, you need to enter the following information.

Information needed	How QuickBooks uses this information
Job name or number	■ Displays on Customer:Job list; sorted alphabetically (or numerically), indented under the customer name ■ Displays on all drop-down lists where you choose the customer and job (for example, on sales forms) ■ Displays on all reports that are by customer or job or that show the customer:job name on a transaction ■ Prints in the Project field of sales forms that have this field
Name, address, and contact information	QuickBooks copies what you already entered for the customer, but you can change it if necessary.
Account number, customer type, credit limit, price level, custom fields (optional)	QuickBooks copies what you already entered for the customer, but you can change it if necessary.
Job status (optional, available in QuickBooks Pro and Premier only)	■ Displays on Customer:Job list ■ Displays on the job progress invoices vs. estimates report and is available as a filter for that report ■ Available as a possible column and as a filter for any customer list report
Start, projected end, and end dates (optional, available in QuickBooks Pro and Premier only)	Available as a possible column and as a filter for any customer list report

Information needed	How QuickBooks uses this information
Job description (optional, available in QuickBooks Pro and Premier only)	Available as a possible column and as a filter for any customer list report
Job type (optional)	Available as a possible column and as a filter for any customer list report

Working with customers and jobs

Viewing and changing customer and job information

The Customer:Job list displays helpful information at a glance:

- Name of each customer and job
- Current balance owed by each customer (and for each job)
- Whether there is an existing note for the customer or job
- Job status of each customer or job (QuickBooks Pro and Premier only)
- Amount of any existing estimate for the customer or job (QuickBooks Pro and Premier only)

Double-click in the Notes column to add or view notes about a customer or job.

The Job Status column shows the job status entered in the Add Job or Edit Job window.

The Estimate Total column shows the amount of the estimate if the job (or customer) has an

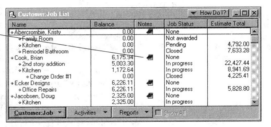

To see further details about a customer or job, you can view the Edit Customer or Edit Job window or you can create a report. You can also change information about a customer or job.

The Address Info tab of this window (not shown) has name, address, and phone information.

In QuickBooks Pro and Premier, you can assign a price level to a customer.

You can set up and fill in any custom fields that fit your needs.

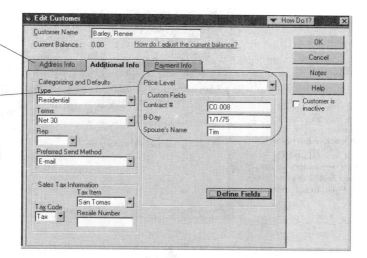

QuickBooks does not allow you to delete a customer or job if there are any transactions associated with the customer or job. To delete a customer or job you have used, you must remove the name from every associated transaction.

On the other hand, you can hide a customer or job on the Customer:Job list without deleting the name by making the customer or job *inactive*. For example, you may have customers who have not done business with you in a long time and who owe you no money. You don't want their names to keep appearing on the list.

When you make a customer or job inactive, QuickBooks keeps the information associated with that customer or job, but hides the customer or job name on the Customer:Job list. The names are removed from any drop-down lists that use customers or jobs. You do not need to change or delete any transaction that uses the customer or job. You can make a customer or job active again at any time.

To see which names are currently inactive, select the Show All checkbox on the Customer:Job list. Inactive names display with a hand symbol to their left.

QuickBooks provides a notepad for recording notes about a customer or job. These notes can help you keep track of important dates and information for a customer or job. You can have a different set of notes about each job for one customer.

You can reach the notepad directly from the Customer:Job list. (You can also write on the notepad when viewing a customer's record or when entering a transaction.)

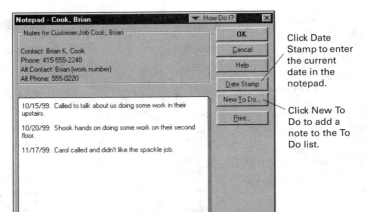

Click Date Stamp to enter the current date in the notepad.

Click New To Do to add a note to the To Do list.

Each customer's notepad can hold roughly 10 windows' worth of text.

Once you fill up this window, use the Up and Down Arrow keys or PgUp and PgDn to see more text.

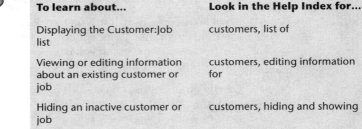

To learn about...	Look in the Help Index for...
Displaying the Customer:Job list	customers, list of
Viewing or editing information about an existing customer or job	customers, editing information for
Hiding an inactive customer or job	customers, hiding and showing
Deleting an unused customer or job	customers, deleting
Creating a note for a customer or job	customers, notes about
Viewing or adding to an existing note for a customer or job	customers, notes about
Displaying all hidden (inactive) customers and jobs	customers, hiding and showing
Making an inactive customer or job active again	customers, hiding and showing

Viewing the customer register

The customer register is something like a checkbook register for just one customer or job. A customer register is available for each customer on your Customer:Job list. It lists all transactions that affect how much the customer owes you: invoices, statement charges, payments, credit memos, and customer discounts. (It does not list any transactions in which the customer pays in full at the time of sale.)

The customer's name appears both at the top of the register and in the **Customer:Job** field.

If you choose a customer name, the register shows transactions for all jobs for that customer.

If you choose a job name, the register shows transactions for that job alone.

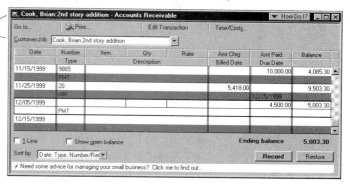

 To locate a particular invoice or payment for a customer, scroll through the customer's register. Sort the register by date, amount, document number, order entered, or paid status.

To learn about...	Look in the Help Index for...
Viewing a customer register	customers, registers for

Contacting customers by mail

You can use your QuickBooks customer data in conjunction with Microsoft Word letters to send various messages to your customers, including collection notices, thank you letters, and change of address notices.

To learn about...	Look in the Help Index for...
Getting your QuickBooks data into Microsoft Word letters	letters using QuickBooks data in Microsoft Word
Printing labels	mailing labels, printing

Changing the opening balance for a customer or job

When you first set up a customer or job, you have a chance to enter the opening (unpaid) balance for the customer or job as of a specific date. The date should be your QuickBooks start date (that is, the date when you enter opening balances for all accounts, customers, and vendors).

When you enter the customer's opening balance (in the EasyStep Interview or New Customer window), QuickBooks creates an invoice for the amount and date you specify. This invoice is probably the first transaction in the customer register. (There should not be any opening balance transaction if the customer had no unpaid balance as of the start date.)

You can change the customer's opening balance invoice by finding it in the customer's register and then editing it.

If you failed to enter an opening balance but want to create one now, enter an invoice dated on or before your start date. To summarize the amount owed as of your start date, enter on the invoice an item set up as a nontaxable other charge, and assign the account Uncategorized Income.

To learn about...	Look in the Help Index for...
Displaying a customer's register	customers, registers for
Editing a transaction displayed in a register	registers, editing entries
Entering an invoice	invoices, creating
Setting up an other charge type of item	other charge items

Changing customer types

If you create customer types to classify your customers, you can rename, reorganize, hide, or delete them.

To learn about...	Comments	Look in the Help index for...
Changing an existing customer type	The changes affect all customers already assigned to the type.	customers, types
Hiding a customer type	The hidden (inactive) name is not visible on the drop-down list in the **Customer Type** field.	customers, types
Making a hidden customer type active	Active customer types are visible on the drop-down list in the **Customer Type** field.	customers, types
Deleting an unused customer type	You cannot delete a customer type currently used for any customer or job.	customers, types

Changing job types

If you create job types to classify your jobs, you can rename, reorganize, hide, or delete them. Job types are available only in QuickBooks Pro and QuickBooks Premier.

To learn about...	Comments	Look in the Help index for...
Changing an existing job type	The changes affect all jobs already assigned to the type.	job types
Hiding a job type	The hidden (inactive) name is not visible on the drop-down list in the **Job Type** field.	job types
Making a hidden job type active	Active job types are visible on the drop-down list in the **Job Type** field.	job types
Deleting an unused job type	You cannot delete a job type currently used for any customer or job.	job types

Changing job status

QuickBooks does not automatically change the job status of any job on the basis of transactions you enter. You must edit the customer or job to change the status (for example, from In Progress to Closed).

You can change the descriptions of the five choices for job status, but you can't delete or hide any of them. Job status is available only in QuickBooks Pro and Premier.

To learn about...	Look in the Help Index for...
Changing the job status of a customer or job	job status
Changing the description of a job status shown on the **Job Status** drop-down list	job status

TRACKING INCOME

If you provide services or sell products, you should be tracking this income using one of the QuickBooks sales forms described in this chapter.

Note: **In QuickBooks, "sales" is a broad term.** It refers to any business action that generates income in exchange for services or products, even if you don't think of what you do as selling. For example, a psychologist with patients, a graphic designer with clients, and a roofing contractor with customers all would track sales in QuickBooks.

On the other hand, if your income is from commissions you receive from a third party or voluntary contributions from the public, you probably don't need to use any of the sales forms in QuickBooks. You can simply record the money you receive as a deposit into your bank account and assign an appropriate income account to track the income. See "Receiving and depositing payments" on page 126.

How QuickBooks can track your income

For any particular transaction, record it only once in QuickBooks, or you will duplicate the income. You can use different methods for different situations.

All the options (except depositing directly into your checking account) require that you enter items from your Item list. It is through the items that you keep track of which income account or accounts each sale affects. For a discussion of items, please read Chapter 8, *Items—your services, products, fixed assets, and more*, beginning on page 75.

 Would you like help choosing the right sales form for your business? In the Help index, enter "sales, choosing the right form for," click Display, and then click "Use an interactive tool to help you decide which one is right for your business"

What are my choices?

Sales Receipts

If your customers pay in full at time of service or sale, you could use sales receipts. If customers pay in advance, either in part or in full, you should not use the sales receipt. A cash sale requires full payment at the time you record the sale.

Invoices

If your customers owe you money at the time you perform your service or provide your product, you need to track how much they owe you— your *accounts receivable,* also called A/R. QuickBooks offers two different ways to record a sale for which you receive any payments at another time: invoices and statement charges.

To learn about creating invoices, see "Invoices" on page 122.

Statements

If you send invoices and your customers need to know how much they owe in total, you can send *reminder statements*. These statements show the previous balance, list new invoice amounts, and show payments received (including advance payments) and the new balance. The details about the sales are only on the invoices, not on the statements, so you would have to send invoices as well as statements.

To learn about printing statements, see "Statements" on page 125.

Should I record estimates?

QuickBooks Pro and Premier allow you to record estimates. You can prepare an estimate, using items from the same Item list you use to record sales.

Bids and proposals

The most obvious use for QuickBooks estimates is to prepare a proposal of work you can do and products or materials you can provide.

Later, if the proposal is accepted, you can turn the estimate into a single invoice or a series of *progress invoices* (if you invoice in phases).

progress invoice

One of a series of invoices all based on the same estimate for the same job. Use progress invoices when you want to invoice for the job in phases—that is, by milestone or by percentage complete.

QuickBooks keeps track of the amount you have already invoiced and the amount not yet invoiced.

Invoicing in phases

Progress invoicing (also called *progress billing* or *partial billing*) is invoicing in phases for the same job, based on the same estimate. When you create a progress invoice from an existing estimate, you can choose from among the following:

- Invoice for the entire estimate (100 percent).
- Invoice for a percentage of the entire estimate.
- Invoice for selected items or for different percentages of each item.

Use estimates and progress invoices if you invoice in phases against a purchase order with a preset amount. For example, if you receive a purchase order (PO) for a large amount of work and then invoice in phases, enter an estimate for the PO. (even if you don't have to submit an estimate). Then create progress invoices for your work against the PO.

On the other hand, if you send a series of invoices all based on actual time and costs, you should not use progress invoices. Instead, you should transfer the time and costs directly to each new invoice.

To learn how to prepare estimates and turn estimates into invoices, see "Estimates and proposals" on page 121 and "Invoices" on page 122. To learn about invoicing for actual time and costs, see "Charging for actual time and costs" on page 130.

Setting up for tracking sales

To record sales, you must set up items on your Item list. Remember, you can have items for services as well as for products or materials.

If you collect sales tax, you set up your sales tax by having one or more sales tax items on your Item list.

You don't need to set up customers on your Customer:Job list if all your sales are cash sales—that is, if people never owe you money. But if customers do owe you money, you'll need to set them up.

QuickBooks provides preset designs for sales forms that you can print on plain paper, letterhead, or preprinted forms purchased from Intuit. But you can customize both the contents and the layout to get the form you want.

If you assess a finance charge for overdue payments, you can set it up with your usual rate.

Finally, there are preferences you can set for such choices as whether to use estimates, do progress invoicing, or automatically apply payments to the oldest invoices first.

Refer to the following for tracking sales of services or products in QuickBooks.

What to set up	Comments	Search Help index for...
Items for services, products, other charges, or sales tax that are relevant to your business	See Chapter 8, *Items—your services, products, fixed assets, and more,* beginning on page 75.	■ items, services ■ items, non-inventory parts ■ items, inventory ■ items, miscellaneous charges ■ items, sales tax
Names and information about customers that don't pay at the time they receive the service or product	See Chapter 9, *Customers and jobs,* beginning on page 97.	customers, adding new
Names and information about the individual jobs for customers (optional)	See Chapter 9, *Customers and jobs,* beginning on page 97.	jobs, adding new
Customized columns, fields, or layout for forms you print: estimates, invoices, sales receipts, credit memos, statements (optional)	You can have alternative versions of the same type of form. See Chapter 6, *Creating a professional image,* beginning on page 49.	entries under: customizing forms

What to set up	Comments	Search Help index for...
Company-wide preferences for sales (for example, how to apply payments, whether to track reimbursed expenses as income) (optional)	Only the QuickBooks Administrator can change company-wide preferences.	sales, preferences
Company-wide preferences for estimates (for example, whether to use estimates, whether to use progress invoicing) (optional, available only in QuickBooks Pro and Premier)	Only the QuickBooks Administrator can change company-wide preferences.	estimates, preferences for
Finance charges for overdue invoices or statements (optional)	Finance charges appear on printed statements.	finance charges, setting up for

Setting up to track reimbursed expenses as income

reimbursed expenses

Expenses you have incurred on behalf of a customer, and for which you request reimbursement.

If you request reimbursement from your customers for expenses you incur on their behalf, and you want this income from reimbursed expenses to show up on profit and loss statements, you need to follow the steps in the next section to track reimbursable expenses as income. Unless you do the following setup, the reimbursed expense will cancel the original expense and won't show up on profit and loss statements at all.

You may want to do this if reimbursable expenses are a significant portion of your business, such as a construction or remodeling business, so that your profit and loss statement accurately reflects the portion of total sales that these reimbursable expenses comprise.

For example, Mary purchases an antique sink for $100 for a customer's home that she is remodeling. She charges the customer an additional $25 for the sink. Her profit and loss statement shows the following, depending on whether or not she tracks reimbursable expenses as income.

Track reimbursable expenses as income	Do not track reimbursable expenses as income
Income........$125 Expense.......$100 ---------------------------- Net Profit.....$25	Income..........$25 ---------------------------- Net Profit........$25

In QuickBooks Basic, Pro, and Premier

In each of these products, you can make direct expenses billable—that is, you record an expense account and dollar amount for a purchase, assign a customer (and job), and mark the expense as billable. Then you can transfer the expense to an invoice. (See "Charging for actual time and costs" on page 130.)

If you want to have separate accounts for the expense and for the income for the reimbursed expense, do the following:

1 Turn on the "Track reimbursed expenses as income" preference in the Sales & Customer preferences.

2 After turning on the preference, edit the expense accounts you plan to use for reimbursable expenses. In the Edit Account window, you can now select an income account to use for the reimbursement.

Note that you must take *both* actions to track an expense and your customer's reimbursement for the expense in separate accounts.

In QuickBooks Pro and Premier only

In addition, in QuickBooks Pro and Premier only, you can use items for any expenses associated with a particular customer or job. For example, you can have an item for a subcontracted service, an object purchased for a customer, or a charge such as shipping.

The advantage of setting up items for reimbursement is that you can use the same items for purchases and for sales. For each item, you can specify a purchase price (what the item costs you) and a sales price (what you charge customers).

When you set up an item for reimbursement in QuickBooks Pro or Premier, you should mark the checkbox that allows you to track purchases and sales separately. When you record the purchase of the item, you mark the item as billable to the customer or job. Later, you can transfer the billable item to an invoice. (See "Charging for actual time and costs" on page 130.)

In QuickBooks, on the other hand, you can't make items billable when recording purchases.

Note: **Invoicing for reimbursable expenses.** For information about invoicing for reimbursable expenses in QuickBooks, see "Reimbursable expenses in QuickBooks" on page 131. For information on invoicing for reimbursable expenses in QuickBooks Pro and Premier, see "Reimbursable time and costs in QuickBooks Pro and QuickBooks Premier" on page 132.

To learn about...	Look in the Help Index for...
Turning on the preference for tracking reimbursed expenses as income	sales, preferences
Setting up items in QuickBooks Pro or Premier for reimbursable expenses	■ items, reimbursable ■ service items

Tracking sales and customer payments

If you are not sure which options are best for your business, see "How QuickBooks can track your income" on page 114.

How to track sales and payments

Sales Receipts

To record a sale in which the customer pays in full and doesn't owe you money, you should record a sales receipt (which you can print if you want).

You do not have to receive payment in cash in order to record a sales receipt. It works equally well with a payment by check, credit card, or debit card. All that matters is that you have received payment for the sale, so you need to record the payment as well as the sale.

Recording a sales receipt does the following:

■ It tracks what you sold (that is, the service or product) so you can analyze your sales on reports and graphs and keep track of inventory (if your business sells inventory).

■ It tracks the sales tax, if any, you collected and increases what you owe for sales tax.

■ It either deposits the amount from the sale in your bank account or records the money with other undeposited funds. (You specify in the window what QuickBooks should do with the money.)

If all you want is a summary of the total services or products for a day or week, you can enter the summary directly on the sales receipt form. (If you don't need to track the services or products, and you don't collect sales tax, don't use a sales receipt. Simply enter the payments as a deposit into your checking account.)

To record what you sold and received full payment for, use the Enter Sales Receipts window.

The **Customer:Job** field can be blank on a sales receipt.

Specify where to record the proceeds from the sale:

- Group with other undeposited funds (for deposit later).
- Or, deposit directly in the account specified.

For QuickBooks Merchant Account Service users

If you use the QuickBooks Merchant Account Service to process credit card payments, either click Swipe Card on the toolbar — if you have the customer's credit card in hand and use a card reader with your QuickBooks merchant account — or select "Process credit card payment when saving" and then enter the customer's credit card information. You should also specify "Group with other undeposited funds" to make matching QuickBooks deposits and bank deposits easier. For more information about services that can help you process customer payments online, refer to "Offering more ways for your customers to pay you" on page 64.

If you aren't processing a credit card payment and don't need to track which customer purchased the items, you're not required to enter a customer's name. You can leave it blank or use a generic name such as "Counter Sales," "Cash Customer," or "Daily Sales Summary."

payment item

A type of item on your Item list. You can set up a different payment item for each method of payment.

Use payment items on sales receipts only when you need to show two or more kinds of payments on the same receipt.

You enter a sale or summary of sales by entering one or more items from your Item list. If the items are taxable, QuickBooks calculates the correct sales tax and adds it to your sales tax liability. Optionally, you can print the form as a receipt to give to the customer.

If a summary sales receipt covers payment by more than one method (for example, checks and credit card charges), you can show the breakdown by using a different payment item for each method. (Otherwise, you don't have to enter any payment items; QuickBooks knows you have received payment.)

To learn about...	Look in the Help Index for...
Creating a sales receipt to record both a sale and its payment	sales receipts
Entering a sales receipt for credit card payment	merchant account service, entering customer payments
Creating a daily sales summary form that you can fill in with quantities and amounts	sales, daily
Tracking sales tax collected on cash sales	■ sales tax, applying to sales ■ sales tax, tracking how much you owe
Tracking daily overages or shortages	overages
Printing a sales receipt	receipts

Estimates and proposals

In QuickBooks Pro and Premier, you create estimates or proposals using the Create Estimates window.

The estimate window displays the cost of each item and the markup, but only the customer's price prints (unless you customize your estimates differently).

To create an invoice based on this estimate, click Create Invoice.

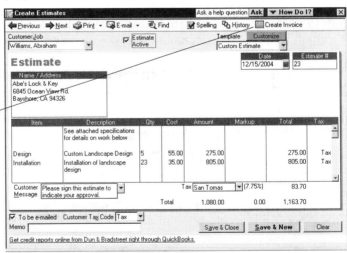

Because estimates represent only potential sales, they do not affect any income accounts or any account balances.

To help you make alternative proposals, QuickBooks Pro and Premier let you create multiple estimates for each customer or each job.

You can create each of these multiple estimates independently or you can create one estimate, duplicate that estimate, and modify it. You can also duplicate an estimate created for one customer and modify it for another customer.

To learn about...	Look in the Help Index for...
Preparing estimates (or proposals) (Pro and Premier only)	estimates, creating
Marking up the cost of items on estimates (Pro and Premier only)	estimates, markups on
Printing an estimate (Pro and Premier only)	estimates, printing
Sending estimates by e-mail	e-mail business forms to customers
Displaying a list of estimates (Pro and Premier only)	estimates, list of

Invoices

You create invoices using the Create Invoices window. On the other hand, if you already have an estimate for the same customer or job, you can create an invoice directly from the estimate.

This invoice design is based on the Intuit Progress Invoice template, one of several preset invoice design templates you can choose.

You can also create your own custom design.

Some fields shown here do not print. You can customize what displays onscreen and what prints.

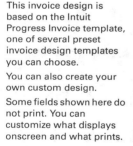

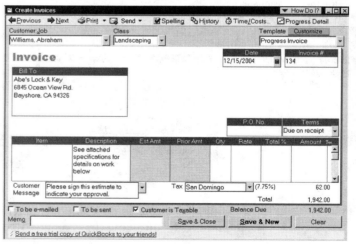

Note: You can't have more than one job on a single invoice. If you create a job for a customer (so you can track multiple jobs for the customer separately), then you should associate each sale with both the customer name and the job name. If you do simultaneous jobs for a customer and want to present the customer with detail for all the jobs on a single statement, consider using statement charges instead of invoices. See "Statement charges" on page 125.

In QuickBooks Pro and Premier, if you are set up to create progress invoices from an estimate, you can display and print additional detail about the estimate and the previous invoices based on the same estimate.

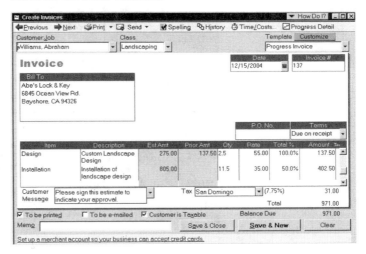

A progress invoice has columns that compare the estimate amounts with the amounts previously invoiced and the amount on the current invoice.

You can customize what displays and what prints on your progress invoices.

When you create a progress invoice from an estimate, you can base it on a percentage of the estimate or on selected items (or different percentages).

In his contracting business, Frank invoices for only 90 percent at the completion of a job. He invoices for the final 10 percent (the retainage) later.

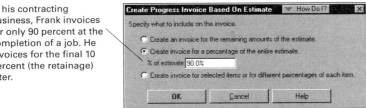

To learn about...	Look in the Help Index for...
Creating an invoice from an accepted estimate (QuickBooks Pro and Premier only)	invoices, basing on estimates
Invoicing in phases from a single estimate (QuickBooks Pro and Premier only)	progress invoicing
Preparing invoices that are *not* based on an estimate	invoices, creating
Adding billable time or costs to an invoice	expenses, billing to a customer
Adjusting the sales tax QuickBooks calculates on an estimate or invoice	sales tax, applying to sales
Recording back-ordered items	pending sales
Printing one or more invoices	invoices, printing
Displaying a register that shows all invoices	accounts receivable, register
Sending invoices by e-mail	e-mail business forms to customers
Displaying a register that shows all invoices, statement charges, or payments for a particular customer or job	customers, registers for
Mailing invoices from QuickBooks	invoices, mailing through QuickBooks

Sales orders

A sales order is similar to an invoice and behaves much like the other sales forms in QuickBooks. You can create a sales order by selecting Create Sales Order on the Customer menu. Sales orders can help you track back orders—items your customers have ordered but you do not have in stock. If you create an invoice and QuickBooks indicates that you do not have enough of an item to sell, you can create a sales order instead. From the sales order you can create a partial invoice for those items you have on hand. The sales order, with the amount not on hand, will remain open.

To learn about...	Look in the Help Index for...
Using sales orders	sales orders, back ordered itemss

Statement charges

You enter statement charges for a customer and job directly in a register that looks like a checkbook register. The register shows previous statement charges and payments, as well as the current balance, for the customer or job.

If you choose a job name as well as a customer name in the **Customer:Job** field, the register shows sales transactions for that job alone.

QuickBooks fills in the Billed Date and Due Date after you print a statement that includes the charge.

You enter a new statement charge on the register's first blank line.

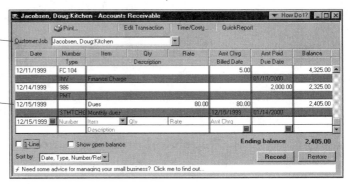

To learn about...	Look in the Help Index for...
Recording individual charges that will be listed on a statement	statements, entering charges

Statements

A QuickBooks statement prints information already recorded. You can't edit what is on a statement. A statement covers a time period and shows the previous balance, new activity, and the new balance.

If you record statement charges, the statement contains the date, description, and amount of each charge. And, if you customize your statement to add columns for quantity and rate, the statement has the quantity and rate of each charge. When you print the statement, QuickBooks sets the date of expected payment for each new statement charge (based on the payment terms you set up for the customer).

On the other hand, if you record invoices, the statement contains only the date, invoice number, and total for each invoice.

- A *billing statement* is a statement that shows new statement charges.

- A *reminder statement* is a statement that shows only the previous and new balances and the dates and amounts of recent payments, invoices, and credit memos.

Do people pay you regularly, without receiving statements?
For example, do you have to keep track of who has paid the monthly condo fee? You can do this by recording statement charges and printing statements but not sending them. You must print the statement in order to make QuickBooks set the date for when the charges on it are due.

To learn about...	Look in the Help Index for...
Creating, previewing, and printing statements	statements, printing
Sending statements electronically	e-mail business forms to customers

Receiving and depositing payments

Use the Receive Payments window to record payments and specify what they are for. You need to use it not only when you have actually received payment for invoices or statements but also when you need to apply any credit to any charge or refund for a customer.

If you track jobs as well as customers, you must choose both the customer name and job name in the **Received From** field.

The checkmark next to the invoice tells QuickBooks to apply the payment to the invoice.

QuickBooks has a preference that determines whether or not it should automatically apply payments.

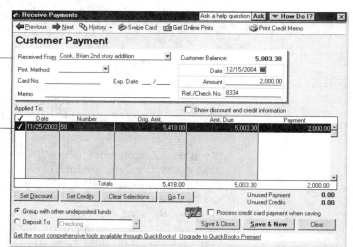

For QuickBooks Merchant Account Service users

If you use the QuickBooks Merchant Account Service to process credit card payments, enter the credit card information in the Receive Payments window, and then either click Swipe Card on the toolbar — if you have the customer's credit card in hand and use a card reader with your QuickBooks merchant account — or enter the customer's credit card information manually. For more information about services that can help you process payments online, refer to "Offering more ways for your customers to pay you" on page 64.

To indicate that you are keeping the payment in a *cash drawer* until you are ready to deposit it, choose "Group with other undeposited funds." To identify similar types of payments so you can deposit them all together, use the **Pmt. Method** field to label the payment.

If you are a QuickBooks Merchant Account Service user, you can more easily match your customers' credit card payments with the lump sum deposit on your bank statement, as well as account for banking fees. When you receive payments or enter sales receipts, you should always select the "Group with undeposited funds" option. For more information, see "Matching bank deposits and credit card deposits (Merchant Account Service users)" on page 69.

?

To learn about...	Look in the Help Index for...
Recording customer payments received and applying them to outstanding invoices or statement charges	■ receiving payments, on invoices ■ receiving payments, on statements
Accepting credit card payments through the QuickBooks Merchant Account Service	merchant account service
Applying a discount for early payment	discounts, for early customer payments
Depositing undeposited customer payments	deposits, bank or checking account
Printing a list of the customer payments in a deposit	deposit slips
Handling a bounced check from a customer	bounced checks
Assessing a finance charge or late payment charge for overdue payment	finance charges, assessing on overdue invoices and statements
Recording an overpayment	overpayments
Recording a bad debt after a customer has failed to make payment	bad debts
Matching bank and credit card accounts	■ reconciling, bank statements ■ reconciling, credit card statements

Down payments, advance deposits, and retainers

If you receive payment before performing a service or providing a product, the way to track the payment depends on your type of business.

To learn about...	Look in the Help Index for...
Recording down payments received in advance of a sale	down payments
Recording and applying legal retainers	retainers

Returns and refunds

To record the return of an item you sold, fill in the Create Credit Memos/Refunds window. Items on a credit memo reduce the sales income for those items.

In the Create Credit Memos/ Refunds window, you can:

■ Record the return of items.

■ Click Refund to create a refund check to pay a customer to whom you owe money.

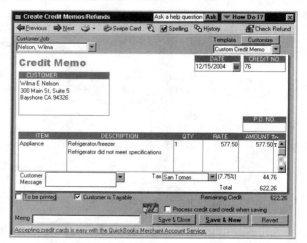

A credit memo reduces the amount that the customer owes you. If the customer has already paid you in full, the credit memo makes the customer's balance negative in the Customer:Job window, in dicating that you owe the customer money.

If there are no returned items (for example, if a customer simply overpays), you don't need to create a credit memo.

If you owe a customer money due to returned items or overpayment, you can either issue a refund check or process a credit card refund.

To issue a refund check, click Refund in the Create Credit Memos/Refunds window.

QuickBooks fills out a refund check for you to record and print.

When you click Refund in the Create Credit Memos/Refunds window, QuickBooks fills in the Write Checks window with information from the credit memo.

A refund to a customer is assigned to the Accounts Receivable account, so that it can increase the customer's negative balance to zero.

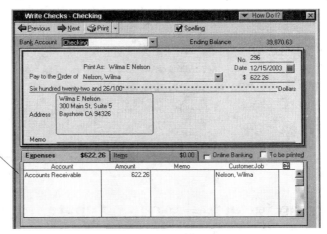

For QuickBooks Merchant Account Service users

If you use the Merchant Account Service, you can issue customers a credit or process a customer refund or return using the Create Credit Memos/Refunds window. The transaction will appear as a debit on the Payments to Deposit window.

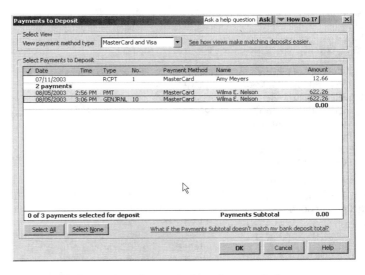

For more information about services that can help you process customer payments online, refer to "Offering more ways for your customers to pay you" on page 64.

If the customer owes you money (for the same job, if you track jobs) after you record a credit memo, simply wait until you receive a payment from the customer. Then, in the Receive

Payments window, apply the new payment to the credit memo as well as to the appropriate invoices or statement charges.

To learn about...	Look in the Help Index for...
Recording returned items	credit memos, creating
Writing a refund check	refunds
Recording credit card refunds	■ refunds, refunds to customers ■ merchant account service, refunds for customer payments
Voiding credit card transactions	merchant account service, voiding customer payments

Charging for actual time and costs

Charging your customer for the actual time and costs for a job is a two-step process:

1 Track the time and costs, assigning them to the specific job.

2 Transfer the time and costs to a sales form (with or without a markup) or to the register for the job (like the one on page 125).

The following table shows what you must do to track time or costs so that you can charge for them.

To track...	You must...	See...
All expenses incurred for the job (QuickBooks only) Miscellaneous costs incurred for this job (costs you prefer not to record by using items) (QuickBooks Pro and Premier only)	Record a bill, check, or credit card charge, using the Expenses tab to identify the accounts and amounts for other costs incurred for this job.	■ "Paying bills" on page 176 ■ "Using checks" on page 183 ■ "Using credit cards" on page 185
Time billable to this job (QuickBooks Pro and Premier only)	Record hours spent on this job, using the Timer, the Stopwatch, or entering time manually into QuickBooks. ■ Assign the hours to the service item that should be used on the invoice. ■ To show the service date for each time entry on the invoice, customize the invoice to add a Service Date column. ■ Be sure to mark the hours as billable.	■ "Setting up and using the Timer" on page 221 ■ "Using the Stopwatch to time an activity" on page 226 ■ "Entering time manually into QuickBooks" on page 227

To track...	You must...	See...
Subcontracted services, products, materials, and other charges billable for this job (QuickBooks Pro and Premier only)	Record a bill, check, or credit card charge, using the Items tab to identify goods and services purchased for this job. Be sure to mark these items as billable.	■ "Items for reimbursable costs in QuickBooks Pro and Premier Editions" on page 86 ■ "Paying bills" on page 176 ■ "Using checks" on page 183 ■ "Using credit cards" on page 185

Reimbursable expenses in QuickBooks

When you have billable expenses in QuickBooks and are ready to invoice for them, click the Expenses button on an invoice for the customer or job. (If you are using QuickBooks Pro or Premier, see "Reimbursable time and costs in QuickBooks Pro and QuickBooks Premier" on page 132.)

QuickBooks displays the Choose Reimbursable Expenses window. It shows the expenses you have marked billable but have not yet billed to this customer or job. In this window you mark which billable expenses to add to the invoice.

This window is in QuickBooks Basic only, not QuickBooks Pro or Premier.

To hide a markup on an invoice, be sure to select this checkbox.

For a percentage markup, add a % sign after the number. QuickBooks prefills your preset markup percentage if you set one up in sales and customer preferences.

Most people use an income account for markup.

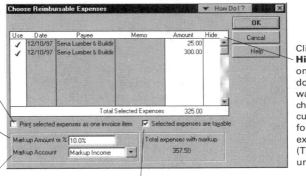

Click the **Hide** field only if you don't ever want to charge this customer for the expense. (The bill is unaffected.)

To make the marked expenses taxable on the invoice, select this checkbox.

After you click OK in the window, QuickBooks puts all the marked expenses on the invoice.

Note: You can set up so that QuickBooks assigns income for a reimbursed expense to an income account. If you don't do this setup, the income cancels the original expense in the expense account. See "Setting up to track reimbursed expenses as income" on page 117.

Reimbursable time and costs in QuickBooks Pro and QuickBooks Premier

In QuickBooks Pro or Premier, when you click the Time/Costs button on an invoice for a customer or job, it displays a window with three separate tabs, one for billable items, billable expenses, and billable time.

On the Items tab, you mark which billable items to add to the invoice.

This window shows all billable but not-yet-billed time and job costs for this particular job.

Time tab displays only if time tracking is on.

Click the **Hide** field only if you don't ever want to charge this customer for the item. (The bill is not affected.)

Each of the three tabs displays the dollar total for the lines that have a mark in the **Use** field. These amounts will be added to the invoice.

To use all lines on this tab, click Select All. To unmark all lines, click Clear All (the button name changes).

Select this checkbox to print only the overall total and a general description for the group of marked items on all three tabs.

To print an overall total but no detail for one tab alone, mark the lines on only one tab, select the checkbox, and click OK.

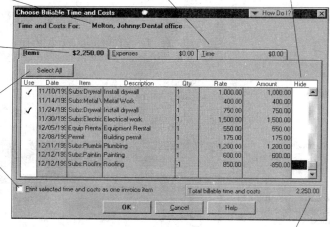

The **Description** and **Rate** fields show the sales description and rate for each item from the item setup. They may differ from the purchase description and rate.

This is the total amount for marked items on all three tabs.

On the sales form, QuickBooks Pro and Premier use the sales price, not the cost, for each inventory part and for each resale non-inventory part, subcontracted service, and reimbursable other charge item. You can change the price on the sales form. If you set up the item with a sales price of 0.00 because costs vary, be sure to enter a sales price on the sales form.

On the Expenses tab of QuickBooks Pro or Premier, you mark which billable expenses to add to the invoice. You may add a markup to your actual expenses.

For a percentage markup, add a % sign after the number. QuickBooks prefills your preset markup percentage if you set one up in sales and customer preferences.

Most people use an income account for markup.

To make the marked expenses taxable on the invoice, select this checkbox.

To hide the markup on an invoice, be sure to select this checkbox.

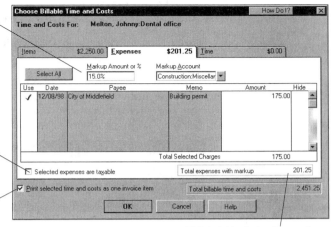

This total includes the markup.

Note: You can set up so that QuickBooks assigns income for a reimbursed expense to an income account. If you don't do this setup, the income cancels the original expense in the expense account. (Your net income is the same in either case.) See "Setting up to track reimbursed expenses as income" on page 117.

Finally, on the Time tab of QuickBooks Pro or Premier, you mark which billable time to add to the invoice.

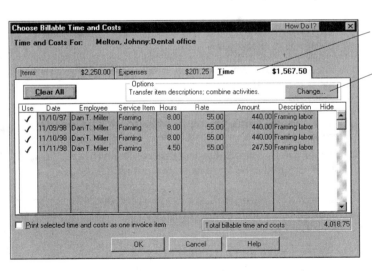

The Time tab shows all time that is billable for this job but has not yet been billed.

Click Change to specify the following:

- Whether to copy your time notes or the description of the service item into the **Description** field of the sales form.

- Whether to show each activity as a separate line or to combine all activities for the same service item.

The rates shown are the rates set up for each service item.

In this window and on the sales form, QuickBooks Pro and Premier use the hourly rate for the service item you assigned to the activity, not the payroll rate of the employee. If the service item has the subcontractor checkbox marked, QuickBooks uses the sales price. You can change the rate on the sales form.

To change how QuickBooks Pro or Premier groups and describes time activities on the sales form, click Change.

After you click OK in the window, QuickBooks puts all the marked time and costs on the invoice. If you return to the window *before* recording the invoice, the items already on the invoice have an invoice symbol in the Use field.

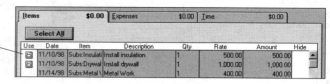

The invoice symbol in the **Use** field indicates that the item has already been added to the invoice.

You can put given job costs on a sales form only once.

If you record a sales form that has actual job costs on it and then discover you made a mistake, the actual job costs you used previously are no longer available to use again. The only way you can reinstate such costs is to go to the original record (that is, weekly timesheet, single activity, bill, check, or credit card charge). Click the Billable field to make the cost billable again.

Making changes while tracking sales

Finding or changing existing sales forms or statement charges

QuickBooks allows you to change a sales form or statement charge you have already recorded.

Don't change sales forms or statement charges to record payments received later.

To enter the payments, use the Receive Payments window, not the original sales form or statement charge.

If the form was among the last ones you recorded, you can move to previous forms in the window where you entered the form by clicking the Previous button.

The easiest way to find a statement charge or an older invoice or credit memo is to scroll through the customer register. You can sort the register by date, amount, number, and so on.

Sales receipts are either in your bank account register or in the register for undeposited funds, depending on how you specified what to do with the payment received. Even if you have already deposited the sales receipt payment with other undeposited funds, the sales receipt remains in the register for undeposited funds. The register will also have the subsequent deposit.

To learn about...	Look in the Help Index for...
Finding and viewing statement charges or older invoices for a customer	customers, registers for
Finding and viewing sales receipts for which payments were deposited with other undeposited funds	Undeposited Funds account

Correcting the application of a payment

After you have recorded a payment, you may discover that you should have applied it to different invoices or statement charges. (Or you may have failed to apply it at all.) You can edit the payment and apply it correctly.

If the payment was originally with other undeposited funds and you subsequently deposited the funds, you must delete the payment from the deposit before you can edit the payment. After correcting the application of the payment, be sure to edit the deposit and add the corrected payment to it to keep your bank balance correct.

To learn about...	Look in the Help Index for...
Correcting a customer payment that is already recorded	receiving payments, fixing misapplied
Editing a deposit of undeposited funds to delete or add a payment	deposits, editing

Voiding or deleting a sales transaction

QuickBooks allows you to void or delete a sales transaction, although you would not want to do either if you have already recorded a payment for it.

You can delete a sales form altogether from QuickBooks; however, there might be better alternatives.

- If you want complete records of all sales, you may want to void a sales form instead of deleting it.
- Don't delete an invoice or receipt if you made an error on the invoice. Just correct the error on the original form and reprint it.
- Don't delete an invoice if you've already applied a payment to it. If a customer cancels an order on which you have received some payment, your records will be clearer if you create a credit memo to reverse all or part of a sales transaction.

To learn about...	Look in the Help Index for...
Voiding or deleting a sales transaction	■ transactions, voiding ■ transactions, deleting
Reversing all or part of a sales transaction with a credit memo	credit memos, creating

Repeating similar transactions

Making a copy to use later

If you need to create similar estimates, invoices, sales receipts, or statement charges, you can make a copy to use later or for a different customer. Then you don't have to start from scratch.

QuickBooks calls making a copy *memorizing*. You can memorize estimates, invoices, or sales receipts without specifying a customer name.

Statement charges work slightly differently. You must memorize a customer or job name with the statement charge. You might memorize a statement charge if you wanted to repeat the same charge, say, every month. If you have similar charges for different customers, you must memorize each one separately.

Scheduling repeated transactions

When you memorize any transaction, you can set up a schedule to record the same transaction again and again. For example, if your organization charges members a monthly fee, you can schedule memorized statement charges for each member. You can specify whether you want QuickBooks to enter the charges automatically or to remind you that it's time for you to enter them.

QuickBooks Merchant Account Service users can use Automated Credit Card Billing to schedule repeated credit card transactions. To do this, from the Customers menu, choose Process Credit Card Payments and then Manage Automatic Credit Card Billing. Note that QuickBooks does not record recurring transactions automatically. But you can use the memorized transaction feature to help automate this process.

Starting from a copy

QuickBooks calls starting from a copy of a transaction *recalling*. You can recall any transaction that has already been memorized, and can make changes on the recalled transaction. For example, if you recall an invoice with no customer name, you'd add the correct name and perhaps add or delete some items.

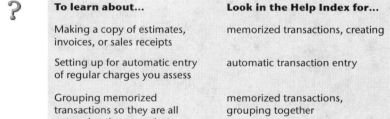

To learn about...	Look in the Help Index for...
Making a copy of estimates, invoices, or sales receipts	memorized transactions, creating
Setting up for automatic entry of regular charges you assess	automatic transaction entry
Grouping memorized transactions so they are all entered at the same time	memorized transactions, grouping together
Using a copy of a transaction	memorized transactions, using
Automatic credit card billing	automatic credit card billing

Managing what customers owe you

The most important part of managing what customers owe you is making sound choices about how much credit you should extend and to whom you should extend it. With QuickBooks Credit Check Services, powered by Dun & Bradstreet, you can get online credit reports for your commercial customers so you can understand their credit history before you extend credit. For additional information, select Credit Check from the Customers menu and click Learn More.

When you keep track of how much a customer owes you—your accounts receivable, also called A/R—it's very important to keep track of *which* invoices or statement charges have been paid and which are still unpaid. You do this by recording each customer payment in the Receive Payments window and specifying what the payment is for. Then QuickBooks can tell you what is overdue.

 Would you like to know how to get customers to pay their bills faster? Customers who pay late or not at all can be a problem for any business. QuickBooks can help you manage your accounts receivable, use A/R reports effectively, establish a credit policy, and devise a strategy for collecting overdue bills. For information on these topics, choose Decision Tools from the Company menu, and then choose Manage Your Receivables.

Connecting related transactions

The most important thing to remember when tracking accounts receivable is to make sure that related transactions are connected within QuickBooks.

- When a customer makes a payment after receiving one or more invoices, you have to tell QuickBooks which invoices the payment is for.

- When a customer makes a payment after receiving a statement with details of statement charges, you have to tell QuickBooks which statement charges the payment is for.

- If a customer makes a down payment ahead of time and you write an invoice after doing the work, you have to tell Quick-Books that the invoice has been partially paid by the down payment.

- If a customer overpays, you have to tell QuickBooks that you are applying the credit to an unpaid invoice, to an unpaid statement charge, or to a refund check.

- If you write a credit memo for some returned items, you have to tell QuickBooks that you are applying the credit to an unpaid invoice, to an unpaid statement charge, or to a refund check.

QuickBooks considers invoices and statement charges still open and due until you connect them to a payment (or credit). If you don't make the connections, a customer can seem to have a zero or negative balance and yet have overdue invoices or statement charges.

To learn how to record the various kinds of customer payments, see "Receiving and depositing payments" on page 126.

Viewing all accounts receivable transactions

Besides the accounts receivable reports and graphs, QuickBooks has an accounts receivable register. This register, like a checkbooks register, shows every transaction that affects how much people owe you. It includes all invoices, payments, credit memos, statement charges, and finance charges. In addition, each customer register shows the accounts receivable transactions for that customer.

The **Number** field shows invoice and statement charge numbers, FINCHG for finance charges, or check numbers for customer payments.

QuickBooks records invoice or statement charge amounts in the **Amt Chrg** field, and payment amounts in the **Amt Paid** field.

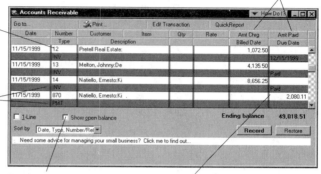

The **Type** field shows whether the transaction was an invoice (INV), a statement charge (STMTCHG), a credit memo (CREDMEM), a payment from a customer (PMT), or a customer discount (DISC).

Select **Show open balance** to show the amount still due for invoices and billing statements.

When a customer pays an invoice or billing statement, QuickBooks replaces the date in the **Due Date** field with the word "Paid."

The Ending balance shows the total amount you are owed (unpaid invoices minus any unused customer credit).

The one-line view of the A/R register displays many more transactions in one window. You can use this view when you want to see more transactions with less detail.

To see the one-line view, select **1-Line**.

When you select a transaction in the accounts receivable or customer register, you can click Edit to display the window for the transaction and see detail.

Do you need to find the payments for a specific invoice?
Select the invoice in the register. Then, from the Edit menu, choose Transaction History. You'll see a list of all the payments for this invoice.

?

To learn about...	Look in the Help Index for...
Viewing the accounts receivable register or a customer register	■ accounts receivable, register ■ customers, registers for
Displaying a list of payments for a particular invoice	invoices, payments toward

The Vendor list in QuickBooks allows you to record information about your vendors (the people or companies from whom you buy goods and services or owe taxes), and track your related accounts payable and 1099-MISC information. You can also create reports and print mailing labels based on your Vendor list. With the Vendor Detail Center, you can get valuable insight on each of your vendors.

Tracking vendor information

How much information should I add for each vendor?

For most vendors, you'll want to add the basic information such as the vendor name, address, and phone number; but you can also add account and terms information, categorize your vendors by types (that you define), create custom fields to track information important to your business, and add notes about conversations, products, or other information about this vendor.

QuickBooks prints this information in the **Memo** field of checks that pay bills from this vendor. Or, it sends it with online payments.

You can classify your vendors by type.

This field tracks bill aging and tells you when payment is due.

If you file a 1099-MISC form for this vendor, fill in the **Tax ID** field and select the checkbox.

If you use ACT! or Microsoft Outlook contact management software to manage vendor data, you can transfer basic vendor information (such as name, address, phone, and so on) from your contact manager to QuickBooks Pro or Premier and vice versa. See "Sharing QuickBooks Pro and Premier information with your contact manager" on page 298.

To learn about...	Look in the Help Index for...
Transferring information from your contact manager to QuickBooks	contact management, synchronizing names with a contact manager

Defining custom fields for vendors

To track additional information about your vendors, you can define up to seven custom fields. You might want to define fields for:

- Web site addresses
- Pager numbers
- Customer service numbers
- Hours open (for example, 9:30 - 5:30)

After you add custom fields, you can customize your forms to include these fields. You can also display and filter for customized field data in your reports.

Categorizing vendors by type

By setting up and using vendor types, you can create reports and send special mailings based on a specific vendor group.

For example, a construction business might set up the following vendor types:

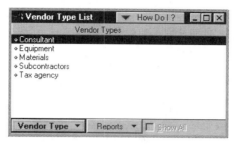

Information you may want to set up for different kinds of vendors

Besides entering the name, address, and phone number for your vendors, use the following table for ideas on additional information that might be useful.

Vendors	Comments	Information you may want to set up
Product suppliers and service companies	N/A	■ Account number ■ Terms ■ Credit limit ■ Product or service information using the notepad
Financial institutions	Financial institutions are considered vendors because they provide services and products (such as loans and credit cards) that you repay.	■ Account number ■ Terms ■ Contact names
Tax agencies	Tax agencies are considered vendors because you owe them money.	Use the notepad to track information about conversations with tax staff.
Contractors, subcontractors, consultants, agents, brokers	These people provide a service for which you owe money, but they are not employees.	■ Tax ID ■ "Vendor eligible for 1099" ■ Pager or cell phone number using a custom field.
Utilities, phone companies, landlords	Besides entering the main phone number for these vendors, consider adding custom fields for pager, customer service, or emergency phone numbers.	Define fields for one or more of the following: ■ Pager or cell phone number ■ Customer service phone number ■ Emergency phone number

Setting up vendors

Note: You might have already set up some of your vendors with the EasyStep Interview.

What to set up	Comments	Search Help index for...
Vendor types (optional)	Use this feature to classify your vendors by the type of service they perform or the items they sell. After you add all your entries to the vendor types list, you can select the appropriate type for each vendor you add.	vendor types
Custom fields for vendors	Use these fields to record additional information about the vendor. Once you've set up the custom fields for one vendor, the fields will appear for all vendors.	vendors, custom fields for
Vendors	If you plan to track accounts payable, you must enter information about the vendors you work with.	vendors, adding
	■ Payment terms The Terms drop-down list is located on the Additional Info tab of the New Vendor window. When you enter a bill from this vendor, QuickBooks uses the terms to calculate when the bill is due.	terms for payment
	■ Credit limit (optional) The Credit Limit field is located on the Additional Info tab of the New Vendor window. Enter the credit limit that your company has with this vendor. QuickBooks warns you when you are about to exceed the limit.	vendors, adding
	■ Tax ID field and 1099 checkbox The Tax ID field is located on the Additional Info tab of the New Vendor window. Fill in the Tax ID field if you send 1099-MISC forms to the vendor. Then select the 1099 checkbox.	1099s
	■ Opening balance Enter the amount you owed this vendor as of your QuickBooks start date.	■ opening balances, entering for accounts receivable and accounts payable ■ historical transactions
Account to track vendor discounts (Optional)	If you receive discounts for early payment, you can set up an expense account called 'Vendor Discounts." Because discounts reduce your expenses, this type of account is sometimes called a *contra-expense* account.	accounts (managing), adding

Using vendor names and managing your Vendor list

Using vendors in QuickBooks

As you create purchase orders, enter bills, and use other forms, you'll choose your vendor from the vendor drop-down list.

If you discover that a vendor is missing from the list, you can enter it in the **Vendor** or **Name** field and add it at this time.

Managing your Vendor list

The Vendor list displays helpful information at a glance:

- Name of each vendor

- Current balance you owe each vendor

Managing your Vendor list includes updating your vendors' records to keep the information current. It also includes making little-used or no-longer used vendors inactive. By managing your list in this way, you make the list much easier to work with.

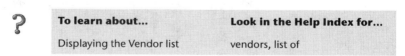

To learn about...	Look in the Help Index for...
Displaying the Vendor list	vendors, list of

Editing vendors

You can edit a vendor record at any time to update vendor information.

To learn about...	Look in the Help Index for...
Editing vendors	vendors, editing information for

Hiding vendors

If you haven't used a vendor for a long time, you can make the vendor inactive. QuickBooks keeps the information associated with that vendor, but hides the vendor from the Vendor list and from any vendor drop-down lists. You do not need to change or delete any transaction that uses the vendor. You can make the vendor active again at any time.

To learn about...	Look in the Help Index for...
Making vendors inactive	vendors, hiding and showing
Making inactive vendors active	vendors, hiding and showing

Merging vendor records

If you have duplicate vendor records stored in your Vendor list, you can use the merge feature to combine the duplicate records into one record.

For example, if your Vendor list included both BayShore Water and BayShore Water Co you'd want to merge them.

To learn about...	Look in the Help Index for...
Merging vendor records	merging, list entries

Deleting vendors

If you add a name to your Vendor list by mistake, you can delete the vendor. QuickBooks allows you to delete a vendor only if there are no transactions associated with the vendor.

To learn about...	Look in the Help Index for...
Deleting vendors	vendors, deleting

Adding notes

The vendor notepad provides a place to record important conversations and product information. You can access the notepad from the Edit Vendor window or anytime you are viewing a transaction related to the vendor. You can also create To Do notes to remind you of a vendor-related task, such as placing an order or making a phone call.

To learn about...	Look in the Help Index for...
Using the vendor notepad	vendors, notes about
Creating To Do notes	To Do notes

Contacting your vendors by mail

You can use your QuickBooks data in conjunction with prewritten Microsoft Word letters to mail your vendors change of address notifications, requests for credit applications, and other messages.

To learn about...	Look in the Help Index for...
Using your QuickBooks data with Microsoft Word letters	letters using QuickBooks data in Microsoft Word

INVENTORY

If you purchase goods for resale, keep them in inventory, and then sell them, QuickBooks can help you track the current quantity and value of your stock. In addition, QuickBooks can handle the accounting associated with buying, holding, and selling inventory.

QuickBooks is not designed to handle certain kinds of inventory. Before you begin to set up inventory in QuickBooks, read the first section of this chapter carefully to determine whether QuickBooks is suitable for your inventory tracking needs.

Is QuickBooks inventory right for my business?

Which types of inventory can I track in QuickBooks?

inventory

The most common kinds of inventory are merchandise or stock in trade; raw materials; work in process; finished products; and supplies that physically become a part of the item intended for sale.

(From the IRS *Tax Guide for Small Business*)

QuickBooks inventory is designed for retail and wholesale businesses that buy items ready for resale or assemble purchased items into items that are sold as units (finished goods). If your inventory meets *all* the following guidelines, you can track it successfully in QuickBooks:

- You purchase and hold multiple copies of the same items. That is, your inventory is not made up of one-of-a-kind items.

- The value of your inventory is based on the purchase price of each item. You don't add any labor or repackaging that increases its value.

- You actually sell all or most of your inventory. You don't simply use it up in the course of your business.

- You keep items in stock rather than ordering just what you need for a specific job.
- When you sell items from inventory (non-assembled items), you want to track the quantities sold in the same units as you track the quantities purchased.
- You are willing to track the value of your inventory according to the average cost method. (See "How Quick-Books calculates the value of your inventory" on page 165.)

Here are some instances in which QuickBooks inventory is probably not suited to your business:

- You have a manufacturing business, and your inventory includes products that you create from different raw materials. Inventory assembly items, which can be created and built using QuickBooks Premier Editions, can be used to combine component items into assembled units you can sell, but QuickBooks is not designed to track inventory through a manufacturing process.
- You stock items that are all unique from one another (for example, antiques, rare coins, gemstones, or items that must be tracked by serial numbers).
- Your inventory consists of items you rent or lease out, rather than sell, to customers.
- You sell items on consignment, so you do not own the items you sell.
- You need to fill orders for back-ordered items automatically as soon as you receive the new shipment.
- You rely on a point-of-sale scanning system to update your inventory.
- You want to track the stock of items you purchase for use in your work (for example, office supplies).
- You need to value your inventory by last in, first out (LIFO) or first in, first out (FIFO).

If you're not sure whether to use QuickBooks to track your inventory

You can set up items that are *not* inventory items for things you purchase, things you sell, or both. QuickBooks calls such items *non-inventory parts* (although they don't have to be a part of anything else). See "Types of QuickBooks items" on page 81.

Here are some advantages of using non-inventory parts instead of inventory parts:

- If you decide you have inventory that QuickBooks can track, you can change a non-inventory part into an inventory part. However, you can't change an inventory part into a non-inventory part, nor can you delete an inventory part that is used in any QuickBooks transaction.

- Because QuickBooks doesn't keep track of how many non-inventory parts you have on hand, you can use them for raw materials or components or anything you do not sell directly.

- You can use non-inventory parts with generic descriptions for one-of-a-kind items you sell (for example, a ring or an antique dresser). You can edit the description or sales price right on the sales form. Using generic non-inventory parts keeps the quantity of items on your list of items from drastically increasing.

If you're still not sure whether or not to use QuickBooks inventory, we recommend that you consult with your accountant.

Should I be using QuickBooks if it can't track my inventory?

Ultimately, the answer depends on how much you need your inventory tracking to be integrated into your accounting software.

Many businesses use QuickBooks for the basic flow of money in and out of the business. They either make periodic accounting entries to show the value of inventory on their books or simply track their inventory in a separate program (such as a spreadsheet).

Talk it over with your accountant to see whether you can use Quickbooks for everything but your inventory.

What QuickBooks inventory can do for you

If you have the kind of inventory that QuickBooks can track, here are some advantages of using the inventory feature:

- You can see at a glance how many items are in stock and how many are on order.

- Every time you receive more items, QuickBooks automatically updates the value and quantity of your inventory of those items. If the items had been on order, QuickBooks reduces the number on order.

- QuickBooks warns you if you try to sell more of an item than you have in stock.

- QuickBooks warns you if you're running low on a certain item and need to reorder.

- When you sell inventory, QuickBooks tracks the cost of the goods you are selling and the income you receive. It also automatically updates the value and quantity of your inventory of those items.

This diagram shows the basic process of tracking inventory in QuickBooks.

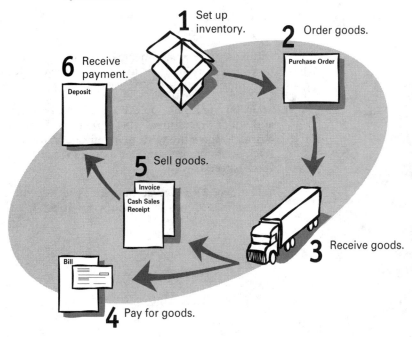

Setting up for tracking inventory

 The level of detail you use while setting up your inventory items and accounts determines the level of detail in your reports. Take some time to determine the level of detail you'd like to track. See Chapter 4, *Organizing data effectively,* beginning on page 23.

List for setting up for inventory tracking in QuickBooks

If you're doing this setup as part of setting up your business in QuickBooks, the goal is to set up your inventory as of your QuickBooks start date. (See Chapter 5, "Setting up your company in QuickBooks," in the *QuickBooks Getting Started Guide*.) Then enter all purchases and sales of inventory as part of the process of entering all historical transactions between your start date and today.

If your business is already set up in QuickBooks but you're just beginning to purchase inventory, you're starting with zero quantities. After setting up items you plan to purchase, you are ready to enter purchase orders, purchases, and sales from now on.

What to set up	Comments	Look in the Help index for...
(If you collect sales tax) Turn on and set up sales tax if you have not already done so.	If your sales tax is set up first, you can indicate which inventory items are taxable when setting them up.	sales tax, setting up
Turn on the preference for using inventory.	QuickBooks automatically turns on this preference if you use the EasyStep Interview to create your company and indicate that you plan to track inventory.	preferences, inventory
Create one or more income accounts for tracking income from sales of inventory.	QuickBooks automatically creates two other accounts you need: ■ Inventory Asset, an asset account for the value of your inventory ■ Cost of Goods Sold, an account for tracking the cost of items you sell See "Accounts for tracking inventory" on page 154.	accounts (managing), adding
Gather the quantity and value for each inventory item you had on hand as of your QuickBooks start date.	You need correct opening quantities and values to set up your inventory items in QuickBooks.	inventory, value of

What to set up	Comments	Search Help index for...
Set up inventory items by adding them to your Item list.	If you didn't have any stock of an item on your QuickBooks start date, enter zero for the quantity on hand and value as of that date. QuickBooks will start calculating the cost of goods sold from the first time you begin purchasing the items to sell.	inventory, items
Enter purchase orders for any items currently on order.	You don't have to enter purchase orders that were received in full between your start date and today.	inventory, ordering
Enter all purchases and sales of inventory between your QuickBooks start date and today.	To bring your quantities and values up to date, you must enter these prior purchases and sales.	■ inventory, receiving ■ inventory, selling

Accounts for tracking inventory

When you set up inventory items on your Item list, you need to associate each item with three different accounts.

QuickBooks automatically sets up the first two accounts for you. Simply indicate that you want to track inventory (either in the EasyStep Interview or in the purchases and vendors preferences). Then set up an inventory item.

- **Inventory Asset account:** QuickBooks uses this *other current asset* type account to track the current value of your inventory.

  Although most businesses need only one such account, you may set up additional other current asset accounts for inventory if you wish.

- **Cost of Goods Sold account:** QuickBooks uses this *cost of goods sold* type account to track the cost to you of the items you have sold. On your chart of accounts, this account is below your income accounts but above your expense accounts. On a profit and loss statement, QuickBooks subtracts the total cost of goods sold from your total income to provide a gross profit before expenses.

  Although most businesses need only one such account, you may set up additional cost of goods sold accounts if you wish.

- **One or more sales income accounts:** You need one or more income accounts to track the income from the resale of inventory. You can associate all or most of your inventory items with the same income account. The number of income accounts you have depends on how much detail you need to see on your profit and loss statements. For guidelines and tips, see Chapter 4, *Organizing data effectively,* beginning on page 23.

Setting up inventory items

If you track inventory, the Inventory Part item type allows you to keep track of how many items remain in stock after a sale, how many items you have on order, your cost of goods sold, and the value of your inventory.

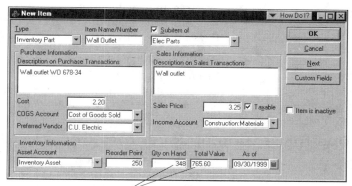

Enter the price you usually pay for this item in the **Cost** field.

Enter the price you charge for this item in the **Sales Price** field.

Enter the quantity on hand and value as of your QuickBooks start date.

Choose an **Income Account** for tracking income when you sell the item.

Setting up subitems, group items, or assembly items

If you have a long list of inventory items, you can organize your list by setting up items for general types of items, such as garden tools. Then you can set up subitems for the items you actually sell (such as shears, trimmers, and spades).

The item you set up for the general type must be an inventory part itself. Subitems must be of the same item type as the parent item. You can make the quantity and value of the parent item zero because you do not buy or sell it.

If you sell or purchase groups of inventory items as one unit, you can set up group items or inventory assembly items to represent the entire unit. This makes it easy to enter the item on purchase orders, purchase forms, and sales forms.

Group items allow you to combine different item types, such as an inventory part with a service item. When you use group items, QuickBooks tracks the inventory of individual items in the group, not the group item itself. The price of a group is the sum of the prices of the individual items, but you can include a discount or an additional charge item in the group to adjust the price.

Inventory assembly items allow you to combine inventory part items or other assembly items and build them into one unit you can sell. When you use inventory assemblies, QuickBooks tracks the assembly items, not the individual components of the assembly. The price of an assembly can be anything you specify. If you want to include a service item with an assembly item (for example, to include installation for an assembled product that you sell), you can do this by combining an assembly item with the service item in a group item.

You must have QuickBooks Premiere Edition(s) to create inventory assemblies and build them. Afterwards, you can use any version of QuickBooks to view, sell, purchase, or report on assembly items that exist in your company file.

Tips for setting up inventory items

- Set up an item for each kind of good you have on hand. Do not try to use the same item for products that have different values (aside from price fluctuations).

- You can use either names or numbers for items.

- If you like to buy an item from a certain vendor, enter that vendor's name in the **Preferred Vendor** field.

- If you want QuickBooks to remind you to order more of an item, fill in the **Reorder Point** field. When the quantity on hand for that item reaches this amount, QuickBooks reminds you to reorder on the Reminders list that appears each time you start QuickBooks. (You can also access the Reminders list by choosing it from the Company menu.)

- For the purchase description, enter the information the vendor needs to know. For the sales description, enter the information the customer needs to know.

- You can use custom fields to provide additional description for your items, such as color, size, or finish of the item.

Once you use an inventory item, you can't delete it or change it to a different type of item.

Before setting up inventory items (inventory part, inventory assembly, non-inventory, and group items or subitems) and using them, be sure that QuickBooks inventory is right for your type of business. If you record purchases or sales of an inventory item, you won't be able to delete the item unless you delete all transactions for the item. As long as the item is on your Item list, you can't set up a new item of the same name but different item type. (However, you can hide unwanted items so you don't see them on your list.)

To learn about...	Look in the Help Index for...
Setting up inventory items	inventory, items
Setting up subitems	subitems
Setting up group items	items, grouped together

Working with QuickBooks inventory

Ordering inventory items

You can write purchase orders for inventory items and send them to your vendors. Or, you can record purchase orders to track orders made by phone.

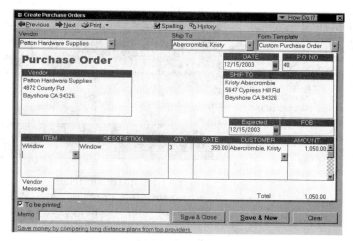

When you record a purchase order for inventory items, QuickBooks tracks the status of the items you have on order. Your accounts aren't affected.

 To see a list of outstanding purchase orders, choose Purchase Orders List from the Vendors menu. The list is alphabetical by vendor.

To learn about...	Look in the Help Index for...
Filling out a purchase order for inventory	inventory, ordering
Viewing inventory items on order	inventory, reports about
Viewing items on order for a particular customer or job	purchase orders, reports about

Receiving inventory items

QuickBooks provides several ways to record the receipt of items. No matter which way you use, QuickBooks always increases the quantity on hand for each inventory item you receive.

If you receive items with a bill

If you receive items with a bill, use the Enter Bills window to record the items received.

Record the items on the Items tab of the bill (shown in front in this example).

If you have additional expenses (such as freight charges), record them on the Expenses tab of the bill.

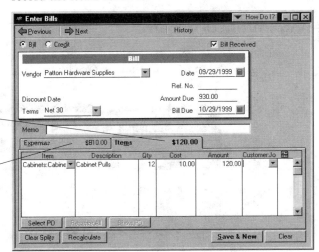

If you have recorded a purchase order for the items, you can receive against that purchase order. When you enter the vendor name on the bill, QuickBooks checks to see if open purchase orders exist for that vendor. If there are, it lets you record which items you have received against one or more open purchase orders.

If you receive items before the bill arrives

If you receive items without a bill, use the Create Item Receipts window to record the fact that they arrived. Later, when you receive the bill, you can turn the item receipt into a bill.

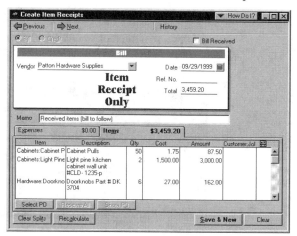

When you record an item receipt, QuickBooks increases the quantity and value of your inventory.

If you have recorded a purchase order for the items, you can receive against that purchase order just as you can for a bill.

When you receive the bill for items received earlier

When you indicate that you want to enter a bill for items received earlier, QuickBooks asks for the vendor name and then displays all item receipts for that vendor. When you choose the appropriate item receipt, QuickBooks displays a bill that matches items on the item receipt.

If the actual costs differ from what you expected, you can edit them on the bill. QuickBooks automatically adjusts the value of your inventory.

You can also add miscellaneous expenses on the Expenses tab of the bill.

To learn about...	Look in the Help Index for...
Recording items received with or without a bill, and entering the bill when it comes	receiving inventory
Paying bills	bills from vendors, paying

Buying inventory items over the counter

When you pay for and receive items on the spot, you record the items and payment in one step.

Paying with a check or cash

If you pay by check or cash when buying inventory items over the counter, use the Write Checks window to enter the purchase.

If you wrote a check, the **Bank Account** field should show your checking account.

If you paid cash, the **Bank Account** field should show the QuickBooks bank account you set up for petty cash.

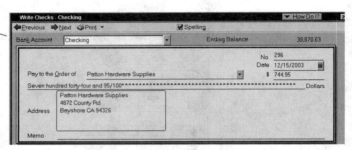

Paying with a credit card

If you pay by credit card when buying inventory items over the counter, use the Enter Credit Card Charges window to enter the purchase.

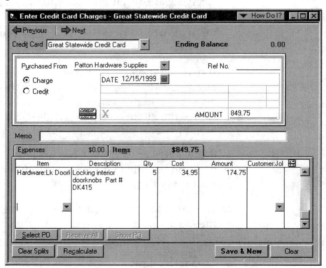

> **Always use the Items tab (not the Expenses tab) on the Write Checks or Enter Credit Card Charges window.**
>
> The Items tab distinguishes inventory items from standard business expenses and allows QuickBooks to increase the quantity and value of your inventory.

To learn about...	Look in the Help Index for...
Buying inventory over the counter	inventory, buying over the counter

Selling inventory items

You record the sale of inventory items the same way you record any sale in QuickBooks. See "How to track sales and payments" on page 119.

When you sell items from inventory, QuickBooks does the following:

- It tracks how many items remain in stock after the sale.

- It enters a line in your Inventory Asset account register for each item sold, and it reduces the value of your inventory by the number of items sold times the average cost per item.

- It increases your sales income by the amount of each line item.

- It increases your cost of goods sold by the result of the quantity sold times the average cost of each item.

You can add shipping charges to a sales form. You need an *other charge* type of item for the shipping charges. (See "Types of QuickBooks items" on page 81.) Then add this item to the sales form along with the inventory items you're selling.

To learn about...	Look in the Help Index for...
Creating invoices	invoices, creating
Creating packing slips	packing slips
Recording sales receipts	sales receipts
Receiving payments	inventory, selling

Tracking back orders and layaways

Depending on your needs, you can track backorders and layaways in one of two ways in QuickBooks.

- Enter invoices and mark them as pending. You can then get reports on backorders or layaways by customer. You can also record any down payments or prepayments. However, pending invoices do not affect your inventory quantities on hand (because a pending invoice is not a sale). You may inadvertently record a sale of an item you have already set aside as a layaway.

- Or, enter postdated invoices (that is, invoices with dates some time in the future). Postdated invoices do reduce your inventory. They don't affect your income on reports as long as the reporting period doesn't extend into the invoice dates.

To learn about...	Look in the Help Index for...
Creating a pending invoice	pending sales

Managing your inventory

Managing your inventory includes such tasks as viewing items you have on hand and on order, recording returns to vendors or from customers, and updating your inventory quantities.

QuickBooks keeps track of how many of each item you have in stock or on order, and warns you if you try to sell something you don't have.

When you record inventory returns to a vendor or from a customer, QuickBooks adjusts the amount you owe the vendor or the amount the customer owes you. It also adjusts the quantity on hand and value of your inventory.

When you record changes to your physical inventory, QuickBooks automatically updates the value of your inventory.

Viewing quantities on hand and on order

View the quantities on hand and on order in several ways:

- To view all quantities on hand, display your Item list. (See the illustration on page 80.)

- To view the reorder points, quantities on hand and on order, and average weekly sales of each item, create a stock status by item report.

- To view a list of purchase orders and quantities still on order for one item, create an item QuickReport.

Returning inventory to a vendor

If you return items to a vendor, you must enter a bill credit to make QuickBooks reduce your inventory of those items. Enter a bill credit regardless of whether you have received a bill and regardless of whether you have paid for the items already.

To create a bill credit instead of a bill, select Credit in the Enter Bills window.

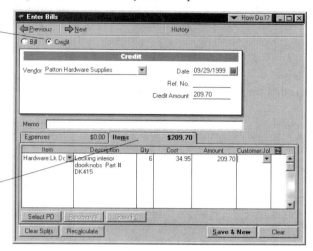

Because you are returning items, record them on the Items tab (not the Expenses tab).

 Enter the bill credit in addition to the original item receipt, bill, check, or credit card charge that includes the items you're returning. When you're ready to pay the bill, apply the bill credit to the full bill in the Pay Bills window. If you have already paid for the items, apply the bill credit against another bill from the vendor or against a refund you receive.

Receiving returns from a customer

When you receive returns from a customer, you enter a credit memo. (See the illustration on page 128.) The credit memo reduces the sales income for the returned items and reduces the cost of goods sold. In addition, it increases the inventory asset account by the same amount and increases the quantity in inventory. QuickBooks doesn't recalculate the average cost of the returned items.

Adjusting inventory

Many companies that have inventory take a physical inventory every 6 to 12 months, often at the end of their fiscal year. For help with taking inventory, print the physical inventory worksheet (an inventory report). The worksheet shows each item name and description, preferred vendor, and quantity on hand, and has blank lines on which you can record the physical count.

Although QuickBooks automatically adjusts your quantities after every purchase and sale, you may need to adjust them yourself from time to time for reasons such as breakage, theft, shrinkage, or fire. If you know about changes to your physical inventory, you should record those changes as they happen rather than at year end.

When you adjust your quantity on hand, QuickBooks assumes that the average cost of the item remains the same and adjusts your inventory value accordingly. If needed, QuickBooks lets you adjust the value of your inventory.

For example, after doing a physical inventory, you find you have seven fewer shirts than you thought you had. You decrease your quantity. QuickBooks then asks you which account you would like to attribute this shrinkage to for your profit and loss statement. As you reduce the quantity, you reduce your inventory asset amount and increase your expense.

?

To learn about...	Look in the Help Index for...
Viewing quantity on hand	inventory, reports about
Viewing items on order	inventory, items
Returning items to a vendor	inventory, returning
Receiving returns from a customer	returns, recording
Taking a physical inventory	inventory, taking stock of
Adjusting quantity on hand	Inventory, adjusting

Inventory and your QuickBooks accounts

As you use QuickBooks to do everyday tasks like receive items, write invoices, and enter sales receipts, QuickBooks automatically updates the accounts associated with your inventory.

When you receive inventory, you affect at least two accounts:

- Your inventory asset account increases in value by the cost of the items you have received.

- If you haven't paid for the items, your accounts payable balance increases. If you paid by check, your bank balance decreases. If you paid by credit card, your credit card balance increases.

When you sell inventory, you affect several accounts:

- QuickBooks automatically calculates the cost of the items you sold. (For details, see "How QuickBooks calculates the value of your inventory" following.) This cost shows up on your profit and loss statement in your cost of goods sold (COGS) account.

- Income from the sale of the item shows up on your profit and loss statement in an income account. As long as you charge more than the cost of the items, you are increasing your gross profit.

- Your inventory asset account decreases in value by the cost of the items you have sold.

- For sales receipts, your bank account or your account for undeposited funds increases. For invoiced sales, your accounts receivable balance increases.

How QuickBooks calculates the value of your inventory

QuickBooks uses the average cost method for valuing your inventory rather than other methods such as last in, first out (LIFO) or first in, first out (FIFO).

That is, QuickBooks calculates the average cost of an inventory item (equal to the total value of the items currently in stock divided by the number of items in stock).

When you purchase more of the same items, the value of the inventory increases by the purchase cost. Purchasing more items may change the average cost per item.

When you sell some items, the value of the inventory decreases by the average cost per item multiplied by the number of items sold. Selling items does not change the average cost per item.

To learn about...	Look in the Help Index for...
How QuickBooks calculates average cost for inventory assembly items	items, inventory assembly

How QuickBooks calculates cost of goods sold

The cost of goods sold (COGS) is the expense to your business of goods you have sold from inventory. QuickBooks calculates the cost of goods sold for an item as the average cost of the item at the time of sale multiplied by the quantity sold.

On your chart of accounts and your profit and loss statement, the cost of goods sold account is below your income accounts but above your expense accounts. Although most people need only one cost of goods sold account, you can set up additional accounts. QuickBooks uses the account assigned to the inventory item in the Edit Item window.

When you sell goods, you're also realizing income. The difference between the income and the cost of goods sold is your profit on the sale.

Tracking expenses in QuickBooks means tracking any money you spend on anything relating to your business. These can be services you purchase, items you plan to keep in inventory for resale, fixtures that will become capital assets of your business, office supplies, coffee filters, desks, computers, cleaning services, plant rental or subcontractor services. Basically, any time money leaves your business, you must decide how you want to track it.

Keep supporting documents—sales slips, paid bills, receipts, and canceled checks. If the IRS ever needs to see your records, you must be able to document all your expense deductions.

Ways to track and pay expenses in QuickBooks

Tracking expenses

By account

The expense accounts you set up to track expenses will determine the level of detail you have on your reports regarding your expenses.

For example, a construction firm may want to capture the information about job expenses using the four subaccounts as shown below, but lump all office supplies into one account.

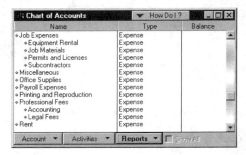

An advertising agency, though, may want to track more detail on its office supplies.

Tax implications

You may want to model your expense accounts after the tax lines that appear on the tax forms you file. For example Schedule C (Profit and Loss from Business) includes the following tax lines:

(line) 8 - Advertising

(line) 9 - Bad debts from sales or services

(line) 10 - Car and truck expenses

If you file this form, you'll want to set up at least one QuickBooks expense account to track "Car and truck expenses," but you could also choose to have subaccounts for this expense area.

Note: If you designate your tax lines for your expense accounts you can simplify your income tax reporting. See "Setting up income tax tracking" on page 209.

By class

While you must have some expense accounts set up for your business, classes are optional, but provide another way to track and look at your expense (and income) information.

For example, you might want to track the income and expenses for each partner in your law firm. You would set up your Class List as follows and then for each transaction (invoice, expense, and so on) specify the appropriate class.

For more information about classes, see "Tracking income and expenses with classes" on page 30.

By customer (and job)

Some businesses using QuickBooks find it useful to track customer information and related job information, parts ordered, and costs.

For example, a construction company may do several jobs for one customer and may want to track the expenses (and income) for them separately.

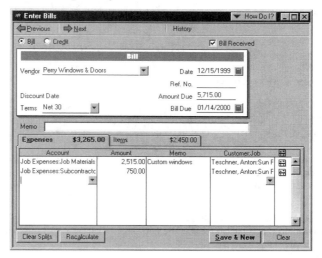

Use the Customer:Job column to track the expenses for a customer, and in this example, a specific job.

You can track the parts you order for a particular customer and job on a purchase order. You'll continue tracking the parts (and the customer:job information) when you receive them and enter the bill (or item receipt).

For more information about customers, see Chapter 9, *Customers and jobs,* beginning on page 97.

Summary of expense accounts, classes, and customers

If you assign the amount of the bill to various expense accounts, customers, jobs, and classes in the detail area of the form or register, your reports will accurately reflect how much you spend within each expense account, for each customer or job, and within each class you have set up.

By purchase order

QuickBooks purchase orders can help you track inventory parts. At any time, you can see items you have on order and when they're due to be received. For more information about inventory parts, see Chapter 12, *Inventory,* beginning on page 149.

If you are a QuickBooks Pro or Premier user, you can also order non-inventory parts, services you order from subcontractors, and other charge items on a purchase order if you set up these items with both an income and an expense account, reflecting that you both buy and sell these items. For more information about these types of items, see Chapter 8, *Items—your services, products, fixed assets, and more,* beginning on page 75.

Paying for expenses

Situation	How to record in QuickBooks	Comments	See...
You purchase an item or service and must pay for it on the spot.	Enter the expense as a check, credit card, or petty cash transaction.	These could include costs of dining out, office supplies, highway tolls, and expenses incurred at the post office.	"Paying bills immediately (non-A/P)" on page 183
You receive a bill and want to track and pay it using accounts payable (A/P).	Enter the bills as soon as you receive them and be reminded of when they are due.	Using A/P can help you pay on time and help you forecast your cash flow. You'll also be able to easily find out: ■ Which vendors you owe money to and how much you owe them; ■ If you've paid a certain bill; ■ If any of your payments are overdue, including which ones and by how much; ■ How much you spent with each vendor last quarter.	"Using A/P to track and pay expenses" on page 176

(continued)

Situation	How to record in QuickBooks	Comments	See...
You receive a bill and want to pay it immediately.	Pay for the expense with a check, credit card, or cash.	It's a simple way to handle paying your bills.	"Paying bills immediately (non-A/P)" on page 183
You purchase an item for your business but pay for it with a personal check or credit card.	We recommend setting up a liability account to track these expenses. You would enter these types of expenses directly in the account's register.	Consider opening business checking and credit card accounts to make your expense reporting simpler for tax purposes.	"Mixing business and personal funds" on page 188
You want to use online payment.	You can pay bills or write checks in QuickBooks as you usually do. Your online transactions are automatically stored in an "outbox" until you're ready to send them.	For information about scheduling payments, see page 175.	"Using online payment" on page 172 and "Setting up online payment" on page 175
You handwrite your checks.	Enter the check information in the check window or register.	On the Write Checks window, you'll need to make sure you clear the **To be printed** checkbox and that the **No.** field has the same number as the check you write.	"Using checks" on page 183.

Paying for expenses on the spot

All businesses incur some expenses that involve immediate payment, such as costs for travel and dining out, and office supplies. For these payments, you'll want to update the appropriate QuickBooks register or form with the expense information.

For example, if you paid for a business lunch with a credit card, enter the expense on the Enter Credit Card Charges window or in the appropriate credit card register, choosing the appropriate expense account.

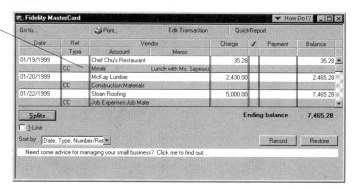

Paying bills at a later time

accounts payable

The record of outstanding bills a business must pay. Called A/P for short.

You can track and pay bills you receive through the mail by using the QuickBooks accounts payable (A/P) feature or by simply paying bills as you receive them with a check, a credit card, or cash.

Note: You should use just one method to avoid duplicating payments.

Using online payment

Whether you use A/P or not, you should consider using the QuickBooks online payment feature. Online payment works with any U.S. account with check-writing privileges. You can:

- Pay anyone, from the electric company to your janitorial service.

- Send remittance information on an online payment check voucher.

- Create online payment instructions for one or more payments, and then send all your instructions in one connection.

- Schedule a payment, up to a year in advance, to arrive on a certain date.

- Inquire about online payments, and cancel them if the need arises.

    Note: For more information on online payments, go to www.quickbooks.com.

How Your Bills Get Paid

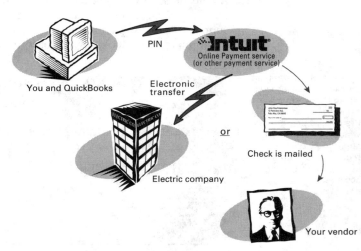

PIN

Intuit
Online Payment service (or other payment service)

You and QuickBooks

Electronic transfer

or

Check is mailed

Electric company

Your vendor

Note: You cannot send paychecks, payroll liability payments, or sales tax checks using online payment.

Delivery date information

Depending on your financial institutions payment processing model, you may be able to specify a delivery date for your online payments. If you can enter a delivery date, QuickBooks calculates the payment delivery date based on the type of online payment that the payee is set up to receive. However, because processing times can vary, it's a good idea to enter a delivery date that's a few days before the due date.

- If the payee is set up to receive an electronic funds transfer (EFT), the financial institution transfers the money directly from your account to the payee on the payment date you designate.

- If the payee cannot receive EFTs, the payment processor prints a check that includes the account number the payee uses to identify you. The processor then sends the check to the payee via U.S. mail.

The number of business days needed for processing the payment is the *lead time*. QuickBooks will calculate the necessary lead time at the time you enter the payment.

Setting up to track and pay expenses

Task	Comments	Look in the Help Index for...
Decide your bill paying scheme.	**Important**. Once you decide whether you'll use A/P tracking or just pay bills as they arrive, you'll want to use the method consistently to avoid duplicate payment of bills!	bills from vendors, tracking bills vs. writing checks
Add additional accounts to the chart of accounts as needed.	The Accounts Payable account is automatically added to your chart of accounts the first time you enter a bill. QuickBooks uses this account to track the money your business owes to others. When you enter a new bill, or pay off outstanding bills, QuickBooks records the transaction in the register for your Accounts Payable account.	■ accounts (managing), adding ■ petty cash account
Set your checking-related preferences.	Checking preferences let you set default accounts for checking, print account names on voucher checks, and warn about duplicate check numbers.	preferences, checking
Set up your printer for check printing.	None	entries under: printing checks
Set the preference for whether to automatically recall the last transaction for a vendor.	When this preference is on, QuickBooks automatically recalls the last bill or check for a vendor when you enter the vendor name on a new bill or check.	automatic transaction entry
If you want to order services or goods, turn on the preference for using purchase orders and inventory.	Even if you don't track inventory, turn on this preference if you want to issue purchase orders to subcontractors and other vendors.	purchase orders, turning on
Set up the Reminders preferences.	You can designate how many days in advance you want to be reminded of due bills and if you want to see a summary or a detailed list of due bills.	preferences, reminders

Setting up online payment

Action	Comments	Look in the Help index for...
Setting up online payment	See "Setting up online banking (account access and payment)" on page 60.	online payments, setting up
Setting up online payees	Online payees can be anyone to whom you need to send payments. Employees cannot receive online paychecks, but they can receive other types of online checks. The **Account Number** field number is used by the payee to identify you. It is printed on the check so a payee can apply your payment to the correct account. If you do not have an account number, enter a note or message to your payee.	payees for online payment
Scheduling online payments	You can schedule payments up to 12 months in advance using the date fields on the Write Checks and Pay Bills windows and on your checking register. For example, you may want to schedule the payment of your monthly rent check. Using the Write Checks window, you enter the appropriate information and a **Delivery Date** of 06/30/00. Click Next when done. Now enter the same information for next month's rent payment changing the **Delivery Date** to 7/31/00, and so on. You'll then need to send these online payments. **Important:** The balance of your checking register will be affected.	online payments, scheduling

Using A/P to track and pay expenses

Paying bills

If you track your accounts payable, paying bills in QuickBooks is essentially a two-step process. You enter the bills in one window and pay them later using a different window. The following steps provide the general work flow:

1 Enter bills in the Enter Bills window as soon as you receive them. This keeps your cash flow reports up to date, and you won't run the risk of setting bills aside and forgetting about them.

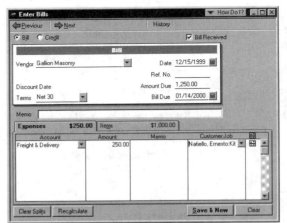

The Expenses tab is used to enter purchases assigned to an expense account. You can also enter shipping charges or tax not associated with any one item.

The Items tab is for entering items you've purchased with or without a purchase order.

You can enter bills directly into the Accounts Payable register instead of using the Enter Bills window. However, if you want to receive a bill or items against a purchase order, use the Enter Bills window.

2 You will be prompted by the Reminder window when bills are due. (If you didn't set up this feature, see the table on page 174.)

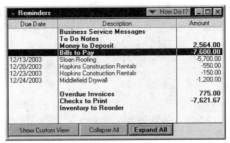

3 Indicate which bills you want to pay in the Pay Bills window. You can apply a discount or credits to any bill. Indicate a payment method to use (check, credit card, or online banking payment). If you don't see a bill you expected to pay, select "Show bills due on or before" and enter the appropriate date. See also "Applying a vendor's discount" on page 178.

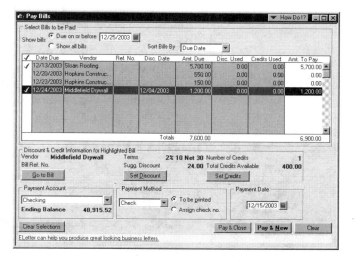

4 If you choose Check as the payment method, you can choose to print the checks or you can assign specific numbers to them if you plan to hand write them. If you have a subscription to an online billpay service through your participating financial institution, or with the QuickBooks Online Payment service, you'll send the payment instructions using that online banking service.

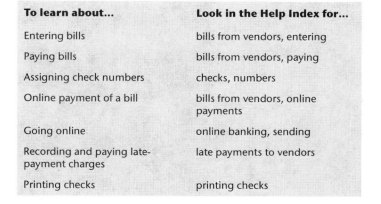

To learn about...	Look in the Help Index for...
Entering bills	bills from vendors, entering
Paying bills	bills from vendors, paying
Assigning check numbers	checks, numbers
Online payment of a bill	bills from vendors, online payments
Going online	online banking, sending
Recording and paying late-payment charges	late payments to vendors
Printing checks	printing checks

Applying a vendor's discount

You can apply a vendor's discount from the Pay Bills window.

- If you entered a vendor's payment terms when you set up the vendor or designated terms on the Enter Bills window, QuickBooks calculates the discount for you and displays it when you highlight the bill. You can change the amount of the discount as needed.

- If you don't specify a vendor's payment terms, calculate the discount manually and enter it in the Discount and Credits window.

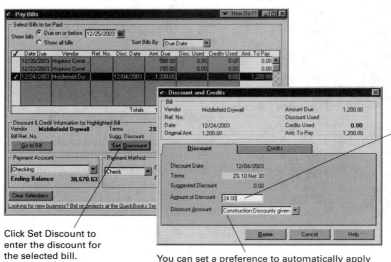

You can enter the suggested discount or enter a different one. When you click Done, the discount is subtracted from the amount you owe.

Click Set Discount to enter the discount for the selected bill.

You can set a preference to automatically apply discounts to any bills you select to pay.

To learn about...	Look in the Help Index for...
Creating an expense account to track your vendor discounts	accounts (managing), adding
Applying a vendor's discount	discounts, from vendors
Automatically applying discounts	preferences, bills
Payment terms	payments you make, terms
Setting up a reminder to pay bills	bills from vendors, reminding yourself to pay

Handling bills you receive regularly

In your business, you probably receive the same bills every month. For example, you may receive phone and utility bills or make loan payments and pay rent at the same times each month. You can memorize these bills and have QuickBooks re-enter them at the intervals you specify.

To learn about...	Look in the Help Index for...
Memorizing bills	bills from vendors, memorizing

Editing bills and payments

You can edit any bill or payment transaction except online payment transactions. Even if you've already paid a bill, you can edit its amount.

If you reduce the bill amount, QuickBooks creates a credit with the vendor you overpaid. If you increase the bill amount, QuickBooks considers the bill not fully paid until you pay the additional amount.

To learn about...	Look in the Help Index for...
Editing bills	bills from vendors, editing
Editing payments	payments you make, editing

Sending an online payment inquiry

With QuickBooks, you can send messages to any financial institution at which you have accounts enabled for online banking. You can inquire about the status of a specific payment, and you may choose to send a message with the inquiry.

To learn about...	Look in the Help Index for...
Online payment inquiries	online payments, inquiring about
Online banking messages	online banking, messages about

Deleting bills and payments

You can delete any bill or payment transaction. If you delete a bill that you have already paid, QuickBooks creates a credit with the vendor. If you delete a payment, the bill or bills it was paying will have unpaid balances.

To learn about...	Look in the Help Index for...
Deleting bills	bills from vendors, deleting
Deleting payments	payments you make, deleting

Viewing an A/P transaction history

A transaction history shows transactions related or linked to the one you selected, so you can move easily to any related transaction. For example, from a bill, you can see any of the payments that paid the bill.

The following table describes the transaction history QuickBooks shows for different types of transactions.

Transaction type	History shows these related transactions, in chronological order
Bill	Payments made on the bill Discounts Purchase Orders
Payment	Bills to which your payment was applied
Credit with a vendor	Bills to which your credit was applied
Item receipt	PO's against which the items were received

To learn about...	Look in the Help Index for...
Viewing the history of a transaction	transaction history

Entering and applying credits from vendors

Use the Enter Bills window to enter a credit from a vendor. Simply change the Bill setting to Credit.

You can easily apply any credit you have with a vendor in the Pay Bills window.

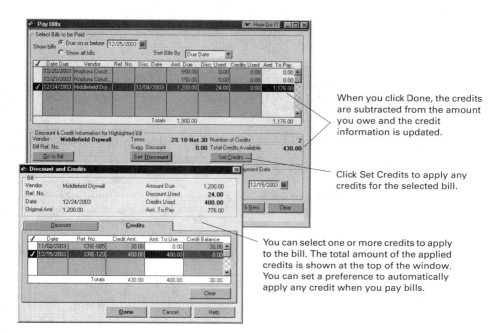

When you click Done, the credits are subtracted from the amount you owe and the credit information is updated.

Click Set Credits to apply any credits for the selected bill.

You can select one or more credits to apply to the bill. The total amount of the applied credits is shown at the top of the window. You can set a preference to automatically apply any credit when you pay bills.

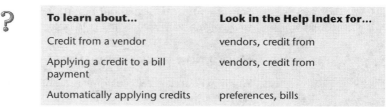

To learn about...	Look in the Help Index for...
Credit from a vendor	vendors, credit from
Applying a credit to a bill payment	vendors, credit from
Automatically applying credits	preferences, bills

Receiving items with a bill

When you receive items with a bill, you can record their receipt and enter the bill at the same time. This feature allows you to associate the items received with the purchase order you entered when ordering them. See also "Receiving inventory items" on page 158.

To learn about...	Look in the Help Index for...
Receiving items with a bill	inventory, receiving

Accounts payable reports

Accounts payable reports can answer questions such as these about your business:

- Which vendors do I owe money to?
- Which of my bills are more than 30 days past due?

QuickBooks has preset A/P reports that give you information about your unpaid bills. You can calculate the aging for the A/P reports and graphs from the due date or the transaction date.

You can filter each preset report so that it shows only the information you want to see. You can also customize each report so that it looks the way you want onscreen and on paper.

Report	Description
A/P aging summary	Shows aging status of unpaid bills in accounts payable, subtotaled by vendor.
A/P aging detail	Lists each unpaid bill, grouped and subtotaled by aging period. Shows how many days a bill is overdue.
Unpaid bills detail	Lists each unpaid bill, grouped and subtotaled by vendor.
Vendor balance summary	Shows unpaid balances for each vendor.
Vendor balance detail	Lists each transaction for a vendor, subtotaled by vendor. Total for a vendor equals that vendor's unpaid balance.

For more information about reports, see Chapter 18, *Tracking your progress with reports and graphs,* beginning on page 285.

Reporting online payments

You'll need to create a custom summary report to report your online activities. After you create the report, you may want to save the settings for future use. See "Saving report settings" on page 292 for more information.

To learn about...	Look in the Help Index for...
Creating a report of online payments	online payments, reports about

Paying bills immediately (non-A/P)

For bills you pay immediately, you'll use check and credit card windows that emulate familiar paper forms. You can also enter these types of transactions in the account's register. For cash purchases, you enter the expense in your petty cash register.

Using checks

If you are not tracking your bills with the accounts payable feature, you can simply write a check when the bill is due. The following steps provide the general work flow:

1 Write the check for the expense using the Write Checks window.

If you are using online payment and you want to include an invoice number or other remittance information, select **Transmit Memo**. A check voucher is printed with the information entered in the **Transmit Memo** field.

The Expenses tab is used to enter purchases assigned to an expense account. You can also enter shipping charges or tax not associated with any one item.

The Items tab is for entering items you've purchased with or without a purchase order.

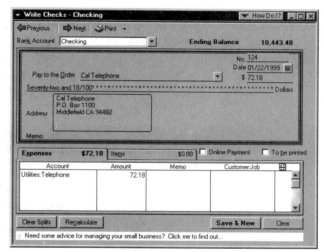

You can write a check directly into the check register instead of using the Write Checks window. However, if you want to pay for an expense connected with a purchase order use the Write Checks window.

2 Either print the checks or send them online if you are using online payment. (If you write checks by hand, you'll need to clear the **To be printed** checkbox on the Write Checks window and make sure the **No.** field has the same number as the check you write.)

To learn about...	Look in the Help Index for...
Paying bills immediately	checks, for expenses and items
Printing checks	printing checks
Online payment of a bill	bills from vendors, online payments
Going online	online banking, sending
Changing information on a check you've recorded	checks, editing

Voiding or deleting checks

Voiding a check changes the amount of the transaction to zero, but keeps a record of the transaction in QuickBooks. If you stop payment on a check or a check is lost, you may want to void it rather than delete it.

 Deleting a check removes the transaction from QuickBooks. Once a check is deleted it can't be recovered.

If you're using online payment, choose Cancel Payment from the Edit menu to cancel a payment that has already been sent to the financial institution.

Note: **This will not stop a payment that has already been issued.** To stop a payment you must contact your financial institution.

To learn about...	Look in the Help Index for...
Voiding checks	checks, voiding or deleting
Deleting checks	checks, voiding or deleting
Canceling an online payment	online payments, canceling a payment

Handling bills you receive regularly

If you repeatedly write similar checks, such as rent or insurance payments, you can save time by memorizing the checks.

To learn about...	Look in the Help Index for...
Memorizing checks	checks, memorizing

Using credit cards

If you're not tracking your bills with the accounts payable feature, you can simply use your credit card to pay for a bill when it's due. The following steps provide the general work flow:

1. Enter the credit card charge in the Enter Credit Card Charges window.

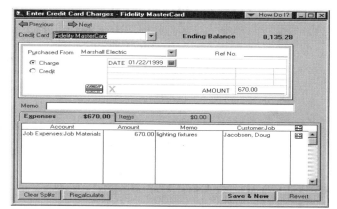

The Expenses tab is used to enter purchases assigned to an expense account. You can also enter shipping charges or tax not associated with any one item.

The Items tab is for entering items you've purchased with or without a purchase order.

You can enter charges directly into the credit card register instead of using the Enter Credit Card Charges window. However, if you want to pay for a bill connected to a purchase order, use the Enter Credit Card Charges window.

2. If you are using online payment, send the payment instructions online. Otherwise, call or visit the company and give them your credit card number.

To learn about...	Look in the Help Index for...
Entering or editing a credit card charge	credit cards you use, transactions
Online payment of a bill	bills from vendors, online payments
Going online	online banking, sending

Voiding or deleting a credit card entry

Voiding a charge changes the amount of the transaction to zero, but keeps a record of the transaction in QuickBooks.

Deleting a charge removes the transaction from QuickBooks. Once a charge is deleted it can't be recovered.

To learn about...	Look in the Help Index for...
Voiding a charge	credit cards you use, voiding or deleting a charge
Deleting a charge	credit cards you use, voiding or deleting a charge

Handling merchandise you return that was paid for with a credit card

If you return merchandise for which you receive credit, you'll need to enter this amount into the credit card account's register or in the Enter Credit Card Charges window. Make sure to assign the credit to the appropriate expense account, class, and customer:job.

To learn about...	Look in the Help Index for...
Credit card refunds	credit cards you use, credits

Using cash to pay for expenses

If you pay for expenses with cash, enter the transaction in your petty cash register.

To enter class and customer:job information, click Splits.

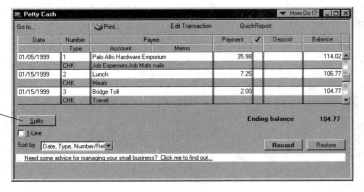

?	To learn about...	Look in the Help Index for...
	Entering cash expenses	cash account, handling expenses
	Handling ATM withdrawals in QuickBooks	ATM withdrawals

Tracking a vendor's discount

You can record a vendor's discount as a negative expense to your Vendor Discount expense account on the appropriate form.

Note: The total amount of the check can't be negative.

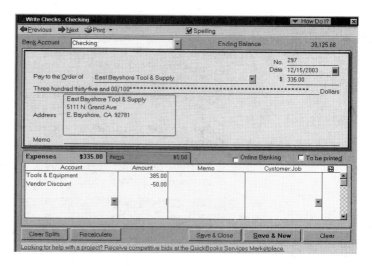

?	To learn about...	Look in the Help Index for...
	Creating an income account to track your vendor discounts	accounts (managing), adding

Mixing business and personal funds

You should keep your business account separate from your personal checking account. -

IRS publication 583, "Starting a Business and Keeping Records"

You should have checking and credit card accounts that are business-only accounts. In fact, the IRS recommends opening a business checking account as one of the *first* things you do when starting a new business. But from time to time you may find it convenient to pay for a business expense with your personal credit card or check, or pay for a personal expense with your business check or credit card.

For owners or partners

The owner's or partner's equity account can track both business expenses you pay for with personal funds and personal expenses paid for with business funds.

Note: **If you track your personal finances in Quicken or in a separate QuickBooks company file, you have to enter the purchase in that file as well.** This section is about recording the purchase in your QuickBooks business file.

Paying for business expenses with personal funds

Enter these business expenses directly in the owner's or partner's equity account register as an increase.

In the Account field, enter the appropriate expense account.

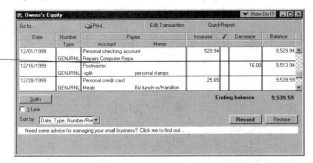

Owners or partners can take a draw (write a check) at any time to reimburse themselves.

To learn about...	Look in the Help Index for...
Creating an owner's draw	owner's draws

Paying for personal expenses with business funds

If you pay for personal expenses with business funds, enter the transaction in the appropriate QuickBooks window (Write Checks, Enter Credit Card Charges, Petty Cash Register) using the owner's or partner's equity account. This will decrease the equity in that account.

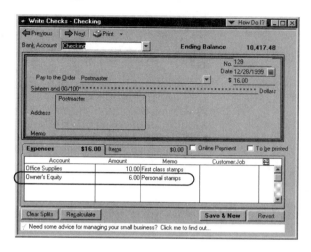

For employees

To reimburse an employee who has paid for a business expense with personal funds, you can do one of the following:

- If you want to reimburse the employee at the time you record the expense, use the Write Checks window.

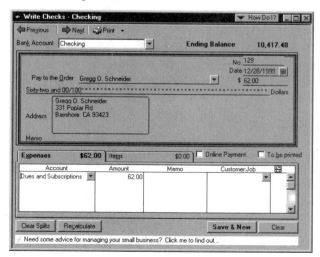

- If you want to reimburse the employee later, enter the expense in an Other Current Liability account as an increase.

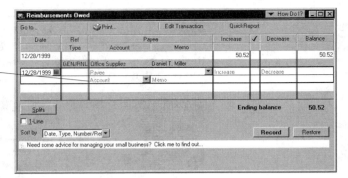

Enter the expense account in the Account field and the employee's name in the Memo field.

When you reimburse the employee, use the Write Checks window. In the Account field, enter the Other Current Liability account, not the expense account, so that the reimbursement check reduces the amount owed.

 Use the To Do Notes feature to keep track of whom you owe.

TRACKING AND
PAYING SALES TAX

QuickBooks helps you determine how much sales tax to collect on each sale, as well as how much you may need to pay when it is due.

This chapter does not intend to be exhaustive on the subject of sales taxes. Tax laws and regulations change frequently and their application can vary widely based on the specific facts and circumstances involved. Be sure to consult your professional tax advisor about your business's specific tax circumstances.

This chapter is about tracking the sales tax you collect from customers, not the sales tax you pay to your vendors.

If you don't collect any sales tax for the services you provide or the products you sell, you don't need to set up sales tax in QuickBooks.

If you need to track the exact sales tax you paid on purchases, you can set up an expense account for sales tax. Most people simply include the sales tax they pay vendors as part of the overall cost of the purchase.

How QuickBooks tracks sales tax

Keeping track of the sales taxes you have to collect from customers and pay to a tax agency can be a challenge. Some things you sell may be taxable while others may not be. Certain customers must be taxed, while sales to others are non-taxable. In addition, different sales may require different taxes. You may even have to collect more than one tax on a sale.

Fortunately, QuickBooks can help you automate your sales tax tracking. You can enter sales quickly and easily, and you'll have more accurate information about the sales taxes you've collected when it is time to pay.

Take the time to set up your sales tax carefully. Then it will be easy to apply the right sales tax to each sale so you will have a better idea of how much sales tax you owe.

The following diagram illustrates the basic steps you perform when tracking sales tax in QuickBooks.

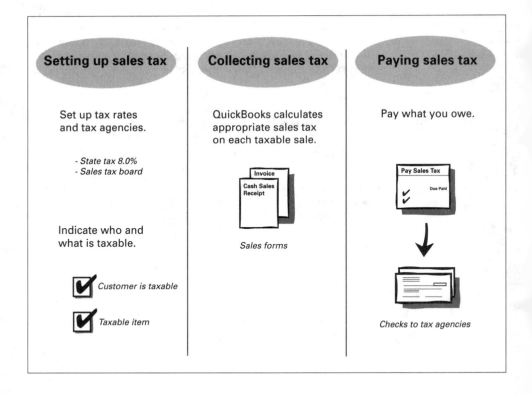

Setting up sales tax

Set up tax rates and tax agencies.

- State tax 8.0%
- Sales tax board

Indicate who and what is taxable.

Customer is taxable

Taxable item

Collecting sales tax

QuickBooks calculates appropriate sales tax on each taxable sale.

Sales forms

Paying sales tax

Pay what you owe.

Checks to tax agencies

Your sales tax rates and tax districts

You collect sales tax for one or more particular sales tax districts. For example, when Stacy sells from her store or makes deliveries within the county, she collects sales tax for the county she is in. If she makes deliveries in the next county, she collects for that county.

For each tax district, you have to tell QuickBooks the tax rate and the name of the agency you pay.

QuickBooks stores the information about your sales tax on your Item list. The Item list has a type of item called a sales tax item, designed exclusively for sales tax. If your rates change, you can update them by editing the relevant sales tax items.

You may be thinking that the Item list is a strange place for sales tax information. Remember that some QuickBooks items are for the services and products you sell, while others are for various calculations on sales forms (subtotals, discounts, credits for payments). Sales tax is just another calculation on a sales form.

Every state with sales tax has a different sales tax structure, so it's hard to generalize. Check with your own state and local sales tax agencies to find out their rules.

The following table describes different sales tax situations you may be dealing with.

Situation	What to use in QuickBooks	See...	Look in the Help Index for...
All taxable sales are in a single tax district.	Sales tax item set up for your tax district	"If your business collects only one tax for one agency" on page 196	sales tax, items
Taxable sales are in two or more tax districts, and you must report sales by district. **Example:** You must report sales by county.	A different sales tax item for each tax district. ■ The districts can be for the same tax agency. ■ The districts can have the same tax rate.	"If your business collects sales taxes based on location" on page 197	sales tax, items

Situation	What to use in QuickBooks	See...	Look in the Help Index for...
You collect a combination of sales taxes on one sale, and you pay the taxes to different tax agencies. **Example:** You pay a statewide tax to one tax agency and a city tax to a different agency.	Sales tax group item that is made up of two or more sales tax items (one for each tax agency)	▪ "Do I need to group individual sales taxes in QuickBooks?" on page 194 ▪ "If your business collects a combination rate" on page 197	sales tax, agencies
You must report sales that are non-taxable because they are outside your state or tax district.	Sales tax codes	▪ "If you report non-taxable sales to out-of-state customers" on page 198 ▪ "Which customers are subject to sales tax?" on page 198	sales tax, out-of-state customers sales tax codes
You must report sales that are non-taxable because the customer is purchasing for resale.	Sales tax codes	▪ "If you report non-taxable sales to resellers" on page 198 ▪ "Which customers are subject to sales tax?" on page 198	sales tax codes
You don't need to report why a sale is non-taxable but you want to make sure the customer is not charged for sales tax.	Sales tax code Non	"Which customers are subject to sales tax?" on page 198	customers, sales tax for

Do I need to group individual sales taxes in QuickBooks?

If you collect a sales tax that combines separate sales taxes, QuickBooks allows you to group the separate taxes together and apply a rate that equals the total of the separate rates.

You may not need to divide your tax into parts in QuickBooks even if the actual tax is a combination of rates. For example, in California, the tax in a county is usually a statewide rate plus some additional taxes levied by the county or a special district. But in QuickBooks, you can simply set up a sales tax item for each county for which you collect sales tax. All sales taxes collected for one county are paid to the same tax agency, and the tax form helps you calculate what you owe for each separate tax.

On the other hand, if you sometimes collect a combination of taxes paid to separate tax agencies, you need to track the taxes separately. For example, suppose you have a county rate plus an additional city rate. In QuickBooks you should set up separate sales tax items (on your Item list) for the county and city taxes. Then you set up a type of item called a *sales tax group* to combine the county and city items. For sales in the city, subject to the combination, you apply the sales tax group item. For sales in the county but outside the city, you apply the county's sales tax item.

Setting up sales tax

The following checklist helps you get ready to track sales tax in QuickBooks.

If you set up your company using the EasyStep Interview and indicated you tracked sales tax, you may have already completed some of these tasks.

What to set up	Comments	Look in the Help Index for...
Add tax agency name or names and information to your Vendor list.	QuickBooks uses this information on the sales tax payment check it writes to each sales tax agency. To print your tax ID number on your payment check, enter it in the Account Number field on the Additional Info tab of the New or Edit Vendor window.	vendors, adding
Turn on sales tax.	Only the QuickBooks Administrator can turn on sales tax.	sales tax, turning on
Indicate the default sales tax codes for your business.	You can set these up in company-wide preferences, or add them later.	sales tax, preferences for
Set company-wide preferences for payment frequency and how sales tax is owed.	You must set these preferences when you turn on sales tax, but you can change them later.	sales tax, preferences for
Indicate the sales tax to prefill when setting up a new customer or starting to enter a new sale.	You must set this choice for "most common sales tax" when you turn sales tax on, but you can change it later.	sales tax, preferences for
Indicate whether to print the letter "T" next to taxable amounts on sales forms.	None	sales tax, preferences for

What to set up	Comments	Look in the Help Index for...
Set up each additional sales tax or component of sales tax as a sales tax item on your Item list.	Most businesses don't need to do this. For more information, see "If your business collects sales taxes based on location" on page 197 and "If your business collects a combination rate" on page 197.	sales tax, items
Set up additional sales tax codes for special situations.	You can add codes at any time to accommodate new situations.	sales tax, codes
To track non-taxable sales, set up a sales tax code for each reason (such as out-of-state, resale).		sales tax, codes
If sales tax has components paid to different tax agencies, set up one or more sales tax groups.	See "If your business collects a combination rate" on page 197.	sales tax, tax assignments
Indicate which existing items on the Item list are taxable and indicate which customers are taxable.	When you turn on sales tax, QuickBooks asks whether to make all existing non-inventory and inventory parts taxable. From now on, when you create a new item, it will automatically be taxable.	items, editing information

If your business collects only one tax for one agency

Most businesses collect only one sales tax for one agency. This is the easiest situation to set up. You need the following:

- The sales tax agency must be a vendor on your Vendor list. Be sure you have entered the agency's address and your sales tax account number, so QuickBooks can print checks with this information.

- You need a sales tax item on your Item list for your sales tax. Your sales tax rate is the rate for this item.

- If you need to report non-taxable sales to out-of-state customers, you need an additional sales tax item for out-of-state sales and a sales tax code to track why the sale is not taxable. See "If you report non-taxable sales to out-of-state customers" on page 198.

- If you need to report non-taxable sales to wholesalers or resellers, you need an additional sales tax item for resale and a sales tax code to track why the sale is non-taxable. See "If you report non-taxable sales to resellers" on page 198.

If your business collects sales taxes based on location

If you deliver, visit customers, or have multiple sales offices, you may need to charge different sales taxes depending on the location of the sale. QuickBooks handles this easily if you do the following:

- For each different sales tax agency you pay, you must have a vendor on your Vendor list. (You need only one agency if you pay all your sales tax to the same agency.)

- For each different sales tax you collect, you need a sales tax item on your Item list. (If you have to report sales and tax by county or district, you need a separate sales tax item for each, even if the rate is the same.)

- If you need to report non-taxable sales to out-of-state customers, you need an additional sales tax item for out-of-state sales. See "If you report non-taxable sales to out-of-state customers" on page 198.

- If you need to report non-taxable sales to wholesalers or resellers, you need an additional sales tax item for resale and a sales tax code to track why the sale is non-taxable. See "If you report non-taxable sales to resellers" on page 198.

- Be sure your customers are set up with the correct sales tax item assigned. Then when you record a new sale to a customer, QuickBooks automatically uses the correct sales tax item.

If your business collects a combination rate

If you collect more than one tax, payable to different agencies, on the same sale but you want to charge your customers one overall tax amount, here is what you must do:

- For each different sales tax agency you pay, you must have a vendor on your Vendor list.

- For each single tax you collect and pay, you need a sales tax item on your Item list.

- For each combination rate you collect, you need a sales tax group on your Item list. A sales tax group includes two or more single taxes set up as sales tax items. The rate for the group is the total of the rates for the items in the group. Group tax items allow QuickBooks to track and report taxes separately, but display them as one combined amount to customers.

- If your most common sales tax is a combination, be sure that the sales tax group item is shown as the most common sales tax in the sales tax preferences. Then new customers and new sales will automatically have the combination rate.

If you report non-taxable sales to out-of-state customers

If you have to report sales that would be taxable had they not been to out-of-state customers, you need to create a sales tax code to identify the out-of-state sale. Then create an out-of-state sales tax item to record the location of the sales. The sales tax liability report will have a separate line showing total non-taxable sales to out-of-state customers.

If you report non-taxable sales to resellers

If you need to identify and report non-taxable sales to resellers, set up a sales tax code for resale and create an out-of-state sales tax item. Then the sales tax liability report will have a separate line showing total non-taxable sales to resellers.

Which customers are subject to sales tax?

After you've set up information about your sales tax, you have to indicate which customers are subject to sales tax. For example, you may sell to retail customers who pay tax and to wholesale customers who are exempt from tax. When you set up or edit customer information, you specify whether the customer is taxable by selecting the appropriate sales tax code.

When you indicate that a customer pays sales tax, you specify *which* sales tax item (if you collect more than one). Then when you write a sales form and fill in the customer name, QuickBooks knows which tax (if any) to apply. (If the taxability of a sale changes for a special case, you can always change it right on the sales form by changing the tax code.)

If a customer does not pay sales tax and you have to report *why* any sales are not taxable, then choose a non-taxable sales tax code.

If you don't have to report the reasons sales are not taxable, assign your most common sales tax. As long as you say the customer is not taxable, QuickBooks doesn't charge sales tax. On reports, it includes sales to non-taxable customers with sales of non-taxable items to taxable customers.

 You can customize the customer phone list report to show the taxability of all your customers. Create the report and then customize it by adding a column for Sales Tax Code. If any customer has the wrong tax code, double-click it on the report to display its Edit Customer window. Then click the Additional Info tab and edit the sales tax information.

Which items are subject to sales tax?

Your sales forms may contain some items that are taxable and some that are not. As part of the information about the items on your Item list, you have to specify whether the item is usually taxable using the sales tax code. The actual tax can vary with the customer and the circumstances of the sale.

When QuickBooks calculates the sales tax on a sale, it includes only the items marked as taxable and ignores the others. You must make sure you have the correct sales tax code for each item.

 The Item Listing report shows the taxability of all your items. Check this report to make sure your items are set up correctly. You can customize the report to remove columns you don't need to see. If any item has the wrong taxability, double-click it on the report to display its Edit Item window. Then correct the sales tax information on the Additional Info tab.

How do I specify when my sales tax is payable?

In some states, you owe sales tax on all sales that occurred before a specified date. For these sales, set preferences to use accrual basis. In other states, you owe sales tax on only those sales for which you have received payment. In this case, you need to set preferences to use cash basis.

You can set a company-wide preference about whether your your sales tax becomes payable as of invoice date or upon receipt of payment. QuickBooks uses this preference to calculate the ending date of sales on which you now owe sales tax. It also uses this preference for the time period covered by the sales tax liability report.

If you collect more than one sales tax, and they differ in which sales they cover or how often you have to pay, don't worry. You can change the preferences any time.

Tracking and paying sales tax

Once you have set up sales tax correctly, QuickBooks automatically adds the correct sales tax to each sale and tracks how much you owe. In addition, if you enter a credit memo for the return of taxable items, QuickBooks reduces the sales tax you owe.

When it's time to pay sales tax, you can use a window that lists all unpaid sales tax for sales through a specified date (such as the end of last month). You tell QuickBooks which taxes to pay, and it writes the check or checks.

There is a report that gives you information you may need in filling out sales tax forms, such as the total gross sales, the taxable sales, and the non-taxable sales.

QuickBooks keeps track of all the sales tax you have collected, all the sales tax you have paid, and your current sales tax liability in an account it sets up for you. This account, called Sales Tax Payable, is a current liability account on your chart of accounts. Your balance sheet always shows the total amount of sales tax you owe.

Applying sales tax to an invoice or sales receipt

QuickBooks automatically calculates the tax on a sale if you've done the following (see "Setting up sales tax" on page 195):

- Set up a sales tax item on your Item list for each sales tax you collect
- Assigned the appropriate sales tax to each customer
- Assigned sales tax codes to the taxable items on your Items list
- Assigned sales tax codes to taxable customers

QuickBooks can't track sales tax for statement charges.

If you enter any taxable items directly in a customer register, QuickBooks can't add sales tax to them. If you collect sales tax, you must enter the sale on a sales receipt or invoice.

When you enter a sale to an existing customer, QuickBooks applies the tax you have assigned this customer to items you've marked with a taxable code.

If the sale is to a new customer (or no customer), QuickBooks automatically fills in your most common tax in the Tax field at the bottom of the sales form. It also adds the default tax code you've specified in Preferences to the **Customer Tax Code** field.

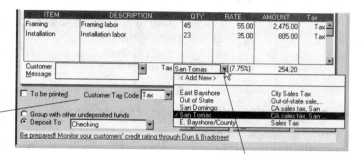

Choose a non-taxable code from the **Sales Tax Code** drop-down list.

To use a different sales tax item or group, choose the item or group from the **Tax** field drop-down list.

You can change an item's taxable status on a sales form by changing the tax code. If the item is normally taxable, but this customer does not have to pay sales tax, then change to a non-taxable code on the sales form. See the following section ("Non-taxable sales").

Non-taxable sales

QuickBooks does not add any sales tax for items that are not taxable. If the customer is taxable, but none of the items on a particular sale is taxable, leave the sales tax item in the **Tax** field, so that the sale is reported as a non-taxable sale for the correct district(s).

If you generally collect sales tax but never tax a particular customer, be sure the customer is set up as non-taxable. See "Which customers are subject to sales tax?" on page 198. Note that even if the customer is non-taxable, you can assign a sales tax code to track the amount of non-taxable sales for each reason (out of state, resale).

On the other hand, if the customer is usually taxable but does not have to pay sales tax on this particular sale, simply change the tax code to one that is non-taxable. See "If you report non-taxable sales to out-of-state customers" on page 198 and "If you report non-taxable sales to resellers" on page 198.

Special tax situations

You may need to change the sales tax that QuickBooks automatically applies when you have an unusual sale. The following table gives examples of special tax situations and how you can handle them.

Special tax situation	How to handle in QuickBooks	Result
Sale to out-of-state or resale customer.	Choose your Out of State sales tax code and assign the out-of-state sales tax item to this sale.	QuickBooks records the non-taxable code on the sales tax liability report.
Some items on a sale are taxed at one rate, some at another rate.	You should do all of the following: ■ Create a placeholder 0.00% tax item to put in the **Tax** field, because you can't record a sale with the **Tax** field empty. ■ List items taxed at the same rate together. ■ Add a subtotal item after each set of same-rate items. ■ On the line after each subtotal of same-rate items, enter the appropriate sales tax item in the **Item** field.	QuickBooks includes the taxable items subtotaled above each tax line item in that tax line item's gross sales and taxable sales. Non-taxable items included in the subtotal above each tax line item are included in that tax item's gross sales and non-taxable sales.
All taxable items on a sale are taxable at one rate; some items are taxable at an additional rate.	You should do all of the following: ■ In the **Tax** field, enter the tax item for all taxable items. ■ List all items taxable at the additional rate together. ■ Add a subtotal item after this set of items. ■ On the line after the subtotal item, enter the sales tax item for the additional rate in the **Item** field.	All taxable items are included in taxable sales for the tax item in the **Tax** field. Items with the additional tax are included in taxable sales for the tax line item.
QuickBooks cannot calculate tax the way you need it calculated (for example, for tiered taxes).	You should do all of the following: ■ Create a placeholder 0.00% tax item to put in the **Tax** field, because you can't record a sale with the **Tax** field empty. ■ If you need to report both non-taxable and taxable sales, add a subtotal item after all the items on the sales form. Otherwise, list all taxable items together and add a subtotal item after them. ■ On the line after the subtotal, enter a sales tax item in the **Item** field. ■ Select and type over the amount of the tax, using an amount you calculate yourself.	QuickBooks reports the amount you type in as the amount of tax you owe your tax agency for the sale. Taxable sales and non-taxable sales amounts are based on the taxable and non-taxable amounts included in the subtotal above the tax line.
Shipping and handling are taxable in your state.	Set up another charge item called "Shipping and Handling" and mark it as taxable.	QuickBooks calculates tax on shipping and handling, because you've marked it as taxable.

Keeping track of how much sales tax you owe

Each time you enter a sale that includes sales tax, QuickBooks tracks the tax information in your Sales Tax Payable account. You can view the sales tax liability you are accruing by displaying the Sales Tax Payable register.

The Sales Tax Payable register shows all sales tax transactions for all sales tax districts.

These two transactions are for a payment to the state collection agency for two different sales tax districts.

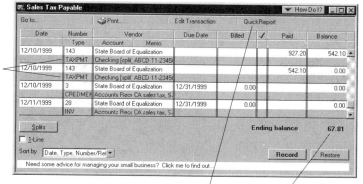

To see a list of all transactions involving a particular tax agency, select a transaction involving that agency; then click QuickReport.

This is the total of all unpaid sales tax.

Note: QuickBooks tracks all sales tax amounts in the same Sales Tax Payable account. If you need to know how much you owe for each sales tax collected, use the sales tax liability report or the Pay Sales Tax window. Also, the register shows the total unpaid sales tax, even if it is not yet due.

To learn about...	Look in the Help Index for...
Displaying the register for the Sales Tax Payable account	sales tax, register
Viewing a vendor QuickReport of all transactions for a particular sales tax agency	report types, sales taxes
Adjusting the amount of sales tax owed, either during initial company setup or to correct an error	sales tax, adjusting your liability

Paying sales tax

Use the Pay Sales Tax window to do the following:

- View how much you owe for each sales tax you collect, through the date shown in the **Show sales tax due through** field of this window.

- Have QuickBooks write or record a payment check to your tax agency or agencies.

- Adjust sales tax for the selected vendor.

QuickBooks takes payment from the account shown here.

You owe sales tax through the date shown here.

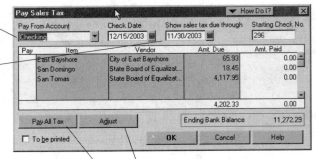

Pay all sales tax or adjust the amount owed.

Use the Pay Sales Tax window even if you don't print checks.

The only way QuickBooks can keep track of how much sales tax you have paid is for you to use the Pay Sales Tax window. If you don't print checks from QuickBooks, just clear the **To be printed** checkbox in the window. (In your bank account register, you can edit the check number if QuickBooks entered a check number different from the one you used.)

QuickBooks displays the unpaid tax owed through the end of your last sales tax period. You can change the date QuickBooks uses by indicating whether you pay monthly, quarterly, or annually in the company sales tax preferences. See "How do I specify when my sales tax is payable?" on page 199.

Similarly, QuickBooks calculates the tax you owe on either a cash basis (that is, as of when you receive payment) or an accrual basis (as of the date of the sale), depending on how the sales tax preferences are set.

If you actually owe less tax than shown because you receive a discount or have a tax credit you have not yet entered, you can enter an adjustment in the Adjust Sales Tax window. Then you must "pay" it in the Pay Sales Tax window. (Because it reduces the total tax you owe, it has a negative sign in the window.)

When you record a payment through the Pay Sales Tax window, QuickBooks writes one check to each vendor you are paying. It updates your Sales Tax Payable account with the payment information. It also reduces the balance in the bank account you specify to use for the payment.

To learn about...	Look in the Help Index for...
Paying sales tax	sales tax, paying
Changing the company's sales tax period or cash vs. accrual basis for paying sales tax	sales tax, accounting basis
Applying a discount to the amount of sales tax owed	sales tax, adjusting your liability
Recording a sales tax credit from the sales tax agency	sales tax, adjusting your liability
Editing the check number of a sales tax payment check written by hand	registers, editing entries

Changing information about your sales tax

You can change any of the following for a sales tax item that is set up to track a particular sales tax:

- Tax rate
- Name (displayed on your Item list, in the **Item** field of sales forms, and in reports)
- Description (displayed and printed in the **Description** field of sales forms)
- Choice of tax agency to whom you pay sales tax
- (For sales tax group items) Which sales tax items are part of the group

When you change a rate, new transactions will use the new rate. However, transactions already recorded will keep the old rate.

To change information about the tax agency, edit the agency on your Vendor list. The agency is set up as a QuickBooks vendor. The Vendor list has information about the vendor address and your tax account number.

To learn about...	Look in the Help Index for...
Changing sales tax information	items, editing information

GATHERING INCOME TAX
INFORMATION FOR THE IRS

You can use QuickBooks to collect and report tax-related income and expense information to help you fill out your tax forms. For a complete tax preparation tool, consider TurboTax® for Business. You can transfer QuickBooks data to this program to give you a head start in tax preparation.

This chapter does not intend to be exhaustive on the subject of taxes.

Tax laws and regulations change frequently and their application can vary widely based upon the specific facts and circumstances involved. Users are responsible for consulting their own professional tax advisors concerning their specific tax circumstances.

For information on payroll (employment) taxes, see "Paying payroll taxes and liabilities" on page 269. For information about sales tax, see Chapter 14, *Tracking and paying sales tax,* beginning on page 191.

Figuring it all out

Here are a few suggestions of experts, programs, books, and software designed to help you with your taxes.

Consulting tax experts

- The Internal Revenue Service (IRS) has information for small businesses. Contact your local IRS office or visit **www.irs.gov.**

- Review the Professional Advisor's Program at **www.quickbooks.com** to find a QuickBooks-savvy tax advisor in your area. (Not all Professional Advisors are tax advisors.)

- Check out software products such as TurboTax for Business (**www.intuit.com/turbotax**), which walks you through paying your business taxes and includes information and publications. A bonus—you can import your QuickBooks data into TurboTax products.

Keeping current with tax information

Even if you rely on a tax expert to complete your forms and keep abreast of tax changes for you, we recommend that you also keep current with tax information. You know your business better than anyone, and only you can make the decision to take advantage of new tax changes.

Stay informed with links to the Internet

Tax alerts in QuickBooks can take you directly to places such as the IRS Web site (**www.irs.gov**) for timely information, or to the TurboTax site (**www.turbotax.com**) for the latest in tax software and electronic filing.

To learn about...	Look in the Help Index for...
QuickBooks alerts	alerts

What QuickBooks can do for you

QuickBooks can help you track your income tax, your payroll (employment) taxes, and your 1099 information.

QuickBooks tracks	Output created
Income tax information, including information for schedules A, B, C, E, F, H, K-1; forms 1040, 1065, 1120, 1120S, 990, 990-PF, 990-T, 4835, 2106, 2119, 8829. This list is not exhaustive. Your options will vary depending on your business entity.	Prints a report detailing all the tax lines for various schedules and forms that you designated when you set up your accounts and company information.
1099-MISC income form information For more information, see "Handling 1099-MISC forms" on page 213.	Prints on the 1099 forms you provide.
Payroll information for W-2, W-3, 940s, and 941s. You can prepare forms 940 and 941 and other payroll tax forms on a Web site accessed from within QuickBooks (if you have an internet connection and subscribe to the QuickBooks Do-It-Yourself Payroll service).	Prints on the W-2 and W-3 forms you provide. Prints government-approved 940 and 941 forms.

Other taxes you may need to pay

Depending on your business situation, you may need to pay Self-employment tax or Excise taxes. Contact the IRS for more information.

Setting up income tax tracking

QuickBooks can track the information you need to report on your income tax forms and help you save time and tax preparation fees.

The following table highlights the income tax tracking information. You may have entered this information during setup using the EasyStep Interview (in the General and Income & Expenses sections). If you ever need to change this information, use the Help Index references.

Task	Comments	Look in the Help Index for...
Change the first month of your company's income tax year. This could be by calendar year or fiscal year.	You must be consistent from year to year.	company, changing information about
Change the income tax form you use for your company.	**Important:** If you change the tax form you use, all associations between accounts and tax lines are reset to <unassigned>. You'll need to reassign the appropriate tax lines.	■ income taxes, changing the tax form you file ■ accounts (managing), tax lines
Enter your federal identification number.	■ If you are a sole proprietor who has no employees and who files no excise or pension tax returns, you can use your **social security number** as your identification number. Otherwise, you must have an **employer identification number (EIN)** if your business fits any of these situations: (1) you are a corporation or partnership; (2) you pay wages to one or more employees; (3) you file pension or excise tax returns. To apply for an EIN, call 1-800-TAX-FORM.	■ company, changing information about
Choose a tax line for each appropriate account in your chart of accounts.	Normally balance sheet accounts do not have a tax line. You may want to add accounts to more closely match your tax forms.	■ accounts (managing), tax lines ■ accounts (managing), adding

Why are tax line assignments important?

If you assign tax lines to your accounts you can:

- Transfer your income tax data from QuickBooks to one of Intuit's TurboTax products

- Get accurate tax reports, which keep you abreast of your tax situation and help you prepare your income taxes (if you're doing your taxes by hand)

The way you set up accounts and their tax line assignments depends on whether you used the preset chart of accounts, added accounts to the preset chart of accounts, or set up your own chart of accounts. Other unique situations may also apply. Look in the Help Index for more information.

> **If you change the tax form you use, all associations between tax lines and accounts are reset to <unassigned>.**
>
> You'll need to reassign the appropriate tax lines.

To learn about...	Look in the Help Index for...
Setting up accounts to track income tax-related income and expenses	income taxes, setting up for

Make sure that you have the latest tax information

Use TurboTax to always have the latest tax information: Intuit provides an updated list of tax forms (the BUSTAX.SCD file) in all TurboTax products for Windows and TurboTax for Business. If you use QuickBooks for Windows, install the *latest* version of TurboTax to update your income tax form information.

Reporting income tax information

The QuickBooks income tax summary report shows the total amount associated for each tax line you specified in your accounts. If you fill out your tax forms by hand, you can print the income tax summary report and use it to aid you in completing your tax forms. Or, to make income taxes even simpler, you can easily transfer your tax information to one of Intuit's TurboTax products. See "Transferring income tax information to TurboTax" on page 212.

Getting the numbers you need to file your income taxes

Whether you fill out your income tax forms by hand or transfer your QuickBooks data to one of Intuit's TurboTax products, you'll want to complete the following steps to make sure your numbers are correct.

- Check and correct tax line assignments. The accuracy of the income tax summary report depends on whether each tax-related account has the right tax line assignment.
- Check that the amounts in your income tax summary report are correct.
- Calculate your sales and returns.
- Calculate the total of your purchases.

To learn about...	Look in the Help Index for...
Checking tax line assignments to ensure the accuracy of your income tax summary report	income taxes, filling out tax forms
Checking the amounts distributed to various accounts	income taxes, filling out tax forms
Calculating sales and returns	income taxes, calculating sales and returns
Calculating the total of your purchases	income taxes, calculating purchases

Income tax summary report

The income tax summary report shows the amount associated with each tax line for the tax form you specified during setup.

Income tax detail report

The income tax detail report shows the individual transactions and the total associated for each tax line you specified in your accounts.

Make sure the reporting preference is set to the accounting method you use for tax reporting: Accrual or Cash.

From the Edit menu, choose Preferences, then Reports & Graphs, and then click the Company Preferences tab.

Transferring income tax information to TurboTax

If you use the current TurboTax for Windows or TurboTax for Business to prepare your taxes, you can import your QuickBooks tax data into the tax software. Once you've set up QuickBooks accounts with the correct tax line assignments, QuickBooks tracks your tax-related income and expenses automatically throughout the year.

Note: QuickBooks Basic 2004, QuickBooks Pro 2004, and QuickBooks Premier Edition(s) 2004 will work only with TurboTax, TurboTax for Business, and ProSeries for tax year 2003.

To learn about...	Look in the Help Index for...
Transferring tax information from QuickBooks to your tax software	TurboTax

Handling 1099-MISC forms

The IRS requires certain 1099-MISC forms of all businesses that make or receive payments. The IRS uses these forms to verify that the recipient has included your payment as income on his or her income tax form. You must give a copy of each information return you file to the recipient or payer.

Setting up to track 1099-MISC information

Tasks	Comments	Look in the Help Index for...
Setting up for reporting payments on 1099-MISC forms	None	1099s
Setting up vendors (recipients)	■ Enter the address in the correct format ■ Enter the federal identification number in the Tax ID field ■ Select the "Vendor is eligible for 1099" checkbox	vendors, adding

Verifying amounts and printing 1099-MISC forms

Before you print your 1099-MISC forms, you should verify information that you'll report to the IRS. After you print your 1099-MISC forms, QuickBooks displays 1096 summary information at the bottom of the window. (It does not print Form 1096.)

To learn about...	Look in the Help Index for...
Verifying 1099 thresholds, vendors, accounts, and amounts	1099s
Printing1099s	1099s

TIME TRACKING

Time tracking, available only in QuickBooks Pro and QuickBooks Premier, allows you to track hours worked by yourself, employees, or subcontractors. You can make the time billable for specific jobs. QuickBooks Pro and Premier can transfer time to paychecks, regular checks, and bills from subcontractors.

QuickBooks Pro and Premier provide time-tracking capability to suit your needs:

- The Stopwatch: When you're working in QuickBooks and want to take a stopwatch approach (that is, turn on a timer, work, and then stop the timer), use the Stopwatch on the Time/Enter Single Activity window.

- The QuickBooks Pro Timer: The Timer is a separate program that runs on Windows on any computer. Because it's separate, you can distribute copies of the Timer to people who don't have access to QuickBooks, such as employees and subcontractors. Then you can merge their time data into the QuickBooks company file.

- You can also enter time data manually into QuickBooks in the Weekly Timesheet window or Time/Enter Single Activity window.

How the Timer works with QuickBooks

The QuickBooks Pro Timer is designed to track and record time data for export to QuickBooks Pro and QuickBooks Premier. Use it when you want to gather time data from people who don't have access to QuickBooks.

You can make copies of the Timer program to give to other people whose work you want to track in QuickBooks. If you distributed the Timer program that came with an earlier version of QuickBooks Pro, replace those copies with the Timer program that comes with the QuickBooks Pro or Premier 2004. The newer version of the Timer can update data files created by the earlier version.

The following flowchart shows the relationship between QuickBooks Pro (and Premier) and the Timer.

The two programs share information as follows:

- QuickBooks Pro and Premier export lists.
- The Timer imports those lists.
- The Timer exports data about time activities.
- QuickBooks Pro and Premier import the time data and makes it part of the company data file.

Note: If you want to time a single activity in QuickBooks, use the Stopwatch on the Time/Enter Single Activity window instead of the Timer. See "Using the Stopwatch to time an activity" on page 226.

Should I track time?

Tracking time can help you make better decisions about work capacity, future hiring needs, and employee productivity.

Furthermore, if you track the time you, your employees, or your subcontractors spend on each job, you'll be able to do the following:

- Invoice customers based on the number of hours of work done for them.
- Automatically fill in hours on paychecks.
- When paying subcontractors, automatically fill in hours on checks and bills.
- Track payroll costs by job, class, or type of work.
- Report hours worked by person, job, or type of work.
- Track billable versus non-billable time.

Should I make time billable?

billable

The status of time worked (or a purchase) for a particular customer or job that allows QuickBooks to charge the customer for the time (or purchase).

After you put the time or purchase on a sales form, QuickBooks marks it nonbillable, so you won't charge twice for the same thing.

When you record time worked for a particular customer or job, one option is to mark it as billable. Then when you invoice the customer, you can add the billable time to the invoice with a few clicks.

If the work done by employees is billable to customers, it becomes billable as soon as you record the time in QuickBooks. It doesn't matter whether you have paid the employees yet.

In some businesses you may want to track time without making it billable. For example, if you agree to do a job at a fixed price, you would not invoice for time.

You may still want to track the time so you can decide after completing the job whether you set the right price.

Also, you can track sick and vacation time, which is normally not billable.

Should I track time for subcontractors?

Most businesses don't need to track time for subcontractors, with a few exceptions:

- On time reports, you want to see all time for a particular job, whether for an employee, a subcontractor, or an owner.

  Glenn's company has only one employee now. By tracking time worked by subcontractors, he'll know what to expect when he has employees doing this type of work in the future.

- You want to track subcontractor time independently of the time subcontractors report on the bills they submit to you.

  Jill gives subcontractors copies of the Timer program and asks them to return time data to her weekly so she can track how many hours have been spent on her project long before she receives the bills.

- You want to pay subcontractors based on time worked, using the time information entered in QuickBooks.

  Eric tracks time for subcontractors and pays them within 30 days. On a weekly basis, Eric enters a bill for each subcontractor and transfers the time worked during the previous week.

How much detail should I track for time activities?

activity

A QuickBooks term for work tracked by the time tracking feature.

You track time based on activities. Each activity needs, at a minimum, the following to describe it:

- Name of person who did the work
- Date the work was done
- Time spent doing the work

The level of detail you include when tracking an activity depends on whether or not it's billable and how much detail you want in your reports.

Describe an activity by specifying ...	Comment
Name of person who did the work	Required.
Date the work was done	Required; each activity can be for only one date.
Time spent doing the work	Required. (If you use the Timer or the Stopwatch to time an activity, they fill in the time spent.)
Customer (and job) the work is for	Required only if you plan to invoice for the time. Even if you don't invoice for the time: ■ Allows you to report on hours worked by customer and job. ■ Allows you to track payroll expenses by customer and job.
Type of work (described by a service item from the Item list)	Required only if you plan to invoice for the time. Even if you don't invoice for the time: ■ Allows you to report on hours worked by type of work. ■ Allows you to track payroll expenses by type of work.

Describe an activity by specifying ...	Comment
Whether time is billable	Time must be billable if you plan to invoice for the time.
Class	If your company does class tracking, you can do the following: ■ Filter time reports by class. ■ If you are set up to split payroll expenses by class, you can assign classes to employee time. Then you can automatically track all payroll expenses by class.

Choosing a method to track time

QuickBooks comes with a separate Timer program that can run on a computer regardless of whether QuickBooks is on the computer. You have a choice between tracking time via the Timer and then transferring the time data to QuickBooks, using the Stopwatch on the Time/Enter Single Activity window, or entering time data directly into QuickBooks manually on the Weekly Timesheet window or the Time/Enter Single Activity window.

Situation	How to track time	See...
You want to use a stopwatch approach to time tracking (in which you turn on a timer, work, and then stop the timer).	Use the Stopwatch on the Time/Enter Single Activity window in QuickBooks (Pro version only).	■ "Setting up QuickBooks for tracking time" on page 220 ■ "Using the Stopwatch to time an activity" on page 226
You want people who don't have access to your QuickBooks company data file to track their own time.	Distribute copies of the QuickBooks Pro Timer to these people, and have them give you their time data.	■ "Setting up QuickBooks for tracking time" on page 220 ■ "Setting up and using the Timer" on page 221
You (and others in your company) have access to your QuickBooks company data file and want to enter time data after the work is done.	You and they can enter the time data manually into QuickBooks (Pro and Premier only) either on a weekly timesheet or as separate activities one at a time.	■ "Setting up QuickBooks for tracking time" on page 220 ■ "Entering time manually into QuickBooks" on page 227
Employees submit paper timesheets.	One person can enter everyone's time data directly into QuickBooks (Pro and Premier only) on a weekly timesheet for each person.	■ "Setting up QuickBooks for tracking time" on page 220 ■ "Entering time manually into QuickBooks" on page 227

Setting up QuickBooks for tracking time

The following list is for tasks you must do in QuickBooks to prepare for tracking time.

 A QuickBooks user must do this preparation before Timer users can set up their own Timers.

What to set up	Comments	Search Help index for...
Turn on time tracking and indicate the first day of your work week.	The weekly timesheet starts with the day of the week you specify.	preferences, time
On the Customer:Job list, names of customers and jobs for which time will be tracked.	If you don't plan to track time by customer or job, you don't need these names on the list now.	■ customers, adding new ■ jobs, adding new
On the Item list, names of service items that describe the types of work that will be tracked	Service items are required only if you make the time billable to a customer or job. Be sure to create separate service items for subcontracted services.	■ service items, setting up ■ subcontractors, service items for
Names of all people whose time will be tracked. Each name must be on one of the following lists in QuickBooks: ■ Employee ■ Other Name (for owners and partners) ■ Vendor (for subcontractors)	If you plan to use time tracking to help with payroll for any employees, you must also set up payroll information for those employees. See: ■ "Setting up to use time tracking with payroll," below ■ "Setting up employees" on page 248	■ employees, adding ■ other names, list of ■ vendors, adding
On the Payroll Item list, names of hourly or salary wage items to be used when paying employees for time tracked	Required only if you will track time for employees and pay them using QuickBooks software.	■ hourly wages ■ salaries
On the Class list, names of classes that apply to the work that will be tracked	Class tracking is completely optional.	classes, adding

Setting up to use time tracking with payroll

As part of the payroll setup for employees, be sure to select the checkbox "Use time data to create paychecks" on the employee's Payroll Info tab.

☑ Use time data to create paychecks

Paychecks will automatically have the employee's time data (including job, class, type of work, sick, and vacation) for the period covered by the paycheck. QuickBooks keeps track of your payroll expenses for hourly or salaried gross pay, employer taxes, and other payroll overhead by job, class, and type of work.

Setting up and using the Timer

Before you can set up the Timer, you must first install it. Also, be sure to do all the tasks on the task list. The task list for setting up the Timer shows whether the QuickBooks user or the Timer user has to do the task (in case they are not the same person).

Task	Which user and which Help index?	Look in the Help index for...
Export QuickBooks lists for Timer into an IIF file and give file to Timer user.	QuickBooks	Timer, exporting lists to
Prepare Timer install disks (if Timer user is unable to use QuickBooks CD-ROM or QuickBooks install disks).	QuickBooks	Timer, creating disks for
Install the Timer on the user's computer.	See the QuickBooks Installation and Conversion Guide.	N/A
Create a Timer data file for the QuickBooks company file that will use the time data.	Timer	data files, creating for the Timer (search the Timer Help)
Import the QuickBooks lists in the IIF file into the Timer data file.	Timer	lists, importing from QuickBooks (search the Timer Help)
Name the person whose work will be recorded in this Timer file.	Timer	default user (search Timer Help)

Exporting lists from QuickBooks Pro and Premier

The first step in getting the Timer ready to use is to prepare a file with the information the timer needs in order to work with QuickBooks Pro and Premier. The Timer must describe activities using the same names that are on the lists in QuickBooks.

Information Timer needs	Source in QuickBooks
Names of possible Timer users	Employee, Vendor, and Other Names lists
Names of customers and jobs (if time will be billable to a customer or job)	Customer:Job list
Type of work that the customer may be invoiced for (if time will be billable)	Service-type items from the Item list
Names of QuickBooks classes (if time will be assigned to classes)	Class list

If the Timer will be used on another computer, the exported list file should be either on a 3.5-inch disk or on a network that both computers can access.

To learn about...	Look in the Help Index for...
Preparing a file of information from QuickBooks lists, for use by the Timer	Timer, exporting lists to

Using the Timer

After you have done the tasks described in "Setting up QuickBooks for tracking time" on page 220 and in "Setting up and using the Timer" on page 221, you are ready to track time with the Timer.

Recording activities in the Timer

You can use the Timer either to time and record an activity while you are doing it or to record it after you have done it.

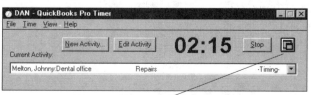

Click this button to switch between a very small window (left) or a larger window (above) that shows detail and provides menu access.

The first time you do an activity for a given customer, job, and type of work, you have to set up the activity in the Timer. To understand how much detail you should include in an activity, see "How much detail should I track for time activities?" on page 218.

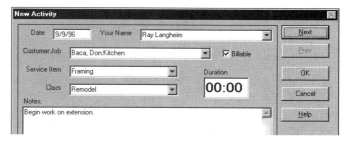

If you have previously set up an activity for a given customer, job, and type of work, you can choose the activity from a drop-down list and use it as a template for the new day's work instead of setting up a similar activity for the new day.

You can add a note while timing an activity or after completing it.

To learn about...	Look in the Timer Help (not the QuickBooks Help) index for...
Timing an activity while you are doing it	■ activities, setting up for timing ■ activities, timing
Recording an activity after doing it	activities, entering time for manually
Recording notes about an activity	activities, adding notes to

Viewing and editing recorded activities

You can view a list of all recorded activities. You can't print this list (or anything else in the Timer). However, after you export time data to QuickBooks, the QuickBooks user can print the list of activities.

To learn about...	Look in the Timer Help (not the QuickBooks Help) index for...
Viewing a list of all recorded activities within a specified date range	activities, viewing data about
Changing information about a recorded activity	activities, editing data about

To learn about...	Look in the Timer Help (not the QuickBooks Help) index for...
Deleting a recorded activity	activities, deleting the record of

Viewing and changing customer information

When you import lists from QuickBooks, you import customer contact information as well as customer names.

You can add a new customer name to use when describing an activity. However, you cannot add a job for a new or existing customer. The Help topic suggests what to do instead.

If a customer is on the list imported from QuickBooks, or if you already exported Timer data using the customer, you can't change information about the customer. Instead, the QuickBooks user must change the information and give you an updated list file.

?

To learn about...	Look in the Timer Help (not the QuickBooks Help) index for...
Viewing contact information about a customer	customers, contact information for
Adding, editing, or deleting a customer	■ customers, adding ■ customers, editing ■ customers, deleting

Sharing Timer information with QuickBooks

You need to export your recorded activities to an IIF file that QuickBooks can import.

Also, from time to time, you will need to update the lists in your Timer data to make them match those in the QuickBooks company file. The QuickBooks user must prepare the updated list file and make it available for importing into the Timer.

For a diagram of how data moves between the Timer and QuickBooks, see "How the Timer works with QuickBooks" on page 216.

?

To learn about...	Look in the Timer Help (not QuickBooks Help) index for...
Copying (exporting) activities to an IIF file that QuickBooks can read	activities, exporting to QuickBooks

To learn about...	Look in the Timer Help (not QuickBooks Help) index for...
Updating the Timer's lists of customers, jobs, service items, and classes to match changes in the QuickBooks file	lists, updating

Managing Timer data files

You can back up a Timer data file. You must restore a backup copy before you can open it in the Timer.

You can reduce the file size by using the Condense feature. The Condense feature in the Timer, unlike the one in QuickBooks, doesn't remove or consolidate any information.

If you track time for more than one QuickBooks company, you must have separate Timer data files.

To learn about...	Look in the Timer Help (not QuickBooks Help) index for...
Backing up your Timer data onto a 3.5-inch disk or your hard disk	data files, backing up
Restoring a backup of Timer data so you can use or view it	data files, restoring from a backup disk
Reducing the size of your Timer file	data files, condensing to save disk space
Creating a new Timer data file to use with a different QuickBooks company file	data files, creating for the Timer
Switching to the Timer data file for a different QuickBooks company	data files, opening

Importing Timer data into QuickBooks

After the Timer user exports the data from the Timer into an IIF file (see "Sharing Timer information with QuickBooks" on page 224), you can import the data into the QuickBooks company file.

When you've finished importing the Timer data, you should check the Timer import detail report (available only from the Import Summary window) to ensure that QuickBooks has assigned the correct payroll item to each activity.

When you've finished importing the Timer data, you should check the Timer import detail report (available only from the Import Summary window) to ensure that QuickBooks has assigned the correct payroll item to each activity.

In addition to activities, QuickBooks imports any items on lists (that is, names, service items, classes) that are not currently on the corresponding QuickBooks lists. You can view reports of the imported list items.

The time reports in QuickBooks report on all activities, including those imported from the Timer. To create a report similar to the Timer import detail report, you can customize a time by job detail report to add columns for payroll item and import date.

?

To learn about...	Look in the QuickBooks Help index for...
Importing Timer data from the IIF file into the QuickBooks company file	Timer, importing timed activities from
Viewing a report of the imported Timer activities or the imported items on lists	Timer, reports about imported activities
Editing an imported activity in QuickBooks	time, entering
Viewing a report on activities exported to or recorded in QuickBooks	time, reports about

Using the Stopwatch to time an activity

Use the Stopwatch on the Time/Enter Single Activity window in QuickBooks Pro or Premier when you want to time an activity—simply start the Stopwatch, work, and stop it when you've completed the work.

Once recorded, the time shows up in both this window and in the Weekly Timesheet window.

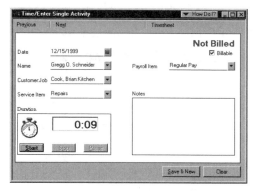

To see how much detail to include when you time an activity, see "How much detail should I track for time activities?" on page 218.

Entering time manually into QuickBooks

If you want to enter time data a week at a time and you generally don't enter a lot of detailed notes about your activities, use the Weekly Timesheet window to enter time data manually.

On the weekly timesheet, the far right column has symbols that indicate whether the time is billable, not billable, or already billed.

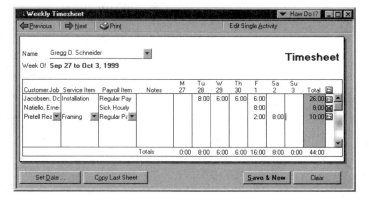

If you tend to enter a lot of detailed notes about your activities or prefer to enter time data as you complete each activity, use the Time/Enter Single Activity window.

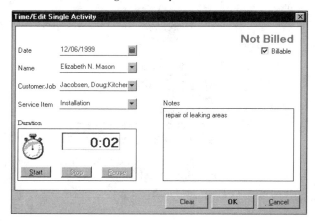

When you fill in and record a Time/Enter Single Activity window, you can later view the information on a weekly timesheet. Conversely, when you fill in and save a weekly timesheet, you can view Time/Enter Single Activity windows that each show the work on one job on one day. The two are simply different views of the same data, similar to views of individual checks versus your check register.

To learn about...	Look in the Help Index for...
Blank timesheets	timesheets
Printing a blank timesheet	timesheets
Filling out a weekly timesheet	timesheets
Entering details for a single activity	single activity entries
Using the Stopwatch to time an activity	Stopwatch

Tasks you can do with time data

Viewing, editing, and printing time data

In addition to creating reports about time data, you can view, print, and edit time data as follows:

- View a timesheet for one person's work during a particular week.

- Print timesheets (each with one person's work for one week or part of a week).

- View the full text of the note entered for a particular activity.

- Edit time data.

?

To learn about...	Look in the Help Index for...
Viewing and printing timesheets	timesheets
Adding notes about an activity to an invoice	invoices, time and cost
Adding notes about an activity to a time report	time, reports about
Editing time data	time, entering

Using time data with payroll

QuickBooks automatically transfers time data when you create paychecks for employees who are set up for transferring time data. That is, it fills in the number of hours for each payroll item for salary or hourly wages included in the time data for the payroll period.

If customers or jobs, service items, or classes are assigned to an employee's time activities, this detail is also included. For example, out of 40 hours altogether, 19 hours may be assigned to Job A, 11 hours to Job B, and the remaining 10 hours to Job C. QuickBooks then splits the payroll expenses for this employee according to how you assigned the time.

Paying nonemployees for time

When you have time data for someone who is not an employee, you may want to pay them based on time worked. QuickBooks can transfer time data for a specified date range to your payment. That is, it can fill in the number of hours worked and the rate for that type of work.

To pay a subcontractor or other vendor, you can either write a check for immediate payment or enter a bill to be paid at a later time. To pay an owner or partner (someone on your Other Names list), you can write a check.

If the person is on your Employee list and is set up for transferring time data to paychecks, then the person's paychecks are always based on the time worked. For further information, see Chapter 17, *Payroll and Employees,* beginning on page 235.

 If you need to report payments for time worked on Form 1099-MISC, be sure the person is set up as a vendor. Always use the vendor name when you track time and when you pay the person. Then when it's time to print 1099-MISC forms, QuickBooks will report the correct amount paid.

To learn about...	Look in the Help Index for...
Setting up an owner or partner	■ owners ■ partners
Adding a name to the Vendor list	vendors, adding
Editing an employee name	employees, editing
Reporting payments on Form 1099-MISC	Form 1099

Service items for the time data

If you plan to transfer time to a check or bill, the time data should have a service item assigned. QuickBooks uses the rate for purchases of the service item when calculating how much to pay a nonemployee for the hours worked.

Service items for owner or partner time

When you pay an owner or partner, the payment is a draw against equity, rather than an expense to the business. Therefore, you need to have at least one service item that affects the person's equity account when used in payments to the person. This service item should not be used for vendors.

When tracking time for an owner or partner, assign the time to a service item set up to track costs in the person's equity account.

Service items for vendor time

When you pay a vendor, the payment is an expense to the business. Therefore, you need to have at least one service item that affects an expense account when used in payments to the person. This service item should not be used for owners or partners.

When tracking time for a vendor, assign the time to a service item set up to track costs in an expense account.

To learn about...	Look in the Help Index for...
Setting up a service item for services with both costs and income	service items

Transferring time to a check or bill

When you write the check or enter the bill, QuickBooks alerts you if there is time data for the payee for dates after the end period for the last-time payment to this payee. If you answer that you want to pay for time, you can specify the date range of the time to pay for. Then QuickBooks prefills the Items tab of the check with the service item, customer and job (if any), rate, number of hours, and amount.

To learn about...	Look in the Help Index for...
Paying nonemployee for time worked	time, paying nonemployees for

---

QuickBooks does not track whether time is paid for.

If you pay for time and then edit the time data (or import data from the Timer), QuickBooks does not track which time has been paid for and which has not. All it tracks is the end date of the last payment for time.

If you always pay for time dated after the end date of the last payment, you will not pay for the same time twice. Other-wise, print a time by job detail report and mark the activities you are paying for.

Charging customers for time

You can transfer time data to invoices and statement charges as long as the time data has a customer:job and service item and is currently marked as billable.

When you're writing an invoice, you can display the unbilled time worked for the job and select which time to include. (See "Charging for actual time and costs" on page 130.) When you record the invoice, QuickBooks marks the time you selected as billed, so you won't bill for it again by mistake. (You can also charge for time as a statement charge instead of writing an invoice.)

To learn about...	Look in the QuickBooks Help index for...
Transferring time to invoices and statement charges	■ invoices, time and cost ■ statements, time and cost
Making time billable again if you billed for it mistakenly	time, making billed time billable again

Costs of work and invoicing for work

When you record time, you are not recording any costs. To record costs, you have to take additional action. The following table shows how you record costs for time worked. The table also shows what you have to do to invoice customers for work.

When work is done by ...	You record the cost of the work when you ...	To be able to invoice for the work, you have to ...
Employees	Pay the employees.	Make the time billable.
Subcontractors (vendors)	Enter bills from the subcontractors (or write checks or enter credit card charges for the work).	On the bills, checks, or credit card charges, make the items or expenses billable. OR Track the time and make the time billable.
Owners or partners	If you pay owners and partners for time worked, the payment is a draw against the person's equity. It is not an expense and therefore does not affect the net profit.	Make the time billable. OR Write a check to pay for the time worked, and make the items on the check billable.

Because recording time has no direct effect on costs, the reports about time show hours but they don't show costs.

If you enter bills for subcontractors or if you pay subcontractors, owners, or partners for time worked, you must guard against making their work billable twice.

Don't make both time and the payment for that time billable.

- If you make a subcontractor's bill for time worked billable, you can invoice for the subcontractor's charges from the Expenses or Items tab (the same one you used on the bill) of the Choose Billable Time and Costs window. (This is the recommended method. See "Charging for actual time and costs" on page 130.)

- If you pay a subcontractor, owner, or partner for time worked by using the Write Checks window, you can make the service items on the check billable. Then you can invoice for the time from the Items tab of the Choose Billable Time and Costs window.

- If you make the time itself billable, you can invoice for the time from the Time tab of the Choose Billable Time and Costs window.

- If you make both the time and the bill or payment billable, you are in danger of invoicing the customer twice for the same work.

PAYROLL AND EMPLOYEES

Paying employees is a big responsibility. You have to keep track of hours, salaries and wages, Social Security numbers and dependents, tax rates and forms, vacation and sick time, bonuses and advances, as well as company payments to government and private pension plans. QuickBooks provides several features and services to help you manage your own payroll quickly and easily.

An overview of QuickBooks payroll

QuickBooks payroll features allow you to track employee information, hours, and compensation. When it comes time to writing paychecks and paying payroll taxes, you have four options:

- Make your calculations manually.
- Subscribe to the QuickBooks Do-It-Yourself Payroll service to receive the latest tax tables and tax forms, allowing QuickBooks to do your calculations for you. Do-It-Yourself Payroll also includes optional add-on direct deposit and e-filing services. (Additional fees apply.)
- Subscribe to QuickBooks Assisted Payroll to receive all the benefits of Do-It-Yourself Payroll, while also having the payroll service prepare and file many of your tax forms for you.

A third payroll service—Complete Payroll—is a full-service solution that manages all your payroll needs for you and downloads your payroll and tax data back into QuickBooks so you can track and report on it there.

For information about Intuit's payroll services and your payroll options in QuickBooks, see "About Intuit Payroll Services" on page 237. Or, in QuickBooks, go to the Employees menu, choose Payroll Services, and then Learn About Payroll Options.

What the QuickBooks payroll feature can do for you

QuickBooks can perform many different payroll tasks, including calculating wages and taxes, managing compensation and liabilities, and processing payments for both employees and payroll tax agencies.

Note: To execute some of the tasks, you need a subscription to either Do-It-Yourself Payroll or Assisted Payroll.

To learn about...	Look in the Help Index for...
Tasks QuickBooks payroll can perform	payroll, overview

If you don't use the payroll features in QuickBooks

If you decide not to use any of the QuickBooks payroll features, you should turn off the payroll features in Preferences. To do so, select Preferences from the Edit menu. Click Payroll & Employees in the left column and then click the Company Preferences tab. In QuickBooks Payroll, select No payroll.

To learn about...	Look in the Help Index for...
Using the Employee list without using the payroll features	payroll, not using

About Intuit Payroll Services

QuickBooks 2004 supports payroll services that can make preparing your payroll easier and help you stay compliant with changing payroll tax laws.

Preparing your payroll in QuickBooks

Two payroll services—Do-It-Yourself Payroll and Assisted Payroll—allow you to prepare your payroll within QuickBooks, using the most current tax rate information and forms available. Assisted Payroll provides additional features that help take the worry out of processing your payroll. Both services require that you have the following:

- An Internet connection from a computer running QuickBooks

- A registered copy of QuickBooks

- A valid subscription to one of the payroll services

- A federal Employer Identification Number for each company you plan to do payroll for

QuickBooks Do-It-Yourself Payroll. For an annual fee, a Do-It-Yourself Payroll subscription enables you to process your own payroll with the confidence that your federal and state payroll tax tables and federal payroll tax forms are current. For more information, select Payroll Services in the Employees menu, then click Learn About Payroll Options.

You can sign up for Do-It-Yourself Payroll, including the add-on services Direct Deposit and E-File & Pay, from QuickBooks. For more information, see "Setting up your payroll" on page 242.

QuickBooks Assisted Payroll. Assisted Payroll is a comprehensive payroll solution that provides all of the features of Do-It-Yourself Payroll, plus makes your tax payments, prepares your W-2 forms, and files W-3 information on your behalf. For more information, select Payroll Services in the Employees menu, then click Learn About Payroll Options.

You can sign up for Assisted Payroll from QuickBooks. For more information, see "Setting up your payroll" on page 242.

Outsourcing your payroll

Complete Payroll, a full-service solution offered by Intuit Payroll Services, is designed for those customers who want the convenience of a fully outsourced payroll service while still being able to download their payroll data into QuickBooks. For more information, from the Employees menu, choose Payroll Services, and then Learn About Payroll Options.

To sign up for Complete Payroll, you must call the payroll service directly. For contact information, from the Help menu, choose Help & Support. Under Contact Intuit, choose Phone Directory, and then click Complete Payroll.

Note: **The information presented in this chapter applies to customers who subscribe to the Do-It-Yourself Payroll or Assisted Payroll service or who do payroll manually in QuickBooks.** For more information about Complete Payroll, contact the payroll service directly.

Choosing the payroll service that's right for you

Determining which payroll service is right for you can depend upon several factors: the size of your company and payroll, the states in which your company is located and your employees work, the pricing and features of each payroll service, the amount of time and energy you want to spend managing your payroll, and so on. QuickBooks has a short questionnaire that can help you make your decision. To try it out, from the Employees menu, choose Payroll Services, then Set Up Payroll. Click Choose a payroll option. Under Help Me Choose, click Answer a few simple questions.

To learn about...	Look in the Help Index for...
Your payroll options	payroll services, description of services
QuickBooks Do-It-Yourself Payroll	Do-It-Yourself Payroll service, overview
QuickBooks Assisted Payroll	Assisted Payroll service
Complete Payroll	Complete Payroll service
direct deposit	Direct Deposit
e-filing	E-File & Pay
Using QuickBooks payroll without a payroll service subscription	payroll taxes, calculating without a payroll service subscription
Using an outsourced payroll service, including Complete Payroll	payroll services, outsourcing your payroll

How QuickBooks payroll works

The importance of payroll items

When you create any kind of payroll transaction in QuickBooks—whether it's a paycheck, a payroll tax payment, or an adjustment at setup time or later—QuickBooks expresses the transaction in terms of payroll items.

QuickBooks uses payroll items to track individual amounts on a paycheck and accumulated year-to-date wage and tax amounts for each employee. There are payroll items for compensation, taxes, other additions and deductions, and employer-paid expenses. You can assign these payroll items to different accounts as needed.

QuickBooks identifies payroll transactions by their use of payroll items:

- Payroll reports include only transactions that use payroll items.

- Payroll liability balances are based on transactions that use payroll items.

- Employee year-to-date amounts are based on transactions that use payroll items.

When the payroll feature is turned on, QuickBooks creates the Payroll Item list with some standard payroll items. You can add payroll items to this list.

To learn about...	Look in the Help Index for...
Payroll items	payroll items, defined

Payroll expense and liability accounts

When QuickBooks creates your initial payroll items, it also adds two accounts to your chart of accounts:

- Payroll Expenses (an expense account)
- Payroll Liabilities (an "other" current liability account)

To keep your balance sheet and your profit and loss statements accurate, QuickBooks associates the appropriate account or accounts with each payroll item.

Whenever you create a new payroll item, QuickBooks helps you assign it to the correct account or accounts by prefilling the account name to use. Of course, you can use a different account if you like.

It is also correct for some types of payroll items (such as a deduction that is a loan repayment) to be associated with an account other than an expense or a liability account.

To learn about...	Look in the Help Index for...
Payroll Liabilities account	payroll liabilities, account
Payroll Expenses account	payroll, expenses account

Payroll items associated with expenses

Common company payroll expenses include gross pay, company-paid payroll taxes, and company-paid benefits for employees. For all payroll expenses, QuickBooks suggests using the Payroll Expenses account. Whenever you run your payroll, QuickBooks keeps track of your company's expenses for each employee. You can then see totals for these expenses on the payroll summary report and on the profit and loss statement.

Keeping track of expenses by customer and job, class, and service item

You can break down company-paid payroll expenses by job, class, and service item. Expenses you can break down include:

- Salary and hourly wages
- Company-paid payroll taxes
- Additions, commissions, and company contributions.

QuickBooks can prorate an employee's company-paid expenses in the same proportions as it prorates the dollar amounts of the employee's earnings. You can also set up QuickBooks to prorate each addition, commission, or company contribution.

To learn about...	Look in the Help Index for...
Keeping track of payroll expenses by customer and job, by class, or by service item	payroll, tracking expenses

Payroll items associated with liabilities

Liabilities are the amounts you owe but have not yet paid. For each type of payroll liability, QuickBooks suggests using the Payroll Liabilities account.

When you do your payroll, QuickBooks calculates how much you owe for each tax, deduction, or company contribution payroll item and records it in this liability account. With each paycheck you write, the balance of the liability account increases.

When you pay your payroll taxes or other payroll liabilities in the Pay Liabilities window, QuickBooks decreases the balance of the liability account.

Some payroll items deduct amounts from the employee's paycheck. For example, federal and state income tax withholding reduce the amount the employee receives. When you write the paycheck, your company is temporarily keeping these taxes, but you will turn them over to the government shortly. In the meantime, you have a tax liability. Payroll items for deductions are usually assigned to the Payroll Liabilities account.

Combinations of expenses and liabilities

Some payroll items are a combination of liabilities and expenses. For example, federal unemployment tax (FUTA) both creates a tax liability and is a company expense at the same time. Payroll items for company-paid taxes and company contributions are usually assigned to both a liability account and an expense account.

Customizing payroll accounts

You may change the names of the payroll liability account and payroll expense account that QuickBooks provides. If you use numbered accounts, you may change the account numbers QuickBooks provides.

You can also use subaccounts of Payroll Liabilities to see more detail on your balance sheet for payroll liabilities, and subaccounts of Payroll Expenses to see more detail on your profit and loss statement of your payroll expenses. For example, corporations may need to report expenses for officer salaries separately from those for non-officer salaries.

To learn about...	Look in the Help Index for...
Adding new accounts	accounts (managing), adding
Changing account information	accounts (managing), editing
Subaccounts	subaccounts

How QuickBooks tracks company-paid taxes and benefits

QuickBooks tracks company-paid taxes with each paycheck you write. It also allows you to track company-paid benefits with each paycheck through company contribution payroll items.

Here are some advantages of tracking company-paid taxes and company-paid expenses with paychecks:

- You always have a record of how much tax you owe at any time, so you can plan to have the cash to pay it.

- For taxes (such as federal unemployment) that have an earnings cap, you can see when QuickBooks reaches the cap for an employee and stops accruing additional tax liabilities.

- When you track company-paid benefits with a paycheck, you can track the total cost to the company for each employee. The total cost equals compensation plus company-paid taxes plus company-paid benefits.

Where this information appears

QuickBooks payroll reports provide you with a list of all company-paid taxes and other payroll expenses. Taxable company-paid expenses also appear on paystubs, the summaries of the details of individual paychecks that you can print separately from checks, if you wanted to keep such summaries in your own records, for example.

Setting up your payroll

The amount of time it takes to set up your payroll information in QuickBooks can vary, depending on the size of your company and the payroll options you choose.

First of all, make sure that QuickBooks' payroll features are turned on. From the Edit menu, choose Preferences, scroll down to Payroll & Employees, click the Company Preferences tab, and then select Full payroll features in the QuickBooks Payroll Features area. You can also use the Payroll & Employee preferences to specify how to sort your Employee list, what prints on the paycheck and its voucher, and other preferences.

To protect your company's payroll data from unauthorized access you can set up user permissions to govern access to payroll features. For information about restricting access to your company file, see "Setting up users" on page 45.

Use the QuickBooks Payroll Setup to choose a payroll option and set up your payroll in QuickBooks. To get there, from the Employees menu, choose Payroll Services, then Set Up Payroll.

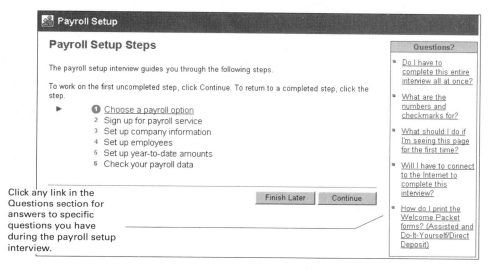

The Payroll Setup provides additional guidance to help ensure that you enter data accurately and completely.

Note: To subscribe to Do-It-Yourself Payroll or Assisted Payroll, you must have a federal EIN—a nine-digit number issued by the IRS. If you don't have an EIN, you can request one by contacting the IRS and obtaining Form SS-4. Call 1-800-TAX-FORM or refer to IRS Publication 15, *Circular E, Employer's Tax Guide*.

The QuickBooks Payroll Setup also includes the Payroll Checkup which reconciles your payroll data with your payroll setup and to reconcile your payroll data with the federal and state payroll tax forms you already filed during the current year.

Payroll Checkup is an optional step for Do-It-Yourself Payroll customers, but a required step for Assisted Payroll customers. The Assisted Payroll service must receive a complete and accurate data file before it can start you on the service.

To learn about...	Look in the Help Index for...
Setting up payroll	payroll setup
Signing up for Do-It-Yourself Payroll	Do-It-Yourself Payroll service, signing up
Signing up for Assisted Payroll	Assisted Payroll service, signing up
Signing up for Complete Payroll	Complete Payroll service
Setting payroll preferences	preferences, payroll

Information you need before you start	Where to find it
Company	
Pay period frequency or frequencies.	Your accountant or company records
State or states for which you file payroll taxes.	Your accountant or company records
Start date for using payroll.	Your company records
Federal Employer Identification Number. **Note:** An EIN is required if you are signing up for one of the Intuit Payroll Services.	Your company records or IRS
Tax information	
State employer tax ID number or numbers.	Your accountant or state tax agency
State unemployment tax (SUI) rate(s) for employer and/or employee.	Your accountant or state tax agency
State disability tax (SDI) rate or rates. **Note:** As of 2000, the rate varies by company for the following states: HI, NJ, and NY.	Your accountant or state tax agency
Miscellaneous state tax rates for your company (selected states).	Your accountant or state or local tax agencies
Local income taxes that you withhold or pay on behalf of your employees.	Your accountant or local tax agency
Whether you qualify for the federal unemployment (FUTA) tax credit.	IRS Publication 15, Circular E, Employer's Tax Guide, your accountant, or the Internal Revenue Service
Compensation, benefits, and other paycheck items	
Which types of compensation you pay employees and officers: hourly wages, salaries, and/or commissions.	Your accountant or company records
Types of deductions from net pay that you withhold. ■ Examples include: union dues, repayments of employee advances or loans, health or life insurance paid by the employee, deductions for pension plans.	Your accountant or company records

Information you need before you start	Where to find it
Types of additions you add to a paycheck. ■ Examples include: bonuses, travel reimbursements, employee advances or loans, tips.	Your accountant or company records
Types of company contributions (that is, company-paid expenses) you need to track with each paycheck. ■ Example: health or life insurance paid by the company.	Your accountant or company records

Employees

Employee names, addresses, and Social Security numbers.	Copies of your employees' Social Security cards
Employee withholding setup.	Employees' Forms W-4 and equivalent state forms
Current employee wages/salaries, additions, deductions, and company contributions.	Paychecks, reports, or payroll ledger
Sick and vacation time policies and hours accrued.	Paychecks, reports, or payroll ledger

Year-to-date amounts

■ Quarterly and pay period summaries of employee payroll amounts from the beginning of this calendar year to your start date. ■ Paychecks from your start date to today.	Payroll service, accountant, or payroll ledger
■ Quarterly and pay period summaries of payroll liability payments from the beginning of this year to your start date. ■ Payroll liability checks from your start date to today.	

Direct Deposit (an optional feature of Do-It-Yourself Payroll and Assisted Payroll. Additional fees apply and Internet access is required.)

For each employee who chooses to use direct deposit: ■ Bank account numbers ■ Bank routing numbers	Employees' direct deposit request forms

Setting up your payroll items

QuickBooks displays your payroll items on the Payroll Item list. You'll also see payroll items on paychecks and in payroll reports.

You can add payroll items to the Payroll Item list at any time. QuickBooks provides extra assistance for setting up common items, such as compensation and benefits, so you can set them up quickly and accurately. For example, some items affect the amount of tax withheld or accrued as a company liability. QuickBooks helps you set up the taxability correctly so you don't have to think about it.

Note: QuickBooks provides preset options for the taxability of a payroll item, based on the most current information from the IRS and other tax agencies. We recommend that you retain the preset taxability of a payroll item, as it is unlikely that it would need to change.

Most states have two or more payroll taxes. The payroll setup interview lets you set up all the taxes for one state at one time.

Depending on your company's payroll, you may need to set up additional payroll items. Refer to the following table for a list of payroll item types.

Note: Federal Tax payroll items are created automatically by QuickBooks. You cannot set them up (or delete them).

Type of payroll item	Use for creating
Salary Wages	■ Compensation to employees whose annual salary is independent of the number of hours actually worked ■ Compensation to salaried corporate officers (with expenses assigned to an expense account for corporate officer salaries) ■ Paid sick time for salaried employees ■ Paid vacation time for salaried employees
Hourly Wages	■ Compensation based on the number of hours worked ■ Paid sick time for hourly employees ■ Paid vacation time for hourly employees
Commission	Compensation based on a percentage of another quantity (such as sales volume) or a flat amount multiplied by another quantity (such as units sold).
Bonus	One-time compensation awarded at the discretion of the employer.
Deduction	Any deduction from gross or after-tax (net) pay. Examples include: union dues, loan repayments, employee-paid insurance, and employee deduction.
Addition	Any addition to gross or after-tax (net) pay.
Company Contribution	Any company-paid benefit or expense that you want to track with each paycheck. Examples include: company contributions to employee benefits, such as health or life insurance or a 401(k) plan.
State Withholding Tax	State income tax withheld from employees' paychecks.
State Disability Insurance Tax	State disability insurance (SDI) based on employee wages of employees working in any of the following locations: CA, HI, NJ, NY, RI; or PR. This tax is sometimes paid by the company and/or employee.

(continued) Type of payroll item	Use for creating
State Unemployment Insurance Tax	State unemployment insurance (SUI) based on employee wages. This tax is sometimes paid by the company alone and sometimes by both the company and employee.
Other Tax	Miscellaneous state or local (county, city, or district) taxes based on employee wages. These taxes may be paid by the company and/or employee.

You can set up payroll items at any time, for example, if you need to add taxes for a new state or to add a new compensation or benefit item.

To do so, you'll use the Add new payroll item wizard, which you can find by going to the Payroll Item list, clicking the Payroll Item button, and then selecting New. The wizard includes an Easy Setup option, which guides you through setting up common compensation and benefits items.

The wizard also has a Custom Setup option for setting up less common items or specifying particular liability or expense accounts. When using the custom setup, if prompted for a tax tracking type, be sure to choose the one that fits your item. The tax tracking type determines whether and how paycheck amounts for the item are reported on payroll tax forms.

When you choose a tax tracking type, QuickBooks provides preset options for the taxability of the item, based on the most current information from the IRS and other tax agencies. We recommend that you retain the preset taxability of the item, when provided, as it is unlikely that it would need to change.

To learn about...	Look in the Help Index for...
Using the QuickBooks payroll setup interview to add payroll items	payroll setup, interview
Changing the name of a payroll item	payroll items, editing
Adding a common payroll item (using the Easy Setup option)	payroll items, adding
Adding payroll items for a local tax	payroll items, other tax
Adding all taxes for a state (using the payroll setup interview)	payroll setup, interview
Adding other payroll items	payroll items, adding
Tax tracking type	payroll items, tax tracking type

Setting up employees

According to the IRS, "anyone who performs services for you is your employee if you can control what will be done and how it will be done." The IRS has more information on how to determine whether an individual providing services is an independent contractor or an employee. See IRS Publication 15, *Circular E, Employer's Tax Guide*, or visit the IRS Web site at www.irs.gov.

Generally, people in business for themselves are not employees. However, if your company is incorporated, corporate officers who work in the business are employees.

Note: If you need to file Form 1099-MISC for an independent contractor, set up the person as a vendor in QuickBooks. Employees cannot receive 1099-MISC forms. See "Information you may want to set up for different kinds of vendors" on page 143 for more information.

To set up employees for payroll, do the following:

- (Optional but recommended) Set up the employee defaults.

- Add new employees to your Employee list and fill in the Payroll and Compensation Info tab, or add payroll information to employees already on your Employee list.

You can add employees to your Employee list at any time— during the QuickBooks payroll setup interview, or after you complete your payroll setup. The interview provides additional help by guiding you, step-by-step, through the setup process.

Employee Defaults: Entering common employee information

The employee defaults help you set up payroll for several employees quickly. You enter payroll information that most employees have in common. These defaults will show up every time you enter information for a new employee. If the information isn't appropriate for an individual employee, you can change it on that employee's record.

You can set up the following information as employee defaults:

- Salary or wage payroll items (with or without rates)
- Pay period
- Class, if you're using classes to track your employees (see Chapter 4, *Organizing data effectively,* beginning on page 23)
- Whether you want to use time data to create checks (except QuickBooks Basic)
- Additions, deductions, and company contributions that appear on paychecks

  Note: The order in which you enter payroll items in the Addition, Deductions, and Company Contributions table can affect the amount QuickBooks calculates for each item and for taxes.

- Whether your employees are covered by a qualified pension plan
- Taxes—Federal, state, and other local taxes
- Sick and vacation time

In QuickBooks Pro and QuickBooks Premier, this checkbox appears only if time tracking is turned on. You can turn time tracking on and off in the Preferences section under the Edit menu.

The **Class** field is available only if you have class tracking turned on. You can turn class tracking on and off in the Accounting section of your Preferences, located in the Edit menu.

To learn about...	Look in the Help Index for...
Using the QuickBooks payroll setup interview	payroll setup, interview
Setting up the employee defaults	employee defaults, creating
Determining how the order in which you add payroll items to employee defaults affects employee pay	employee defaults, order of payroll items in

Adding employees

If you've already set up your employee defaults, QuickBooks can prefill much of the information when you start to set up individual employees.

The Employee list contains the names of all your employees. When you add or edit an employee, you may fill out three sections:

- Personal Info
- Payroll & Compensation Info
- Employment Info

Use the "Change tabs" drop-down list to switch between sections.

You'll need payroll items for all the taxes you enter, as well as for other payroll information. If you have not already set up all the payroll items you need, QuickBooks gives you a chance to add them as you work.

Each of your employees needs to fill out a Form W-4 and its state equivalent to tell you what filing status they will use and how many personal exemptions they will claim. You can get blank forms from the IRS and state agencies.

To learn about...	Look in the Help Index for...
Using the QuickBooks payroll setup interview	payroll setup, interview
Adding employees	employees, adding
Setting up payroll information for existing employees	employees, payroll information about
Categorizing employees by class	employees, grouping by department or location
Types of employees	employees, types

Summarizing amounts for this year to date

Note: Skip this section if you've used the Pay Employees feature in QuickBooks to issue all your employees' paychecks for this calendar year.

If you are about to start using QuickBooks for payroll for the first time but have issued paychecks this calendar year using an application or method other than QuickBooks, you need to enter the following year-to-date information into QuickBooks:

- Enter payroll transactions (paychecks and liability checks) for the period between your QuickBooks start date and today.

- Enter year-to-date information to summarize payroll transactions from January 1 through your QuickBooks start date. For a description of start dates, see Chapter 5, "Setting up your company in QuickBooks," in the *QuickBooks Getting Started Guide*.

After you've entered this information, QuickBooks updates your year-to-date amounts every time it issues paychecks during the remainder of the calendar year, and it keeps your payroll tax amounts correct.

You must enter two types of year-to-date information: summaries for each employee and summaries of payments of payroll taxes and other liabilities. You enter year-to-date summaries when you first set up your payroll (see "Setting up your payroll" on page 242). To access this step, from the Employees menu, choose Set Up Payroll. In the Payroll Setup window, click step 5 and follow the onscreen instructions.

Year-to-date summaries for each employee

Enter summaries of earnings, taxes, and other amounts for every employee (both current and former) that you paid during the current calendar year—January 1 through your start date.

For each employee, you must enter both taxes withheld *and taxes that are a company expense,* as long as you owed them as a result of the employee's earnings. For example, you must enter federal and state unemployment tax summaries for each employee, as well as company taxes.

QuickBooks collects year-to-date information on a quarter-by-quarter basis. We recommend that you use this same method to organize your year-to-date information before you begin entering year-to-date summaries. This will help if you plan to sign up for the Assisted Payroll service, because the service also collects this information on a quarter-by-quarter basis.

When you select an employee and click Enter Summary, QuickBooks displays each payroll item you entered in that employee's record.

Enter summaries for the period specified here.

In this area, enter totals for salary or hourly wages paid during this period.

Enter hours worked during the period, if you want hour totals for reports. QuickBooks displays a message if hours are required for your state.

In this area, enter totals for all other earnings, withholdings, and company-paid taxes or payroll expenses for this employee. Include taxes regardless of whether you have paid them.

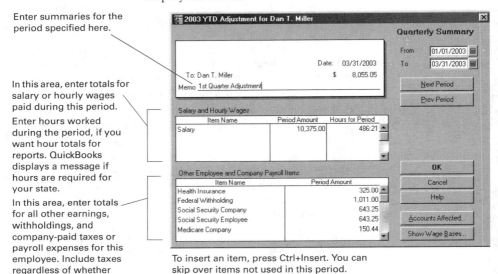

To insert an item, press Ctrl+Insert. You can skip over items not used in this period.

- In the Other Employee and Company Payroll Items area, leave the Period Amount field blank if there was no amount for a payroll item during this period.

- In the Salary and Hourly Wages area, enter payroll items for sick and vacation time taken during this period. You should enter sick and vacation hours and their corresponding wage amounts. Do not include these hours and wage amounts in your totals for regular salary or hourly wages.

- Add payroll items for one-time payroll amounts, such as bonuses, that occurred during this period. You must enter anything that affects compensation or payroll taxes. You are not required to enter non-payroll adjustments—such as reimbursements for office supplies—but you may do so if you would like to track them in QuickBooks.

- Enter an amount for the employee or company portion of Social Security and Medicare. When you enter one portion, QuickBooks fills in the other portion for you, because the amounts should match. QuickBooks uses the separate amounts to track totals for employee withholding; it uses both portions to track your total tax liability.

- You must enter all tax liabilities created because of the compensation paid, even if the taxes were paid later and even if they were company expenses. For example, if the compensation was subject to state unemployment tax, enter the amount of tax.

- If you decide to track company-paid expenses, such as insurance, as a payroll expense for each pay period, you must enter amounts for the employee in the YTD Adjustment window. Later, in the Set Up YTD Amounts wizard, you must also enter the amounts you've already paid, so that QuickBooks can keep track of how much you owe.

Wage bases

For every tax payroll item in the lower half of the YTD Adjustment window for an employee, QuickBooks tracks the wage base for reports and for Form W-2. The wage base is the total amount of employee wages or earnings on which a payroll tax is calculated. You can view the wage bases by clicking Show Wage Bases.

QuickBooks calculates the wage base for a tax as follows:

- First, it totals all salary, hourly wages, and commissions.

- Then it adds those additions and company contributions that are subject to that specific tax.

- Finally, it subtracts those deductions that are deducted prior to calculating that specific tax.

If the total of the wage base year-to-date exceeds the maximum annual earnings limit for this tax, the wage base equals the maximum earnings limit. If you entered amounts for earlier periods this year, QuickBooks counts the wage base from the earlier periods towards the maximum. For example, if the FUTA tax wage limit is $7,000 and you paid an employee $5,000 in each of the first two periods, the wage base for FUTA tax for the second period is only $2,000 ($7,000 - $5,000 = $2,000, the amount left in the wage base).

To learn about...	Look in the Help Index for...
Entering YTD amounts for employees	year-to-date amounts, employee
Wage bases	wage base

Year-to-date summaries of payments of payroll taxes and other liabilities

Note: Skip this section if your company has not made any payments for payroll taxes or other liabilities incurred during this calendar year.

For this adjustment, you'll need to know how much you paid for each of the following:

- Each payroll tax (whether withheld or paid as a company expense)

- Each deduction paid (employee-paid dental insurance, for example)

- Each company contribution you paid (company-paid health insurance, for example)

This adjustment is just for payroll liabilities you paid. It is not for expenses (such as salaries, bonuses, or hourly wages) paid directly to employees.

Enter the ending date of the period you are summarizing.

Enter the date you made the liability payment.

Prior Payments of Taxes and Liabilities

Payment Date 04/15/2003   For Period Ending 03/31/2003

Next Payment
Prev Payment
Done
Cancel
Help
Accounts Affected...

Taxes and Liabilities

Item Name	Amount	Memo
Federal Unemploym...	105.74	
Federal Withholding	1,743.00	
Medicare Company	240.59	
Medicare Employee	240.59	
Social Security Com...	1,028.71	
Social Security Empl...	1,028.71	

?

To learn about...	Look in the Help Index for...
Entering YTD liability payments	year-to-date amounts, liability payments
Checking YTD amounts by running the Payroll Checkup	payroll, checkup

Checking your payroll data

Because QuickBooks bases new payroll transactions on existing data, it's extremely important that you enter all of your payroll data into QuickBooks accurately. To help ensure that your payroll data and year-to-date transactions are accurate, QuickBooks provides you with the following tools.

Running Payroll Checkup

Payroll Checkup is a diagnostic tool within QuickBooks that helps you verify your current setup by scanning payroll data for any discrepancies. The checkup verifies new or modified data against your current payroll setup and displays the results, which you can print and use to review your payroll data.

Note: **Running the Payroll Checkup doesn't verify whether or not your payroll data is complete.** It compares the wage base and tax amount totals with your current payroll setup in QuickBooks and summarizes any discrepancies.

For Assisted Payroll customers: Use Payroll Checkup when signing up for the payroll service. In step 6 of the payroll setup interview (see the image on page 243), QuickBooks uses the payroll checkup to scan the payroll setup and provide possible solutions to any discrepancies. To complete the sign-up process, Assisted Payroll customers **must fix all problems** in their payroll data.

For Do-It-Yourself Payroll customers: Payroll Checkup is optional, but QuickBooks recommends using it for the following tasks:

- During the Payroll Setup.
- Any time you add a new payroll item or edit payroll data in QuickBooks. For example, when you change the taxability of a payroll item or enter year-to-date information, a prompt appears recommending that you run the Payroll Checkup to verify new or modified entries.

    To run Payroll Checkup, choose Run Payroll Checkup from the Employees menu.

Do not delete any zero-tax amount adjustments resulting from the Payroll Checkup.

While scanning your payroll data, the Payroll Checkup may make some wage base adjustments, which can take some time and result in some zero-tax amount adjustments. QuickBooks marks these adjustments by adding "Payroll Checkup" to the Memo field for the payroll item. Do not delete any payroll items with a zero-tax amount adjustment if "Payroll Checkup" appears in the Memo field.

Making sure that your data is complete

Use the following procedures to make sure your data is complete:

Procedure	Comments	Search Help index for...
Review your Employee list.	The Employee list includes the names of all employees on your payroll at any time during the current calendar year.	lists, printing
Review your Payroll Item list.	The Payroll Item list should list everything you need to track on any employee's paycheck.	payroll, reports about lists, printing
Review an employee contact list report.	The employee contact report displays contact information for all employees.	employees, reports about
Review your payroll summary for all employees for this entire calendar year.	You should be able to match the amounts for payroll items with the amounts for payroll accounts on prior payroll reports.	employees, reports about
Review your payroll liabilities as of December 31 of **this** year.	You should be able to match the amounts for payroll items with the amounts for payroll accounts on prior liability reports.	payroll liabilities, report

Managing payroll and employee information

As your business grows and changes, you will probably find it necessary to add payroll items to your list, hire and release employees, and track additional information about your payroll.

Changing payroll item information

By default, the Payroll Item list is organized by payroll item type. Earnings items (for yearly salaries, hourly wages, and commissions) are at the top of the list. To re-sort the list, click a column header.

To view your payroll items:

■ From the Employees menu, choose Payroll Item List.

If you don't need an item in the list, you can mark it inactive.

The icon beside the name indicates that this payroll item is marked inactive.

You can't delete the payroll items for federal taxes (or some of the items that QuickBooks creates), but you can rename or mark them inactive.

Use the menu buttons to add, edit, or perform other activities on payroll items.

To re-sort the list by name or type, click the column header.

To display names of payroll items marked inactive, click Show All. To hide these items, clear the checkbox.

You can use the same payroll item for many employees. For earnings, local taxes, and all other non-tax items, you can always customize the amount or percentage in the setup window for each employee.

You can change the information for existing payroll items, although you probably do not want to change the tax tracking or taxability of an item. You may want to change a payroll item for the following reasons, for example:

■ Your state unemployment tax rate changes.

■ You realize that you're eligible for the federal unemployment (FUTA) tax credit.

■ Your accountant wants you to assign an item to a different account.

?

To learn about...	Look in the Help Index for...
Changing payroll item information	payroll items, editing

What the changes affect

Changes you make to payroll items are reflected in the new checks you write. Certain changes can also affect how payroll amounts are classified historically on tax forms, reports, and check details. When items are changed, the change appears on payroll tax forms and check details.

Employee information and existing checks are affected when you change any of the following information for payroll items:

- Payroll item name
- Account assigned (liability and expense)
- Tax tracking (such as Compensation or Reported Tips)

Changing the following information only affects future paychecks or current paychecks that you change in such a way that QuickBooks must recalculate them:

- State unemployment (SUI) or state disability (SDI) tax rates
- Eligibility for federal unemployment (FUTA) tax credit
- Taxes affected (for additions to or deductions from gross pay)

Deleting, removing, or merging payroll items

You can delete a payroll item from the Payroll Item list if it is not currently used in:

- the employee default setup
- any employee record
- payroll transaction

If you cannot delete a payroll item, you can still hide it on your Payroll Item list by making it inactive. Mark inactive those payroll items you used in the past but no longer need to use.

When you make a payroll item inactive, QuickBooks keeps the information associated with that payroll item, but hides it on the Payroll Item list and removes it from any drop-down lists that use payroll items. You can make a payroll item active again at any time.

If you find that you are using two payroll items to track the same thing, you can combine the payroll items as long as they are of a similar type. This is true for all payroll items except for federal and state taxes. Merging payroll items is an irreversible operation.

Changing payroll item information while using the QuickBooks Assisted Payroll service

If you're using Assisted Payroll, you cannot change the tax tracking classification or taxability of payroll items that are reported on federal and state forms because the service is filing your tax forms based on these items. If you need to change this information, call the number listed in the phone directory. From the Help menu, choose Help & Support. Under Contact Intuit, click Phone Directory, then QuickBooks Assisted Payroll.

You cannot merge a payroll item that is used by the service.

To learn about...	Look in the Help Index for...
Merging payroll items	lists, merging two entries
Hiding and showing inactive payroll items, or Making payroll items active	lists, hiding and showing entries
Deleting payroll items	payroll items, deleting

Changing employee information

Use the Employee list to store information about your employees, including each employee's name, Social Security number, address, and phone number. QuickBooks also provides a notepad with which you can make notes about an employee.

To view your employees:

- From the Employees menu, choose Employee List.

Use the menu buttons to add, edit, or perform other tasks for your employees.

To learn about...	Look in the Help Index for...
Viewing current information about an existing employee	employees, editing

Hiring and releasing employees

When you hire a new employee, add the employee to the Employee list. If you have set up your employee defaults (page 249), this information is copied from the defaults into your new employee record. Then, if you need to, you can change any of the information for this particular employee.

When an employee leaves the company, you need to enter the employee's release date in QuickBooks. If the employee is deceased, you should check the Deceased checkbox; this status is shown on the employee's W-2 form.

After you designate an employee as released, the employee's name stops appearing in the Select Employees to Pay window once the pay period end date is later than the release date. The employee's name will, however, appear when you create W-2 forms, as long as the employee was paid during that year.

You can't delete a released employee if there are transactions associated with that employee. You can, however, hide the employee's name from your Employee list.

To learn about...	Look in the Help Index for...
Hiring a new employee	employees, adding
Releasing an employee	employees, releasing
Hiding the name of a released employee	employees, hiding and showing

Changing employee payroll information

You can change employee information whenever necessary.

Note: **Changes in employee information affect all the employee's paychecks that you create or edit after you record the change.** This includes existing paychecks. Changes you make to an employee's name, address, Social Security number, and sick and vacation balances are reflected in existing paychecks.

The following types of information must be changed individually for each affected employee. Changing the payroll item doesn't affect existing employees:

- Annual limits for a deduction
- Rate or amount changes for a deduction, addition, or company contribution
- Rate changes, if they vary by company, for a miscellaneous state or local tax

Changing employee information while using the QuickBooks Assisted Payroll service

If you're using Assisted Payroll, you cannot change an employee's tax-exempt status because the service prepares Form W-2 based on this information.

If you need to change this information, call the number listed in the phone directory. From the Help menu, choose Help & Support. Under Contact Intuit, click Phone Directory, then QuickBooks Assisted Payroll.

To learn about...	Look in the Help Index for...
Changing information about an existing employee	employees, editing
Adding custom fields for an employee	employees, custom fields for
Giving an employee a raise	employees, raises
Adding notes for an employee	employees, notes about

Hiding or showing employees

You can't delete an employee who has existing payroll transactions. Instead, you can hide an employee on the Employee list by making the employee inactive.

When you make an employee inactive, QuickBooks keeps the information associated with that employee but hides the employee's name in the Employee list and removes it from most drop-down lists that use employees. However, the employee's payroll figures still appear on payroll reports. You do not need to change or delete any transaction that uses the employee. You can make an employee active again at any time.

For example, one of your employees is taking a six-month leave of absence. You don't want his name to appear in Employees to Pay during that time. You can hide it by making the employee inactive, and then reactivating him when he returns to work.

To learn about...	Look in the Help Index for...
Hiding and showing an inactive employee, or making employees active	employees, hiding and showing
Deleting an employee	employees, deleting
Running a QuickReport for your Employee list	employees, reports about

Contacting your employees by mail

In all QuickBooks editions except Basic, you can use your QuickBooks data in conjunction with prewritten Microsoft Word letters to mail your employees notices about such matters as accrued vacation and sick time.

To learn about...	Look in the Help Index for...
Using your QuickBooks data with Microsoft Word letters	letters using QuickBooks data in Microsoft Word

Setting up employees for direct deposit of paychecks

Before you set up Direct Deposit, you must first sign up for one of the Intuit Payroll Services.

Direct Deposit is an add-on service offered with the Do-It-Yourself Payroll and Assisted Payroll services that enables you to deposit employees' paychecks directly into their bank accounts. After you sign up for Direct Deposit, you can use either the payroll setup interview or individual employee records to set up bank account and routing information.

Note: Intuit's outsourced payroll solution, Complete Payroll, also offers direct deposit services. (Additional fees apply.) For information about features in Complete Payroll, contact the Complete Payroll service.

For information on all Intuit Payroll Services, select Payroll Services in the Employees menu, then select Learn About Payroll Options.

After you've signed up for direct deposit, QuickBooks automatically creates a new payroll item for Direct Deposit. This payroll item appears in the Payroll Item list (page 257) and in the Employee Summary area of the Preview Paycheck window.

You can modify your employee's bank account information by clicking Direct Deposit on the Payroll & Compensation Info tab of the employee's record. QuickBooks displays the Direct Deposit window.

You can deposit into two bank accounts; for example, a checking and a savings account.

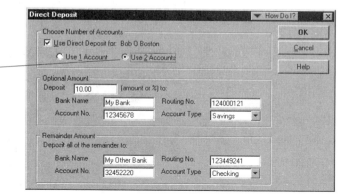

To learn about...	Look in the Help Index for...
Setting up employees for direct deposit	direct deposit, setting up employees for
Adding the Direct Deposit feature to Do-It-Yourself Payroll	direct deposit
Where to find routing numbers	routing numbers

Running payroll and paying taxes

Paying your employees

Before you begin writing paychecks, make sure that you do the following:

- Sign up for either Do-It-Yourself Payroll or Assisted Payroll.

  QuickBooks cannot compute payroll taxes unless you sign up for Do-It-Yourself Payroll or Assisted Payroll.

  Note: New Do-It-Yourself Payroll subscribers can get one free payroll update* that allows you to download and use the latest tax tables and federal forms for a limited time. For more information about Do-It-Yourself Payroll or Assisted Payroll, see page 237.

- Go online to get the latest payroll update, which includes the most current tax information available.

---

* Internet access is required to download the free update. Terms, conditions, offers, pricing, features, and service options subject to change without notice. For the most current information, visit the following Web site: www.payroll.com\services

- Set up your payroll items.
- Enter payroll information for your employees.
- Specify your payroll and employee preferences.
- Enter bank information for employees who want direct deposit.

To learn about...	Look in the Help Index for...
Getting payroll updates	payroll, update
Subscribing to the Intuit Payroll Services	payroll services, description of services
Setting up payroll items	payroll items, adding
Payroll information for employees	employees, payroll information about
Setting up employees for direct deposit	direct deposit, setting up employees for

Selecting employees to pay

To select the employees you want to pay:

- From the Employees menu, choose Pay Employees.

If you print checks, select To be printed. Otherwise, select To be handwritten or direct deposited and enter a check number or note in First Check Number

QuickBooks records the checks in this bank account.

To enter hours worked, sick or vacation time, commission bases, or other variations from pay period to pay period, select this option.

You specify a check and pay period date on the paychecks.

QuickBooks creates a paycheck for each employee marked with a checkmark.

Click here for tips, advice, or information about using the payroll feature in QuickBooks.

When you create a check, this date changes to the next pay period end date.

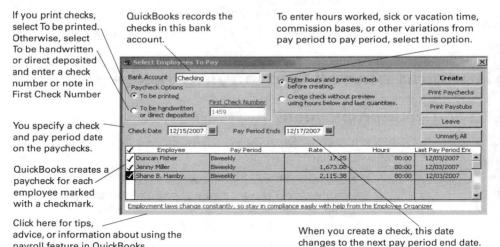

When you've finished selecting the employees to pay, click Create to display paycheck information about the first employee.

You can pay employees in groups. For example, first select all of your salaried employees whose paychecks you don't need to review, and pay them. Then select your hourly employees and preview paychecks so that you can enter their hours.

Previewing, adjusting, and creating paychecks

When you select "Enter hours and preview check before creating" in the Select Employees To Pay window, and then click Create, QuickBooks displays the Preview Paycheck window.

In the Preview Paycheck window, you can do all of the following:

- View the amounts QuickBooks calculated for each payroll item (including gross earnings, taxes, and all other additions, deductions, and company contributions) for the paycheck.

- Enter or edit the number of hours worked.

- Enter sick or vacation hours, as well as prevent sick and vacation hours from accruing for this particular paycheck.

- Enter the base quantity on which to calculate commissions and other additions or deductions based on quantity.

- Add or delete wage, commission, addition, deduction, or company contribution payroll items.

  Note: **To suppress payment of regular salary on a bonus check, delete the salary item in the Preview Paycheck window.** (Select it and press Ctrl+Del.)

- Break down salary amounts by customer jobs.

- Review all company-paid taxes and contributions that do not affect the amount on the check.

- Assign different rates to different sets of hours for hourly employees.

- Edit the amount for any payroll item.

  Note: **You usually will not want to edit payroll items for flat-rate taxes.** This is because QuickBooks detects if your totals for certain flat-rate taxes are not correct for the year or quarter and fixes them automatically. If one or more or these taxes are wrong, it might be because your payroll item taxability or YTD wage base for the tax is wrong.

  Note: **If you're using Assisted Payroll,** you cannot change tax amounts except for state and federal withholding.

To prevent sick and vacation hours from accruing for this paycheck (for example on a bonus or commission check), select this checkbox.

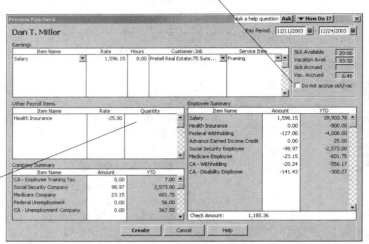

If a commission, addition, deduction, company contribution, or other tax is based on quantity, enter the quantity here.

For Assisted Payroll and Do-It-Yourself Payroll with Direct Deposit customers. After you enter all of your employees' paychecks and click Create, QuickBooks displays a message asking if you want to send your paychecks now. When you see this message, click OK to go online and send your paychecks to the payroll service.

When QuickBooks creates a paycheck, it does the following:

- Updates the pay period end date of the last check written for the employee, and clears the checkmarks in the Select Employees To Pay window.

- Writes a paycheck for your employee made out for the net amount, showing the deductions in the voucher area.

- Increases or decreases sick or vacation hours available based on number of hours accrued and/or used.

  If you selected the "Do not accrue sick/vac" checkbox in the Preview Paycheck window, you prevent the sick and vacation hours from accruing on this particular paycheck.

- Updates year-to-date balances for the employee.

- Records the check in your checking account register and reduces the account balance.

  If you are using the Direct Deposit feature of Do-It-Yourself Payroll or Assisted Payroll, QuickBooks does not reduce the amount in your checking account register until you go online and send the paycheck to the service.

- Records an increase in each affected liability account, showing the extra liability resulting from the payroll transaction (for both employee paycheck deductions and company contributions).

If you are using the Direct Deposit feature of Do-It-Yourself Payroll or Assisted Payroll, QuickBooks first records the increase in the Direct Deposit Liabilities account. Then after you send your payroll, QuickBooks decreases the amount in the Direct Deposit Liabilities account and increases the amount in the appropriate checking account.

- Updates and tracks your payroll expenses in expense accounts.

- Updates any other accounts you have assigned to any payroll items used in the payroll transaction.

To learn about...	Look in the Help Index for...
Previewing and adjusting paychecks	paychecks, checking amounts in

Reviewing and correcting paychecks

After you've recorded a paycheck, you can review it at any time and make changes to it, if necessary.

Sometimes it's necessary to void or delete a paycheck; for example:

- You might want to void a paycheck if there was a payroll error in a recent paycheck that your employee has not yet cashed.

  If the paycheck was in a previous quarter or year for which you've filed your payroll tax forms, you may have to refile these payroll tax forms when you void the paycheck and issue a new one. Consult your professional tax advisor for more information.

- You may want to delete a paycheck if it is a duplicate and you haven't printed it yet.

After you send a paycheck to the payroll service (Do-It-Yourself Payroll with Direct Deposit or Assisted Payroll), you can only change the following items:

- Memo
- Check number
- Print status / Cleared status (for reconciling)
- QuickBooks bank account you wrote the check from
- Expense and liability accounts affected (if you edit the payroll items)
- Class
- Customer:Job

If you change a paycheck, the edited check information will be sent again to the service.

You can void a paycheck that you've already sent to the service. This will reduce the amounts in your tax liability accounts. However, if the paycheck was deposited directly to an employee's account, voiding the paycheck does not prevent the money from being transferred to the employee's account. You will need to get the money from the employee directly.

Note: You cannot delete a paycheck once you've sent it to the service.

To learn about...	Look in the Help Index for...
Editing existing paychecks	paychecks, changing
Voiding paychecks	paychecks, voiding
Deleting paychecks	paychecks, deleting

Printing paychecks and paystubs

When you print paychecks, you use the same printer setup as you do for your other checks in QuickBooks. However, QuickBooks requires you to print your paychecks separately from other checks.

If you don't print your paychecks on voucher checks, you can print paystubs to provide your employees with the information that normally appears on a paycheck voucher.

Both a printed paycheck and a paystub voucher provide all the information required for a legal paystub including:

- Employee's full name, address, and (optional) Social Security number
- Employer's legal and/or DBA name and address

- Pay period start and end dates
- Salary and hourly rate, hours, and amount of pay for the pay period
- Employee taxes
- Deductions from and additions to wages
- Taxable company contributions—such as the taxable portion of company-paid group term life insurance and (optional) all other company contributions
- Federal and state allowances and exemptions
- (Optional) Sick and vacation time used and available
- Net pay
- Year-to-date amounts for the preceding items

Employees who are set up for Direct Deposit can receive an advice of deposit. Intuit offers Advice of Deposit forms, which are personalized with your company name and address. You cannot use Advice of Deposit forms with a continuous-feed printer unless the printer has a single-feed attachment.

For information on purchasing voucher checks, paystubs, and Advices of Deposit from Intuit, visit the Web site at **www.intuitmarketplace.com**.

To learn about...	Look in the Help Index for...
Printing paychecks	paychecks, printing
Printing paystubs	paystubs
Creating and printing direct deposit checks	paychecks, direct deposit

Paying payroll taxes and liabilities

When it comes to paying your payroll taxes, QuickBooks offers several options:

- You can pay your liabilities manually.
- You can e-file federal tax payments from QuickBooks using E-File & Pay for QuickBooks Do-It-Yourself Payroll (an optional feature of Do-It-Yourself Payroll. Additional fees apply and Internet access is required).
- You can subscribe to Assisted Payroll or Complete Payroll, which will calculate and pay many of your taxes for you.

    If you use Assisted Payroll, the payroll service makes federal and state tax deposits for you from your payroll accounts. (State deposits and filings are subject to availability.) However, if you have liabilities to other vendors and agencies, such as insurance payments or local taxes, you need to use the Pay Liabilities window to pay them.

Note: You must have an EIN to pay your payroll taxes. For information about EINs and how to obtain one for your company, see page 243.

When it's time to pay taxes or other payroll liabilities, QuickBooks shows you your current liabilities, lets you choose which ones you want to pay, and creates checks to pay them. You can also add penalties, expenses, and discounts to these checks.

> **Always use the Pay Liabilities window to write checks for your liabilities and taxes.**
>
> Do **not** use the Write Checks window. If you do, your payroll reports will not be accurate.

To display the Pay Liabilities window:

■ From the Employees menu, choose Process Payroll Liabilities then Pay Payroll Liabilities. Enter the date range for the liabilities that you want to pay, then click OK in the Select Date Range For Liabilities window.

Note: **If you subscribe to E-File & Pay**, an "E-Pay" tab also appears on the Pay Liabilities window. Use this tab to create payments for federal taxes you want to pay electronically.

You can modify this date range in the Pay Liabilities window.

This is the date the transaction affects the checking account.

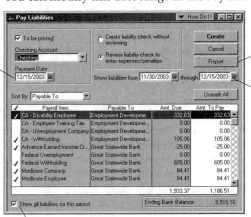

Click here to generate a payroll liability balances report for the specified period.

QuickBooks displays this date on the liability check as the paid-through date.

QuickBooks writes a single check to each different payee for whom you mark payroll items to pay.

To add a name that is missing in the Payable To column of this window, edit the payroll item.

Select this checkbox to show all payroll liabilities for the period, including any credits and zero amounts.

Note: If you are using Assisted Payroll, federal and state taxes do not appear in this window.

Filing your payroll tax forms

When it comes to filing your tax forms, QuickBooks offers several options:

- You can complete federal tax Forms W-2, W-3, 940, 941, and Schedule B (Form 941) in QuickBooks and then print them and file them by mail.

- You can subscribe to the E-File & Pay service and then file those forms electronically from within QuickBooks. (The E-File & Pay service is an optional feature of Do-It-Yourself Payroll. Additional fees apply and Internet access is required.)

- You can subscribe to Assisted Payroll or Complete Payroll, which will prepare many of your payroll tax forms for you.

Regulations for your type of business and geographic location may require you to complete and file other federal forms as well as state and local payroll tax forms. Always be sure to review the payroll regulations for your particular business to ensure you are in compliance.

Federal forms

This section describes various federal tax forms you can create in QuickBooks for your company and your employees.

Form 941
(Employer's Quarterly Federal Tax Return)

Form 941 is a quarterly tax form on which you report federal income tax withheld, Social Security tax, Medicare tax, and advance earned income credit paid to employees. These amounts are usually based on total wages you pay out. However, the amounts may not exactly equal the amounts you've paid or withheld because of rounding errors.

If your amounts need to be adjusted, create a company liability adjustment instead of editing the amount on the Form 941. See "Adjusting the liability balance for a payroll item" on page 276.

Preparing Form 941 in QuickBooks. QuickBooks helps you prepare and print your Form 941. You can print your form on either blank paper or preprinted forms.

To learn about...	Look in the Help Index for...
Preparing and printing Form 941	941s
How numbers are calculated on Form 941	941s
Creating a liability adjustment	payroll liabilities, adjusting

Schedule B (Form 941)
(Employer's Record of Federal Tax Liability)

Schedule B (Form 941) is a quarterly tax form on which semiweekly schedule depositors (or other depositors whose tax liability on any day is $100,000) report their daily tax liability for the quarter.

Check with your professional tax advisor to see if you need to file a Schedule B with your Form 941.

Preparing Schedule B (Form 941) in QuickBooks. QuickBooks helps you complete Schedule B (if required) when you complete Form 941. IYou can print your form on either blank paper or preprinted forms.

To learn about...	Look in the Help Index for...
Preparing and printing Form Schedule B (Form 941)	Schedule B (Form 941)

Form 940
(Employer's Annual Federal Unemployment
(FUTA) Tax Return)

Form 940 is an annual tax form on which you report federal unemployment tax. This tax is generally based on total wages you pay out. Most employers are eligible for a FUTA tax credit. Check with your professional tax advisor or the IRS to see if you are eligible.

Note: QuickBooks does not create Form 940-EZ. The IRS will accept a Form 940 instead.

Preparing Form 940 in QuickBooks. QuickBooks helps you prepare and print your Form 940. If you subscribe to the Do-It-Yourself Payroll service, QuickBooks lets you print the form on blank paper. Otherwise, you must use preprinted forms.

?

To learn about...	Look in the Help Index for...
Preparing, editing, and printing Form 940	940s
Receiving credit toward FUTA tax	FUTA credit

Forms W-2 and W-3

Form W-2 (Wage and Tax Statement) is the end-of-year form you send to each employee and submit to the Social Security Administration. Each form is for a single employee and shows wages and taxes withheld for the year for that employee. Form W-3 (Transmittal of Wage and Tax Statements) is a summary of the W-2 forms you are submitting to the federal government.

Preparing Forms W-2 and W-3 in QuickBooks. The government will accept Form W-2 and Form W-3 printed either on blank paper (available if you subscribe to Do-It-Yourself Payroll) or on preprinted forms. For information on purchasing preprinted forms from Intuit, visit the Web site at **www.intuitmarketplace.com**.

?

To learn about...	Look in the Help Index for...
Preparing and printing W-2 forms	W-2s
Preparing and filing W-3 forms	W-3s

If you use QuickBooks E-File & Pay, QuickBooks will ask you additional questions when you prepare your forms.

The questions request additional information required by tax agencies when you e-file and confirm that your form qualifies for e-filing.

Gathering information for other tax forms not available in QuickBooks

You may be required to file state payroll tax forms or other federal tax forms, such as Form 943 (Employer's Annual Tax Return for Agricultural Employees). Though you cannot prepare these forms within QuickBooks, you can generate reports that help you gather the information you need to prepare the forms.

You can also summarize your payroll data in a special Microsoft Excel® workbook template that is included when you install QuickBooks. The template contains several worksheets, each with a different report. One report is designed to capture payroll data required by most states when you file your quarterly state tax forms. Another gathers information for federal Form 943, and another for federal Form 8846 (Credit for Employer Social Security and Medicare Taxes Paid on Certain Employee Tips). There are additional default reports. You can customize any of them to your liking. For more information about these reports, see the section starting on page 277.

Note: To use this feature you must have Microsoft Excel 97 Service Release 1 (SR1), 2000, 2001, or 2003 installed on your computer.

For more information about these reports, see the section starting on page 277.

Following are the QuickBooks reports and features you can use to gather the information you need:

Report	Description
Payroll summary	Shows the total wages, taxes withheld, deductions from net pay, additions to net pay, and employer-paid taxes and contributions for each employee on your payroll.
Payroll item detail	Lists the payroll transactions on which each payroll item appears. For example, you could use this report to find out which paychecks had deductions for disability insurance.

(continued) Report	Description
Payroll detail review	Provides detailed information about how QuickBooks calculates tax amounts on employee paychecks and in year-to-date transactions. You can use this report as a research tool to see exactly what numbers QuickBooks used to calculate the tax amounts.
Employee earnings summary	Shows information similar to the payroll summary report, but in a different layout.
Employee state and taxes detail	Lists wage information and state taxes withheld for each employee.
Payroll transactions by payee	Lists payroll transactions, grouping them by payee. For example, you could use this report to create a listing of the paychecks your company paid to each employee.
Payroll transaction detail	Shows the line item detail that appears on each payroll transaction
Payroll liability balances	Lists the payroll liabilities your company owes to various agencies, such as the federal government, your state government, insurance plan administrators, and labor unions.
Employee withholding	Shows federal and state withholding information for each employee.
Employee QuickReport	Lists chronologically the transactions related to a particular employee.
Payroll item listing	Shows detailed information about each payroll item you use to track payroll-related expenses and liabilities.
Payroll item QuickReport report	Lists chronologically the payroll transactions that contain a particular payroll item

To learn about...	Look in the Help Index for...
E-filing federal tax forms	E-File & Pay, about
Gathering information for state tax forms you prepare yourself	payroll tax forms, state
QuickBooks reports that help you prepare your state tax forms	report types, payroll
Sending payroll data to the Microsoft Excel Workbook	Excel (Microsoft Excel), summarizing payroll data in

Adjusting the liability balance for a payroll item

If you are using the QuickBooks Assisted Payroll service, you cannot adjust the liability balance for liabilities paid by the service (federal and state tax liabilities).

However, you can adjust the liability balance for local or other taxes not supported by the service and for benefit payments to a third party.

After you prepare a payroll tax form, you may discover that your balance for a liability payroll item (the amount you owe according to QuickBooks) needs to be adjusted. For example, you may have a small discrepancy due to rounding, or you may have failed to take the credit that reduces what you owe for federal unemployment (FUTA) tax.

You can enter an adjustment at any time in the Liability Adjustment window.

Enter the date here that you want your payroll liability account to be affected.

A positive amount increases what you owe for the item. A negative amount reduces what you owe for the item.

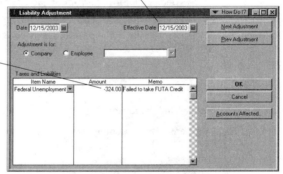

To learn about...	Look in the Help Index for...
Adjusting payroll liabilities	payroll liabilities, adjusting

Getting information about your payroll

This section offers a few examples of how reports and spreadsheet templates can answer questions about your company payroll. For a complete list of all payroll-related reports, see the table on page 274.

Finding out how much you owe for payroll tax liabilities

Let's say you want to see how much you currently owe for each payroll tax for the current quarter. You know that if you have less than a $1,000 tax liability for taxes filed with your Form 941 during the quarter, you can wait and make a payment when you file your Form 941.

You can find out quickly by creating a payroll liability balances report. The report shows liabilities incurred during the date range specified that are still unpaid.

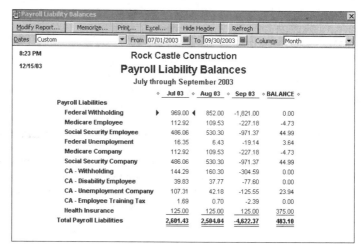

Finding out how much you spend on your payroll

Let's say you want to know how much money you spend on your payroll. You can run a payroll summary report to see your payroll totals by employee and for the whole company for a single payroll period.

You can change the date range to cover this year to date, last quarter, or any period you want.

The gross pay includes commissions and additions to gross. This represents the total payroll expenses, not including the employer-portion for employment taxes and other contributions.

The adjusted gross pay equals gross pay minus deductions from gross.

The net pay is the actual amount of money the employee(s) received. This amount is usually less than gross pay due to taxes withheld and other after-tax deductions.

```
11:43 PM                    Rock Castle Construction
12/15/03                     Payroll Summary
                            December 1 - 15, 2003
                                                TOTAL
                                   Hours   o   Rate   o  Dec 1 - 15, 03  o
Employee Wages, Taxes and Adjustments
     Gross Pay
        Salary                      88                      3,192.30
        Overtime Pay                                            0.00
        Regular Pay                156                      2,491.00
        Sick Hourly                  8                        138.00
        Vacation Hourly                                        0.00
     Total Gross Pay                                        5,821.30

  Adjusted Gross Pay                                        5,821.30

  Taxes Withheld
     Advance Earned Income Credit                              25.00
     Federal Withholding                                     -605.00
     Medicare Employee                                        -84.41
     Social Security Employee                               -360.93
     CA - Withholding                                       -105.06
     CA - Disability Employee                               -332.63
  Total Taxes Withheld                                    -1,463.03

  Deductions from Net Pay
     Health Insurance                                        -25.00
  Total Deductions from Net Pay                             -25.00

  Net Pay                                                  4,333.27

Employer Taxes and Contributions
     Federal Unemployment                                      0.00
     Medicare Company                                         84.41
     Social Security Company                                 360.93
     CA - Unemployment Company                                 0.00
     CA - Employee Training Tax                                0.00
  Total Employer Taxes and Contributions                    445.34
```

For taxes and company contributions, the amounts are liabilities accrued during the period.

Figuring out what wage amount each tax is based on

For each tax amount on employee paychecks, you want to check the amount of wages it is based on. You can generate the payroll detail report to see the amount for every wage base and tax transaction on paychecks.

```
11:26 PM                        Rock Castle Construction
12/15/03                         Payroll Item Detail
Accrual Basis                   December 1 - 14, 2003
```

Type	Date	Num	Name	Payroll Item	Wage Base	Amount
Medicare Company						
Paycheck	12/10/2003	286	Elizabeth N. Mason	Medicare Company	590.00	-8.56
Paycheck	12/10/2003	287	Gregg O. Schneider	Medicare Company	1,311.00	-19.01
Paycheck	12/10/2003	288	Dan T. Miller	Medicare Company	1,596.15	-23.14
Total Medicare Company					3,497.15	-50.71
Social Security Company						
Paycheck	12/10/2003	286	Elizabeth N. Mason	Social Security Company	590.00	-36.58
Paycheck	12/10/2003	287	Gregg O. Schneider	Social Security Company	1,311.00	-81.28
Paycheck	12/10/2003	288	Dan T. Miller	Social Security Company	1,596.15	-98.96
Total Social Security Company					3,497.15	-216.82
CA - Withholding						
Paycheck	12/10/2003	286	Elizabeth N. Mason	CA - Withholding	590.00	-5.52
Paycheck	12/10/2003	287	Gregg O. Schneider	CA - Withholding	1,311.00	-47.47
Paycheck	12/10/2003	288	Dan T. Miller	CA - Withholding	1,596.15	-24.98
Total CA - Withholding					3,497.15	-77.97

Finding out how flat-rate taxes are calculated on paychecks

Suppose you suspect that Social Security tax was under withheld on some employees' paychecks during the last payroll run, and you want to see exactly how QuickBooks calculated Social Security and other flat-rate taxes.

You can generate a payroll detail review report and see the detail behind each flat-tax calculation on every employee paycheck. This report helps you identify when QuickBooks adjusts a tax amount (to correct an error in the payroll data, for example), when your payroll administrator makes manual adjustments, or when a tax has encountered an annual wage base limit.

10:47 AM			**Larry's Landscaping & Garden Supply**				
12/15/03			**Payroll Detail Review**				
			August 1 through October 30, 2003				
◇ Date ◇	Entered/Last Modified ◇	Income Subject To Tax ◇	Wage Base ◇	Payroll Tax Rate ◇	Amount ◇	Calculated Amount ◇	Amount Difference
10/09/2003	12/15/2003 14:02:30	1,380.00	1,380.00		-20.01	-20.01	0.00
10/23/2003	12/15/2003 14:08:17	1,574.10	1,574.10		-22.83	-22.83	0.00
Total Medicare Employee		8,597.03	8,597.03		-124.66	-124.66	0.00
Social Security Employee							
08/14/2003	08/11/1999 15:39:57	1,380.00	1,380.00	6.2%	-85.56	-85.56	0.00
08/28/2003	08/11/1999 15:40:11	1,477.05	1,477.05	6.2%	-91.58	-91.58	0.00
09/11/2003	08/11/1999 15:40:25	1,405.88	1,405.88	6.2%	-87.16	-87.16	0.00
09/25/2003	08/11/1999 15:40:39	1,380.00	1,380.00	6.2%	-85.56	-85.56	0.00
10/09/2003	12/15/2003 14:02:30	1,380.00	1,380.00		-85.56	-85.56	0.00
10/23/2003	12/15/2003 14:08:17	1,574.10	1,574.10		-97.60	-97.60	0.00
Total Social Security Employee		8,597.03	8,597.03		-533.02	-533.02	0.00
Federal Unemployment							
08/14/2003	08/11/1999 15:39:57	1,380.00	0.00	0.8%	0.00	0.00	0.00
08/28/2003	08/11/1999 15:40:11	1,477.05	0.00	0.8%	0.00	0.00	0.00

Getting information for state payroll tax forms

Suppose you want to get a head start on preparing state payroll forms, and you need detailed information about wages and state tax withholding for each employee. You can generate the employee state taxes detail report to see all state-related payroll items for each employee.

11:05 PM			**Rock Castle Construction**		
12/15/03			**Employee State Taxes Detail**		
Accrual Basis			November 2003		
◇ Type ◇	Date ◇	SSN/Tax ID ◇	Num ◇	Payroll Item	◇ Income Subject To Tax
Dan T. Miller					
Paycheck	11/13/2003	333-44-5555	239	CA - Withholding	1,596.15
Paycheck	11/13/2003	333-44-5555	239	CA - Disability Employee	1,596.15
Paycheck	11/13/2003	333-44-5555	239	CA - Unemployment Company	1,596.15
Paycheck	11/27/2003	333-44-5555	256	CA - Withholding	1,596.15
Paycheck	11/27/2003	333-44-5555	256	CA - Disability Employee	1,596.15
Paycheck	11/27/2003	333-44-5555	256	CA - Unemployment Company	1,596.15
Total Dan T. Miller					9,576.90
Elizabeth N. Mason					
Paycheck	11/12/2003	569-87-1234	237	CA - Withholding	619.56
Paycheck	11/12/2003	569-87-1234	237	CA - Disability Employee	619.56
Paycheck	11/12/2003	569-87-1234	237	CA - Unemployment Company	619.56
Paycheck	11/26/2003	569-87-1234	254	CA - Withholding	590.00
Paycheck	11/26/2003	569-87-1234	254	CA - Disability Employee	590.00
Paycheck	11/26/2003	569-87-1234	254	CA - Unemployment Company	590.00
Total Elizabeth N. Mason					3,628.68

Working with your payroll data in Microsoft Excel

You can also get a summary of your payroll data and display it in a Microsoft Excel workbook that uses a specially prepared template installed with the QuickBooks software. Because the workbook extracts payroll data requested by most states, you can also print and send the information with your state payroll tax forms.

When you first open the workbook, Excel uses sample data to set up the worksheets.

To import your payroll data from QuickBooks, click Get QuickBooks Data, then specify date filters and other options in the dialog box that appears.

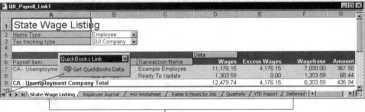

This worksheet shows state wage information for each employee. To display additional information, click any of these tabs.

 Microsoft Excel 97 Service Release 1 (SR1), 2000, 2001, 2002, or 2003 is required.

Though you access this feature from within QuickBooks, you must have one of the versions of Excel listed above installed on your computer to display the workbook template.

To learn about...	Look in the Help Index for...
payroll reports	payroll, reports about

Employee administration

Employee tracking and management in QuickBooks

Managing critical employee information is a big responsibility. You need to stay on top of changing laws and regulations about hiring, establishing time-off, terminations and much more. You also must have correct, up-to-date state and federal forms. QuickBooks Employee Organizer can take the worry out of even the most complex HR and compliance tasks. This fast and easy add-on tool streamlines the management of employee information and key employment laws and regulations. Employee Organizer keeps employee data in your existing company file and provides you with critical employee reports. You get the information you need, when you need it.

QuickBooks Employee Organizer is available as an add-on feature in QuickBooks Pro and QuickBooks Premier. Internet access is required to activate Employee Organizer and to receive updates from the Employment Regulations Update Service. Terms, conditions, pricing, features and service offerings are subject to change without notice.

An Overview of the QuickBooks Employee Organizer

QuickBooks Employee Organizer puts employee information, compliance guidance, and critical reports right at your fingerprints. Employee Organizer helps you:

- Access current information on key state and federal employment laws and regulations.

- Stay in compliance and avoid costly penalties and lawsuits.

- Keep employee data integrated with payroll information in QuickBooks where it's easy to access, update and generate reports.

- Get answers to your employment questions using our e-mail help service.

QuickBooks Employee Organizer also includes step-by-step processes for key employment activities including hiring, leaves of absence compensation tracking and terminations. Plus, it includes downloadable state and federal employment forms, templates, letters, employee management forms, and much more.

What QuickBooks Employee Organizer can do for you

Guidance through key employment processes

Use Employee Organizer step-by-step processes when hiring or terminating an employee or to track employee raises, promotions and leaves. With centralized employee information that is seamlessly integrated with QuickBooks, you can manage your employees more efficiently and effectively.

Each process helps you remain in compliance by asking you to enter the information you need to track and by providing guidance, in the form of frequently asked questions, about the laws that govern your relationships with your employees.

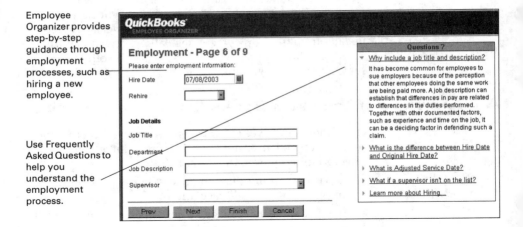

Employee Organizer provides step-by-step guidance through employment processes, such as hiring a new employee.

Use Frequently Asked Questions to help you understand the employment process.

QuickBooks®
EMPLOYEE ORGANIZER

Employment - Page 6 of 9

Please enter employment information:

Hire Date 07/08/2003

Rehire

Job Details

Job Title

Department

Job Description

Supervisor

Prev   Next   Finish   Cancel

Questions ?

▼ Why include a job title and description?

It has become common for employees to sue employers because of the perception that other employees doing the same work are being paid more. A job description can establish that differences in pay are related to differences in the duties performed. Together with other documented factors, such as experience and time on the job, it can be a deciding factor in defending such a claim.

▶ What is the difference between Hire Date and Original Hire Date?

▶ What is Adjusted Service Date?

▶ What if a supervisor isn't on the list?

▶ Learn more about Hiring...

Easy-to-run management reports

QuickBooks Employee Organizer integrates with payroll information in QuickBooks so it's easy to access, update and run management reports. The following additional reports are available in the Employee Organizer:

- Employee Profile
- Employee Compensation Review
- Year-to-date Payroll Summary
- Company Compensation Review
- New Hire List
- Paid Time Off List
- Emergency Contact List

Get human resources information and employment forms, letters and templates

QuickBooks Employee Organizer includes an Employment Regulations Guide that has detailed information on employee issues including recruiting, hiring, compensation and employee relations.

The Employment Regulations Guide also contains selected state and federal government forms and other documents, employee management forms and checklists to help during meetings such as interviews and performance evaluations. The forms and letters can be used as is or modified as required to fit your business needs.

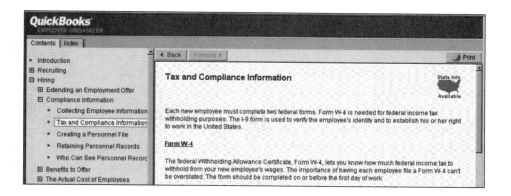

Employment Regulations Update Service

This service provides regular updates to critical employment laws and regulations, important state and federal employment forms, and access to our e-mail help line where your employment questions are answered online within two business days.*

We recommend you check for compliance updates at least every 45 days. You'll download updated laws and regulations through a secure Internet connection.**

How to Access the Employee Organizer

From the Employee Navigator, click on the Manage Employees icon to open the Manage Employees screen. From this screen you can begin any guided process, or access the Employment Regulations Guide or the Employee Summary.

If you have not yet purchased the Employee Organizer, you can get more information and access a demonstration of Employee Organizer in QuickBooks by clicking on the Employee Organizer link from the Business Services Navigator.

---

* Answers to e-mail questions for Employment Regulations Update Service are provided by CCH INCORPORATED, a leading provider of tax and business law information, on average within two business days.
**Upgrade Guarantee – so long as you remain an active subscriber to the Employment Regulations Update Service, you will continue to have access to the Employee Organizer at no additional cost, whenever you upgrade your QuickBooks software.

TRACKING YOUR PROGRESS
WITH REPORTS AND GRAPHS

The purpose of any report or financial statement is to communicate information about your business—for you and others to get valuable insight into your company finances and performance and make informed decisions about a course of action.

QuickBooks provides a wide variety of preset reports and graphs designed to give you quick and easy access to your company's information. For example, besides a standard profit and loss statement, you also have five other variations of this report. In addition, you can create your own versions of reports, changing both the look and layout, as well as the scope of the information reported.

Setting up for reporting and graphing

What to set up	Comments	Look in the Help Index for...
Select cash or accrual-based summary reporting	The IRS requires that certain business entities use the accrual method for tax reporting purposes. Please check with the IRS or your tax accountant to assess which method is appropriate for you. Regardless of the method you use for tax reporting, you can view most reports on a cash or accrual basis at any time by customizing the report when you create it. **Important:** The cash/accrual preference does not affect the 1099 reports (which are always cash based) or the sales tax reports.	■ accrual basis, changing reports to ■ sales tax, turning on
Set your aging preference	Aging is the tracking of due dates and amounts of outstanding invoices or your own unpaid bills. Because you can change the starting point for aging reports, you can age from the due date or from the transaction date.	aging
Choose your report and graph refresh option: ■ Refresh automatically ■ Prompt you to refresh ■ Don't refresh [automatically]	When a change to your data affects what you are viewing, QuickBooks automatically adjusts the report or graph if it can do so quickly. If QuickBooks can't make a quick adjustment, the only way to bring the report back into agreement with your data is to refresh the report or graph. Refreshing can be slow. If up-to-the-minute accuracy is unimportant to you, you may want to refresh reports and graphs at your own discretion instead of having QuickBooks refresh them automatically. All reports and graphs have a Refresh button that you can click at any time. This option can be uniquely set for each user.	refreshing reports and graphs

Generating reports and graphs

Your reported data can become inaccurate if new information is entered by you or another user. To make sure you have up-to-date, accurate data, click Refresh. For more information, see "Choose your report and graph refresh option:" on page 286.

 If you need to run reports on a large company file while in multi-user mode, try to run them when other users aren't using the company file. The reports will display faster and will not become inaccurate due to new data others may enter.

Finding the right report

You can generate a preset report from several convenient places in QuickBooks, including the Report Finder (accessible from the Reports menu) and list displays, such as your Customer:Jobs list.

With the Report Finder, you can quickly review and choose among the many preset reports that QuickBooks provides. To help you choose an appropriate report, the Report Finder displays a sample of each report, as well as a summary of what the report conveys about your business.

Choose a report category and view a general description of your choice.

The specific reports available to you are based on your report category selection.

QuickBooks provides details about a report's content to help you decide whether the report is right for you.

View a thumbnail picture with sample data to see a report's content. You can customize a report before or after you generate it.

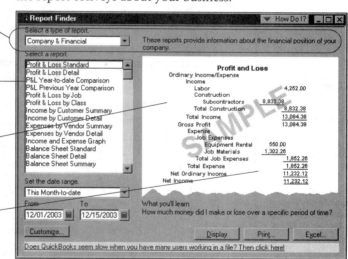

To learn about...	Look in the Help Index for...
Finding a report	reports, finding
Creating a report	reports, creating
Preset reports	report types, all

Customizing the look of the report

Most reports can be customized for unique presentation of your data. For example, you can do the following:

- Change the typeface (font)
- Adjust the width of a column
- Add or remove columns
- Change how numbers display
- Create or change subtotal groupings
- Change the sort order of transactions
- Change what displays in the report header and footer

The following examples show how one user decided to customize a report.

Nora at Rock Castle Construction clicked Modify Report to change the columns her report included.

Nora decided that the **Date** and **Num** columns were not crucial to her. All she wanted to see was the transaction type, due date, aging information, and the open balance for the vendor.

In the Display page of the Modify Report window, she cleared the **Date** and **Num** columns.

The results are shown here.

After Nora removed the **Date** and **Num** columns, she also resized the **Type** column to make the report more readable.

In addition she used the Header/Footer option to remove the company name at the top of the report.

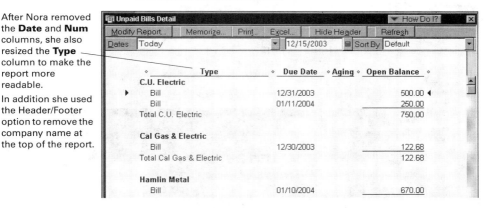

After you customize a report to your satisfaction, you can save your changes. See "Saving report settings" on page 292.

To change column titles or rearrange the order of columns, export the report to a Microsoft Excel spreadsheet. For further information, see page 296.

Changing the scope of the information in the report

Creating your own version of an existing report can also include *filtering* or changing the scope of the information that displays on a preset report.

For example, Nora at Rock Castle Construction wanted to see a Collections Report limited to commercial customers. She clicked the Modify Report button in the buttonbar. From the Modify Report window, she selected the Filters tab. Then she selected Customer Type, then Commercial.

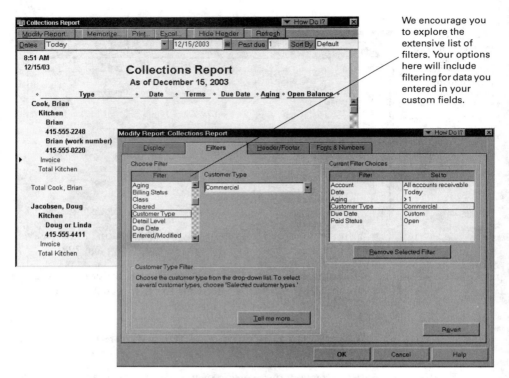

We encourage you to explore the extensive list of filters. Your options here will include filtering for data you entered in your custom fields.

Nora also shortened the report's title by accessing the Header/Footer page of the Modify Report window.

Nora can choose to "memorize" this report to save her settings. See "Saving report settings" on page 292.

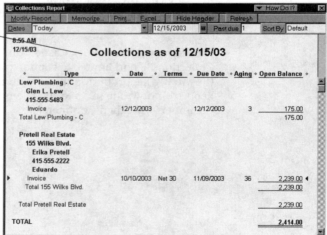

To learn about...	Look in the Help Index for...
Generating a report	reports, creating
Changing date ranges	reports, dates in
Customizing a report	report customization
Adjusting, adding, or deleting columns on a report	report customization, columns
Changing fonts	reports, fonts for
Tailoring the data in the report (filtering)	reports, changing the scope of
Changing headers and footers	report customization, headers

Creating a report from scratch

If QuickBooks doesn't provide a preset report with the information you need, you can create your own custom reports.

From the Reports menu, choose either Custom Summary Report or Custom Transaction Detail Report, depending on the level of detail you want as your starting point.

You can choose from a variety of reporting options (date ranges, accrual vs. cash) and information to report on by column and row. Choose the detail you want and click OK. You can create as many custom reports as you need.

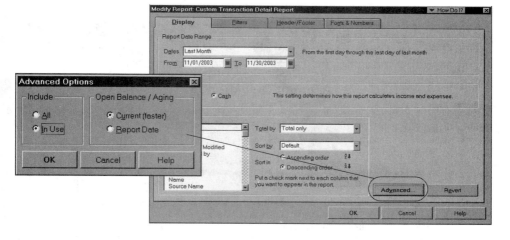

Saving report settings

After you have customized or filtered a report, you may want to save the settings for future use. Saving report settings is called *memorizing*.

Memorizing the report saves all your customizing and filtering changes. It also saves the print orientation (portrait or landscape) of the report. The next time you generate a memorized report, QuickBooks recreates the format of the report, but uses your latest financial data.

When you memorize a report, QuickBooks adds it to the Memorized Report List. To display this list, from the Reports menu, choose Memorized Reports, and then choose Memorized Reports List.

To learn about...	Look in the Help Index for...
Saving the settings of a customized report	reports, memorizing

QuickReports: reports at your fingertips

QuickReports display all the transactions you have recorded in QuickBooks for a specific list entry. For example, you can generate a QuickReport for an account on your Chart of Accounts list, like your savings account, or generate one for a customer, a vendor, for an item, and so on.

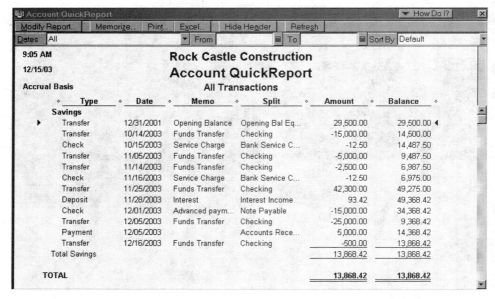

You can create a QuickReport from the Reports menu button on a list.

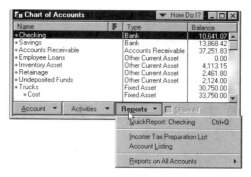

Portraying your data with graphs

QuickBooks can also display your company's data in bar graphs and pie charts. Graphs are helpful if you're looking for a visual summary of your company's finances.

QuickBooks provides six types of preset graphs: income and expenses, sales, accounts receivable, accounts payable, net worth, and budget vs. actual. Using these graphs you can:

- Analyze your income and expenses
- Study sales income
- Examine customer and vendor aging
- Determine changes in your net worth
- Develop better budgets

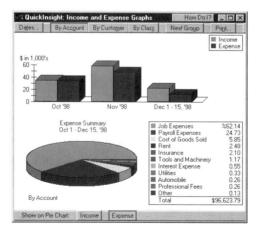

Most graphs you create cover the current fiscal year to date, unless you change the date range.

To learn about...	Look in the Help Index for...
Creating graphs	graphs, creating
Customizing graph appearance	graphs, customizing
Interpreting data on a graph	graphs, how to interpret

Using decision tools

QuickBooks decision tools provide information to help you manage and make decisions about your business. Using decision tools, you can compare alternatives, analyze your financial position, and set policies.

To display the complete list of decision tools, choose Decision Tools from the Company Menu. In centers, click on a tool name to perform an analysis of your financial statements and learn how to interpret it.

Investigating transactions or values on reports and graphs

From time to time, you may want to investigate a particular transaction or value on a report. You can do this easily by using QuickZoom, which is available on most reports. QuickZoom displays the original transaction or a report showing the transactions that contributed to that value. You can change values that are in error.

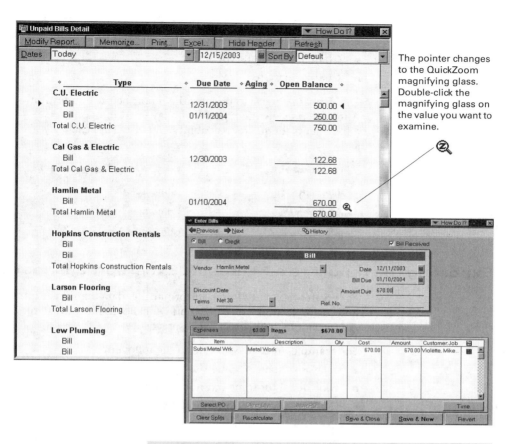

The pointer changes to the QuickZoom magnifying glass. Double-click the magnifying glass on the value you want to examine.

To learn about...	Look in the Help Index for...
Using QuickZoom on summary reports	QuickZoom, seeing the detail behind a summary amount
Using QuickZoom on graphs	QuickZoom, expanding detail in a graph

Printing reports and graphs

When you print reports and graphs, you can choose to:

- Print in portrait (vertical) or landscape (horizontal) orientation
- Print in color (particularly useful for graphs)
- Control widows and orphans (prevent headings from printing near the bottom of a page or single lines at the top of a page) (reports only)
- Fit the report to __ page(s) wide (reports only)
- Have a page break after each major grouping (reports only)

- Print a range of pages (reports only)
- Enter the number of copies
- Change fonts and type size
- Change margins

You can also choose to preview the report before you print it. After you preview the report, you may want to make adjustments for greater readability and visual appeal.

To learn about...	Look in the Help Index for...
Printer setup	printer setup
Printing reports	printing, reports
Printing graphs	printing, graphs

Exporting the report to a Microsoft Excel spreadsheet

For greater flexibility in report formatting, data manipulation, and customization, you can export QuickBooks Pro and Premier report data to a Microsoft Excel spreadsheet.

For example, in Excel you can do the following:

- Take advantage of extensive filtering options
- Hide detail for some but not all groups of data
- Combine information from two different reports
- Experiment with "what if" scenarios
- Add comments
- Change the titles of columns
- Change the order of columns
- Save the report as a file you can e-mail to anyone with Excel
- Save a snapshot of the report data for future reference

The export feature allows you to preserve many QuickBooks report formatting features, such as fonts, colors, and formulas. At the same time, it allows you to take advantage of all the features of Excel.

Note: You must be using QuickBooks Pro or Premier and Microsoft Excel 97 or higher.

To learn about...	Look in the Help Index for...
Exporting a report to a Microsoft Excel spreadsheet (QuickBooks Pro and Premier only)	Microsoft Excel, exporting to reports

STAYING IN TOUCH WITH IMPORTANT CONTACTS

QuickBooks has many features that help you keep in contact with the people who are important to your business.

With these features, you can do the following:

- Share information between QuickBooks Pro or QuickBooks Premier and ACT! or Microsoft Outlook contact management software.
- Create reports about contacts on your Customer:Job, Vendor, Employee, and Other Name lists.
- Send business forms by e-mail to customers.
- Write and send letters (created in Microsoft Word) using data from your Names lists (for customers, vendors, employees, and other names).
- Make To Do notes that remind you of upcoming events or of tasks that you want to complete by a certain date.

Sharing QuickBooks Pro and Premier information with your contact manager

You can configure QuickBooks Pro and Premier so that your Customer:Job, Vendor, and Other Name lists share information with Microsoft Outlook 97, 98, or 2000 and ACT! (versions 3.0.8 and 4.0.2, or 2000) contact management software. You no longer need to enter names, addresses, and phone numbers twice in an effort to keep information in QuickBooks and your contact manager up to date. QuickBooks provides a way for you to transfer information between the two applications so that both are synchronized with each other.

When synchronizing information with QuickBooks and ACT! or Microsoft Outlook, you have three data transfer options:

- QuickBooks to contact manager
- Contact manager to QuickBooks
- QuickBooks to contact manager *and* contact manager to QuickBooks

Note: **QuickBooks currently can't accommodate the direct transfer of contact information from a personal digital assistant (PDA, such as a Palm Computing or Microsoft Windows CE device).** To get contact information from your PDA into QuickBooks, first export the PDA data into ACT! or Microsoft Outlook. At that point, you can synchronize QuickBooks with your contact manager.

Setting up and synchronizing QuickBooks with ACT! or Microsoft Outlook

Setting up for synchronization

Before you begin synchronizing, you must define the parameters for synchronization. During setup, you do the following:

- Choose which contact manager you want to synchronize with QuickBooks.

- Decide which direction you want to transfer information: From QuickBooks to contact manager? From contact manager to QuickBooks? Both ways?

- Select the QuickBooks lists that you want to synchronize with your contact manager. Because of the complex way in which QuickBooks handles employee information, your employee list is not available for synchronizing.

- Select the default method by which QuickBooks will resolve conflicts and discrepancies with your contact manager data.

Following the initial setup, you don't need to go through the setup process again unless you want to change your synchronization settings. To begin setup, choose Synchronize Contacts from the Company menu. Follow the instructions provided by the synchronization setup wizard.

Synchronizing QuickBooks and your contact manager

After completing the setup process, you can synchronize the information between QuickBooks and your contact manager at any time. During synchronization, QuickBooks identifies records where the information in QuickBooks and the contact manager do not match. At that point, you will have several options for resolving conflicts and discrepancies.

Depending on the number of contacts and the type of information you track for each one, the initial synchronization may take a fair amount of time. In most cases, the process will go faster when you synchronize in the future—unless you change the data in QuickBooks or the contact manager *and* change the synchronization settings each time you synchronize. The frequency with which you synchronize depends on how often you make changes to your contact information in either QuickBooks or your contact manager.

Note: **Only a subset of your contact manager information can be synchronized.** Contact managers store much more information about a contact than QuickBooks needs. However, you can synchronize the most vital contact information (including name, address, phone, and fax).

To learn about...	Look in the Help Index for...
Synchronizing QuickBooks with a contact manager	contact management, synchronizing names with a contact manager
Changing synchronization settings	contact management, synchronizing names with a contact manager
Transferring data from a personal digital assistant, such as a Palm Computing® or Microsoft® Windows CE device	personal digital assistants

To learn about...	Look in the Help Index for...
Fixing synchronization problems	contact management, synchronizing names with a contact manager

Creating reports about contacts

You can create reports that list the contact information you need to reach your key customers and vendors.

If you created custom fields such as pager numbers and hours of operation for your customers and vendors, you can customize the report to include this information as well.

List Report	Description
Customer contact list	Shows each customer's name, balance, phone and fax number, contact name, and billing address.
Vendor contact list	Shows each vendor's name, balance, phone and fax number, contact name, address, and account number.
Employee contact list	Shows each employee's name, phone number, social security number, and address
Other name contact list	Shows the name, address, phone and fax numbers, and contact for each name

To learn about...	Look in the Help Index for...
Creating custom fields for customers and vendors	custom fields, for customers, vendors, or employees
Creating list reports	report types, lists
Adding additional columns of data to list reports	report customization, columns

Keeping in touch by e-mail

You can send invoices or statements to customers by e-mail directly from QuickBooks. If you have QuickBooks Pro or Premier, you can also send any form by e-mail. To offer this service to your customers, you must sign up for QuickBooks Billing Solutions. For more information, see page 64.

To send a form (for example, an invoice, statement, or estimate) by e-mail, all you need is an Internet connection and an e-mail account. You don't have to sign up for a new account or pay additional fees. Your customer receives the form in seconds, along with a cover note that you can customize for your own business needs. When you e-mail an invoice, statement, or estimate, your customer receives the form as a PDF file e-mail attachment along with a cover note.

As an option, you can have your customers pay you online from a Web site when you send invoices or statements by e-mail. If you sign up for QuickBooks Billing Solutions, you can track when your customers view the forms you send them by e-mail. Knowing whether a customer has opened your message can help you decide when to follow up with a second message or payment reminder.

To learn about...	Look in the Help Index for...
Sending invoices, statements, or estimates by e-mail	e-mail business forms to customers
QuickBooks Billing Solutions	online billing of customers

Writing letters

From time to time you may need to send a letter to a customer, vendor, or employee, or to a group of customers or vendors. With QuickBooks you can easily add the pertinent QuickBooks data (name, address, balance information, and so on) to a standard letter without having to retype it.

QuickBooks provides a number of business letters focusing on collections, news, and announcements. You can edit these letters as needed to suit your business and style of communication.

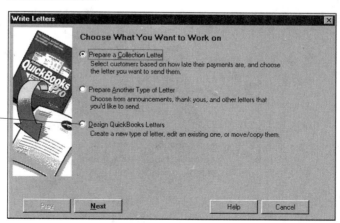

You can convert any existing letters you use to work with QuickBooks or design new ones.

Note: You must be using QuickBooks Pro or Premier 2004 and Microsoft Word 97 or 2000.

?	To learn about...	Look in the Help Index for...
	Getting your QuickBooks data into Microsoft Word	letters using QuickBooks data in Microsoft Word

Printing labels and Rolodex cards

You can print mailing labels and Rolodex cards for customers, vendors, employees, and others sorted by name or nine-digit zip code. You can select names according to criteria you set.

Choose whether to print mailing labels, shipping labels, or Rolodex cards in the Printer setup window. Names and addresses print on mailing labels; names, alternate contact names, addresses, and phone numbers print on Rolodex cards.

Format	Description
self-adhesive labels	QuickBooks can print on a variety of Avery standard mailing labels. Click Help in the Label Printer Setup window for a list of supported label formats.
	For sheet-fed printers, the labels are arranged in columns of two or three on an 8.5-inch-wide backing.
	For continuous-feed printers, the labels are arranged in columns of one or two on an 8.5-inch-wide backing.
Rolodex cards	Prepunched card stock is designed for your computer's printer.
	QuickBooks can print on either 3-inch by 5-inch cards or on 2.25-inch by 4-inch cards.

?	To learn about...	Look in the Help Index for...
	Choosing a format	mailing labels, choosing a format for
	Sorting labels by zip code and printing labels and Rolodex cards	mailing labels, printing

Making To Do notes

You can enter notes to help keep track of phone calls you need to make, tasks that you want to complete by a certain date, or upcoming events, such as a lease expiration.

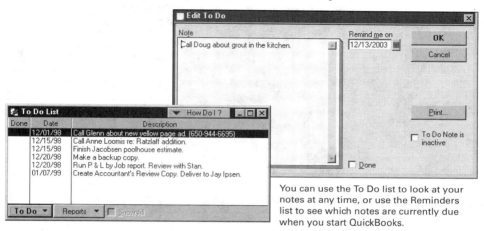

You can use the To Do list to look at your notes at any time, or use the Reminders list to see which notes are currently due when you start QuickBooks.

You can create a To Do notes report that shows the status, date, and description for each To Do note.

To learn about...	Look in the Help Index for...
Using and printing To Do notes, and creating a To Do notes report	To Do notes

Remind me!

You can use the QuickBooks Reminders list to display those tasks you need to take care of now or in the near future, including those tasks you list on your To Do notes.

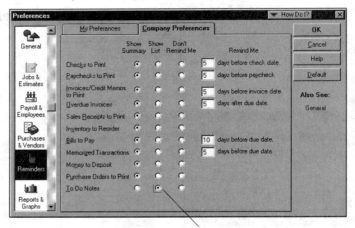

Set up your Reminder Preferences to
Show List for your To Do notes so you'll
see the individual note information.

?	To learn about...	Look in the Help Index for...
	Using reminders	preferences, reminders

With QuickBooks Pro and above, you can share data with a variety of general and industry-specific third-party software applications to allow easy sharing of key data. You can also use import and export commands to move data between QuickBooks and spreadsheets, word processors, and other software. And, you can transfer data between QuickBooks company files.

Using QuickBooks with integrated applications

QuickBooks Pro and Premier can exchange data with applications designed for your business or industry. Sharing data with other applications can help:

- Save time
- Reduce data entry
- Increase accuracy

These applications enable you to share important list and transaction information. Modifications are supported for all names lists: customers, vendors, other names, and employees. Data transfer is more secure than manual importing and exporting, and the shared data is validated by QuickBooks. You control access by any of the third-party applications by setting various levels of permissions. You can also restrict permissions on a third-party application by using existing QuickBooks user permissions features.

Finding integrated applications

A significant number of software companies design their applications to share data with QuickBooks. You can learn about these companies and their products by looking at the QuickBooks Solutions Marketplace site. (http://marketplace.intuit.com).

At QuickBooks Solutions Marketplace you can:

- Find third-party applications designed for your business that share data with QuickBooks.
- Read reviews, written by customers and accountants, of companies and integrated products.
- Learn about product features.
- Rate and review integrated applications.
- Link to sites from which you can buy integrated applications.
- Request an application specific to your business.

You can link to Solutions Marketplace from Quickbooks.com or by using the Business Services navigator in QuickBooks.

Security with integrated applications

Authentication procedures help protect your data from access by unauthorized programs. When a third-party program attempts to access your data, you have the choice of allowing the application to access your company file once, always, or not at all. You can also restrict permissions on a third-party application so that it can access only the portions of QuickBooks data that you specify. QuickBooks also checks to see if an application has a certificate telling you who created the program. You can read certificates to learn more about the application's origin. However, be aware that certificates are supplied by the application developer and not all applications have them.

Importing and exporting to other software programs

QuickBooks exports and imports data in Intuit Interchange Format, called IIF. This format is different from QIF (used by Quicken). QuickBooks imports only IIF data.

When you export information from QuickBooks, the program formats the data into IIF. You can then import the IIF file into spreadsheets, word processors, and database programs.

If you want to import data from other software applications, you need to create an IIF file from scratch or reformat data you already use to conform to IIF standards.

Note: **Creating an IIF file from scratch or changing data from another accounting program into an IIF file is technically complex.** It's not recommended for those who don't have programming experience. However, you don't need to learn about the IIF format to export lists and import them back into QuickBooks.

Unless you have a very large customer database or more than 200 transactions, it may be easier and less time-consuming to enter the data directly into QuickBooks.

You can't export transactions from QuickBooks.

However, you can create a report based on transactions and print the report to a file that can be read by a spreadsheet, database, or word processor.

If you use Microsoft Word, Microsoft Excel, Microsoft Outlook, or ACT!

You can export QuickBooks Pro or Premier data to Microsoft Word or Excel. You can synchronize Microsoft Outlook and ACT! contact data with QuickBooks Pro or Premier.

- If you use Microsoft Word 97 as your word processing program and are using QuickBooks Pro or Premier, you can use the Write Letters feature. See "Writing letters" on page 301.

- If you use Microsoft Excel 97 and are using QuickBooks Pro or Premier, you can export your QuickBooks report data to Excel for further customization and filtering. See "Exporting the report to a Microsoft Excel spreadsheet" on page 296.

- If you use Microsoft Outlook or ACT!, you can synchronize contact information with QuickBooks Pro and Premier. See "Sharing QuickBooks Pro and Premier information with your contact manager" on page 298. (You should not import or export data from your contact manager to QuickBooks because of formatting problems that may occur.)

- If you use QuickBooks Pro and above, you can export report data to a Microsoft Excel spreadsheet and perform calculations on the data. You can also import some types of data from Microsoft Excel and Comma Separated Value (.csv) format. You can first preview the data to identify any potential import problems.

Importing customer names from a list

If you already have information about your customers in software such as a spreadsheet, you can prepare a file for import into your QuickBooks company file. The import file must be in Intuit Interchange Format (IIF), which is a type of ASCII text file with special headings to identify to QuickBooks the type of information it contains.

If you choose to import customer names from such a file, you will probably have to edit each customer to add additional information, such as payment terms or sales tax information.

Also, if you have unpaid balances for such customers, you will need to enter an invoice for each that, at the minimum, tells the total amount owed.

To learn about...	Search the Help index for...
Creating an IIF file for importing list information into QuickBooks	importing data
Creating invoices for customer balances that were unpaid as of the start date	invoices, creating

Transferring QuickBooks lists between company files

QuickBooks allows you to export most lists and their related information. You simply mark the lists that you would like to export and QuickBooks creates a file that can be easily imported into another QuickBooks company.

Importing list information with duplicate entries.

When you import lists into an existing QuickBooks company, QuickBooks considers the import file's entries more recent. It replaces any duplicate entries with ones from the import file.

This table compares the different methods of transferring data.

Method	What it does	Advantages	Disadvantages
Copying a file (through DOS or Windows)	Makes an exact copy (in QuickBooks.QBW format)	QuickBooks can open the copy without extra steps.	A large company file may not fit on one disk. Only QuickBooks can read the file.
Backing up a company file	Makes a compressed copy of everything in the original company file	More data fits on one 3.5-inch disk. Backup allows you to divide very large files among more than one 3.5-inch disk.	QuickBooks must restore the backed-up copy before it can open the file.
Printing to disk	Makes a copy in a format common to other software programs	You can use the file in a spreadsheet or word-processing program.	Only certain information can be printed to disk, such as lists and reports. QuickBooks cannot read files printed to disk.
Exporting	Puts lists into a file in IIF format, with one record per line and one column for each field	You can share lists with other company data files or use a list in a database, word processor, or spreadsheet program. You can add to the list and import it back into QuickBooks.	QuickBooks can export only lists, not transactions or reports.

?

To learn about...	Search the Help index for...
Importing data from other software programs	importing data
The import and export files that QuickBooks creates	■ importing data ■ IIF file format
Exporting lists to another QuickBooks company	exporting data
The process of backing up your company file	backups

GLOSSARY

This appendix provides a list of common QuickBooks terms.

Accounts Payable

The record of the outstanding bills of a business. Accounts Payable is called A/P for short. (Even though the word accounts is plural, QuickBooks uses a single account on the chart of accounts to track all outstanding bills.)

QuickBooks automatically adds an Accounts payable account to your chart of accounts the first time you enter a bill. QuickBooks uses this account to track the money your business owes to others. When you enter a new bill, or pay off outstanding bills, QuickBooks records the transaction in the register for your Accounts Payable account.

Your chart of accounts lists the type of this account as "Accounts Payable." If you need to use more than one of this type of account in your business, you can add additional accounts payable accounts to the chart. When you have more than one accounts payable account, QuickBooks lets you choose the account you want to use when you enter and pay bills.

Accounts Receivable

The record of money owed to a business, that is, invoices for which a business has not received payment. Accounts Receivable is called A/R for short. (Even though the word "accounts" is plural, QuickBooks uses a single account on the chart of accounts to track all outstanding invoices.)

QuickBooks automatically adds an Accounts Receivable account to your chart of accounts the first time you write an invoice. QuickBooks uses this account to track the money owed to your business. When you write an invoice or receive a payment from a customer, QuickBooks records the transaction in the register for your Accounts Receivable account.

Your chart of accounts lists the type of this account as "Accounts Receivable." If you need to use more than one of this type of account in your business, you can add additional "accounts receivable" accounts to the chart. When you have more than one accounts receivable account, QuickBooks lets you choose the account you want to use when you write an invoice or enter a customer payment.

Accrual basis

A method of bookkeeping in which you regard income or expenses as occurring at the time you ship a product, render a service, or receive a purchase. Under this method, the time when you enter a transaction and the time when you actually pay or receive cash may be two separate events.

In QuickBooks, an accrual basis report shows income regardless of whether all your customers have paid, and expenses regardless of whether you have paid all your bills. You can put all your reports on an accrual basis by selecting Accrual in the Reports and Graphs Preferences window.

Aging

Aging refers to the tracking of outstanding invoices and unpaid bills. For both A/R (accounts receivable) and A/P (accounts payable), QuickBooks offers preset aging reports that show how much is currently due, and how much is overdue. For example, an A/R aging summary report breaks down what your customers owe so that you can see how much is:

- Currently due
- 31 to 60 days overdue
- 61 to 90 days overdue
- Over 90 days overdue

Assets

Your company assets are the things that your company owns. QuickBooks distinguishes between two types of assets:

- **Current assets:** Assets you are likely to convert to cash within one year. They include the cash you have on hand, the money in your checking and savings accounts, and the money your customers owe your business.

- **Fixed assets:** Assets you do not expect to convert to cash during one year of normal operations. A fixed asset is usually something that is necessary for the operation of your business—like a truck, cash register, or computer.

Average cost

For an inventory item, average cost is the total cost of the items currently in stock divided by the number of items in stock. QuickBooks uses average cost -- and not another method such as LIFO or FIFO -- to determine the value of your inventory.

QuickBooks recalculates the average cost of an item every time you record the purchase of more units of the item. It adds the cost of the new items to the cost of the old stock and then divides by the total number of new and old items.

Example

You originally bought 100 T-shirts at $5.00 each. When you have 10 shirts left in stock, you order 100 more shirts, but the price has gone up to $6.00 each. Here's how QuickBooks calculates the average cost:

- The cost of your old stock is $50 (10 shirts x $5.00)
- The cost of the new inventory is $600 (100 shirts x $6.00)
- The combined cost of the old and new inventory is $650
- The average cost of your entire inventory is $5.91 ($650/110 shirts)

Balance sheet

A report that summarizes the financial position of a business. A balance sheet shows the value of your company's assets, liabilities, and equity as of a particular day. It is called a balance sheet because the value of the assets is always exactly equal to the combined value of the liabilities and equity.

QuickBooks offers four different preset balance sheet reports. You'll find these reports under Company & Financial on the Reports menu.

Cash basis

A method of bookkeeping in which you regard income or expenses as occurring at the time you actually receive a payment or pay a bill. A cash-basis report shows income only if you have received it, and expenses only if you have paid them. For example, if you have not yet received a payment for an invoice, a cash-basis report on your sales will not include the amount of the invoice.

In QuickBooks, you can put all summary reports on a cash basis by selecting "Cash" in the Reports & Graphs Preferences window. (Summary reports summarize groups of transactions; they have the word "Summary" in their titles.) On the other hand, reports that list individual transactions always appear as accrual basis reports when you create them from the Reports menu. You can change a transaction report to cash basis, however, by clicking Modify Report in the report window and then selecting "Cash" under "Report basis."

Chart of accounts

A complete list of a business's accounts and their balances. You use it to track how much money your company has, how much money it owes, how much money is coming in, and how much is going out. When you set up your QuickBooks company, you chose a preset chart of accounts designed especially for your business.

The accounts that appear on the balance sheet are called "balance sheet accounts." Other accounts track particular kinds of expenses or income.

To display the chart of accounts, choose Chart of Accounts from the Lists menu.

Classes

In QuickBooks, classes give you a way to classify your transactions. You can use QuickBooks classes to classify your income and expenses by department, business office or location, separate properties you own, or any other meaningful breakdown of the business you do.

For example, if you had a restaurant with three locations, you might create an Uptown, a Midtown, and a Downtown class for tracking income and expenses by location. A farmer might create a class for each enterprise—for example, "Corn," "Hogs," and "Soybeans." At the end of an accounting period, you could create separate reports for each restaurant location. Likewise, the farmer could create separate reports for each farm enterprise.

The classes you create appear on your Class list. The "Use class tracking" preference in the Accounting Preferences window adds a Class field to windows where you enter invoices, checks, bills, credit card charges, or other transactions.

Cost of goods sold (COGS)

The cost of goods and materials held in inventory and then sold.

Credit

In accounting, the deduction of a payment made by a debtor from an amount due. In the General Journal Entry window, you enter credits in the Credit column.

Customer type

Customer types let you categorize your customers in ways that are meaningful to your business. For example, you could set up your customer types so that they indicate which industry a customer represents, a customer's geographic location, or how a customer first heard about your business.

You can create reports and do special mailings that are based on your customer types. For example, if you use customer types to categorize your customers by location, you could print mailing labels for all the customers in a particular region.

Depreciation

Fixed assets such as furniture, computers, vehicles, and buildings contribute to the operating capacity of a business over many years. Because of their long-term value, fixed assets are treated differently than other business expenses. Typically, you expense the purchase price of a fixed asset over its useful life, not just the year in which you made the purchase. This business expense is known as depreciation.

EIN (Employer Identification Number)

The EIN is a nine-digit number that the federal government (IRS) assigns to employers. The EIN uses the format 99-9999999. If you do not have an EIN, you can obtain one by submitting Form SS-4. Call 1-800-TAX-FORM to get this form.

You can use your Social Security number as your identification number *if you do not*:

- Pay wages to one or more employees
  OR
- File pension and excise tax returns

Equity

Equity is the net worth of a company. If you sold all your assets today, and if you paid off your liabilities with the money received from the sale of your assets, the money you would have left would be equity. Equity comes from two sources:

- Money invested in your company
- Profits or losses from your business

Of course, an owner can also take money out of the company. Such withdrawals, called owner's draws, reduce the company equity.

Expense account

An account that tracks what your company is spending. (You can think of expenses as money that leaves the company.) They work like categories do in Quicken.

Unlike balance sheet accounts, expense accounts do not have a register of their own. You can get a list of the transactions posted to an expense account by selecting the account in the chart of accounts and clicking QuickReport.

Fiscal year

Your fiscal year is a twelve-month period that you choose to help you track the finances for your business. Many businesses choose a fiscal year that starts in January. Other businesses might choose a different fiscal year to match up with seasonality for customers or vendors. Choose January if your fiscal year matches the calendar year.

QuickBooks uses your fiscal year to set the default date range for certain reports and graphs. For example, if your fiscal year begins on July 1, the beginning date for reports based on your fiscal year is July 1. You can change the date range for any individual report or graph to cover other fiscal years when you create it.

General ledger

A report that shows the activity in your accounts over a specific period of time. For each account in your chart of accounts, the report shows all the transactions that occurred in that account. Initially. QuickBooks General Ledger report covers the current month to date, but you can change the period of time covered by choosing a different date range from the Dates list.

Historical transactions

A listing that shows you which transactions are related or "linked" to a transaction you have selected. For example, a transaction history for a customer payment shows the invoices to which you applied the payment (and the bank deposit, if you deposited the payment).

In QuickBooks, you can display transaction histories for:

- Invoices
- Customer payments
- Deposits
- Credit memos
- Sales receipts
- Bills
- Payments to vendors
- Credits with vendors
- Item receipts
- Journal entries
- Purchase orders
- Progress invoices (Pro, Premier only)
- Estimates (Pro, Premier only)

Income account

An account that tracks the source of your company's income. (You can think of income as money that comes into the company.) They work like categories do in Quicken.

Unlike balance sheet accounts, income accounts do not have a register of their own. You can get a list of the transactions posted to an income account by selecting the account in the chart of accounts and clicking QuickReport.

Inventory part item

In QuickBooks, an inventory part is one of the types of line items you can use when you are filling out a sales or purchase form. You use inventory items to track merchandise your business purchases, keeps in stock as inventory, and then resells. For each inventory item, QuickBooks tracks the current number in stock and the value of your inventory after every purchase and sale.

Invoice

An invoice lists what you sold to a customer and shows the quantity and cost of each item. Use invoices if:

- You sell goods or services and need to keep a detailed record of each sale.
- You use sales tax, discounts, or any other item that is calculated as a percentage of charges.
- You use group items or payment items.

Each invoice stores information that you can draw from later when you analyze your business. For example, if you want to know the sales income for each item you sold, you can create a report (Sales by Item Summary) that provides those numbers. The line item detail on your invoices makes this possible.

Item

In QuickBooks, an item is anything that your company buys, sells, or resells in the course of business, such as products, shipping and handling charges, discounts, and sales tax (if applicable).

Items help you fill out the line item area of a sales or purchase form quickly. When you choose an item from your Item list, QuickBooks fills in a description of the line item and calculates its amount for you.

QuickBooks provides eleven different types of items. Some—such as the service item or the inventory part item—help you record the services and products your business sells. Others—such as the subtotal item or discount item—are used to perform calculations on the amounts in a sale.

Note to retail businesses: Set up your items according to how you enter your sales, either every sale or sales summaries.

Jobs

An optional way to keep track of larger orders, such as those placed by different departments within the same organization. Another name for a job that might have more meaning for your business is project, policy (insurance), or case (legal).

Journal entry

In traditional accounting, a record of a transaction in which the total amount in the Debit column equals the total amount in the Credit column, and each amount is assigned to an account on the chart of accounts. For day-to-day transaction entry, QuickBooks uses familiar forms (invoices, bills, checks).

QuickBooks has a General Journal Entry window that you can use for special transactions (such as selling a depreciated asset) or for all transactions if you prefer the traditional system.

Also, when you enter a transaction directly into an asset, liability, or equity account register, QuickBooks automatically labels the transaction "GENJRNL" in the register and "General Journal" on reports that list transactions.

Liabilities

Liabilities are your company's debts. In a sense, liabilities represent the credit extended to your business. Liabilities include the bills you've received, money you owe on credit cards, sales tax you owe the government, employee withholdings you owe the government, and both short-term and long-term debts. QuickBooks distinguishes between two types of liabilities:

- **Current liabilities:** Debts your company expects to pay within a year, such as a short-term loan or a bill.

- **Long-term liabilities:** Debts your company expects to pay off in more than one year.

Net worth

Same as equity. QuickBooks has a net worth graph that shows assets, liabilities, and their difference (net worth).

Non-inventory part

In QuickBooks, a non-inventory part is one of the types of line items you can use when you are filling out a sales or purchase form. You use non-inventory part items to track merchandise that:

- You purchase but do not resell

- You sell but do not purchase

- You purchase and resell but do not track as inventory

Opening balance

1 The amount of money in, or the value of, an account as of the start date of your records in QuickBooks.

2 On a bank statement, the amount of money in your account at the beginning of the statement period.

Opening Bal Equity account

QuickBooks creates this account the first time you enter an opening balance for a balance sheet account. As you enter the opening balances, QuickBooks records the amounts in Opening Bal Equity. This ensures that you get a correct balance sheet for your company, even before you've entered all your company's assets and liabilities.

Owners draw

Money that the company owner withdraws from a company account. These withdrawals reduce the company equity.

Payroll item

QuickBooks maintains a list of everything that affects the amount on a payroll check or that is for a company expense related to payroll. The entries on this list are called payroll items.

QuickBooks creates payroll items for federal taxes and advance EIC for you. To fully track your payroll, you may need to add more payroll items to the list. For example, you can add payroll items for state withholding, state disability, state unemployment, other state taxes, local taxes; employee deductions of any kind; additions (such as employee loans); commissions; and company-paid expenses (such as company-paid health insurance).

Preset chart of accounts

QuickBooks provides complete lists of accounts for many different types of businesses. When you choose a preset chart of accounts, QuickBooks automatically supplies other lists—such as payment methods, customer and vendor types, and payment terms—that are suited to your type of business.

The accounts and lists that QuickBooks creates are to help you get started. After QuickBooks sets up your company, you can add additional accounts, delete accounts you don't need, and modify your company lists.

Reconciliation

The process of verifying financial entries made in your company file with those on a statement sent by a third party (for example, checking a bank statement against your own records).

Register

A list of transactions, similar to the register of your checkbook. Unlike your checkbook, you can sort the transactions in several ways. QuickBooks has a register for each balance sheet account (except the equity account called Retained Earnings).

Reimbursable expenses

Expenses that your business incurs on behalf of customers. You can charge a customer for reimbursable expenses by assigning the expense to the customer when you incur it and then transferring the expense to an invoice.

Retained earnings

Retained earnings are profits from earlier accounting periods that have not been distributed to the company's owners. At the end of your fiscal year, QuickBooks computes your profit (or loss) into an equity account named Retained Earnings.

Retained Earnings account

An equity account that QuickBooks automatically adds to your chart of accounts when you set up a new QuickBooks company. QuickBooks uses the account to track profits from earlier periods that have not been distributed to owners. At the beginning of a new fiscal year, QuickBooks automatically transfers net income into your Retained Earnings account.

Start date

A date you choose as the starting point for your financial records in QuickBooks. This is the date by which QuickBooks has complete information. The balance for each balance sheet account must be correct as of the start date.

The start date can be in the past if you enter historical records, it can be the current date, or it can be a future date if you prefer to enter information gradually.

Undeposited funds

Money you've collected but have not deposited into a bank account. QuickBooks automatically adds an Undeposited Funds account to your chart of accounts the first time you receive a payment from an invoice or sales receipt.

Vendor type

Vendor types let you categorize your vendors in ways that are meaningful to your business. For example, you could set up your vendor types so that they indicate which industry a vendor represents, or a vendor's geographic location.

You can create reports and do special mailings that are based on your vendor types. For example, if you own a construction company and use subcontractors, you might want to use the ones closest to each job. You could create a QuickBooks report that shows the subcontractors in each geographic area.

Wage base

A wage base is the total amount of employee wages or earnings on which a payroll tax is calculated.

An employee's wage base can be different from total gross wages if the employee has pre-tax deductions, such as a 401(k) contribution. If there is an annual wage limit for the tax (for example, $7000.00 for FUTA) the wage base for the calendar year doesn't exceed this limit.

If a discrepancy exists between the wage and tax amounts in your payroll data, QuickBooks will adjust the wage bases as necessary to ensure the taxes are tracked and reported accurately.

Index

Numbers

1096 forms
  summary information for, 213
1099-MISC forms
  printing and verifying, 213
  setting up for, 213
  vendors, specifying for, 144
3846 forms, gathering information for, 274
90% of job, invoicing for, 123
940 forms, preparing and filing, 273
941 forms
  preparing and filing, 272
  preparing Schedule B, 272
943 forms, gathering information for, 274

A

account numbers
  bill payment checks, printing on, 142
  chart of accounts, 35
  online payees, 175
accountant's review feature, 18–21
accountants
  making adjustments, 17
  using a backup copy, 22
  working onsite, 21
  working with, 15
accounting
  method, defined, 6
accounting software, transferring data to QuickBooks
  from, 307
accounts (types)
  accounts payable, 8
  accounts receivable, 8
  asset, 8
  balance sheet, 8
  bank, 8
  cost of goods sold, 154
  credit card, 8
  equity, 9
  expense, 10
  fixed asset, 8
  income, 10
  inventory asset, 154
  liability, 8
  long term liability, 8

non-posting, 7
other asset, 8
other current asset, 8
other current liability, 8
sales tax payable, 200
accounts (working with), 174
  1099 categories, 213
  alphabetical order, 35
  automatically-created accounts, 7
  balances, viewing, 9
  fees and interest, entering, 68
  hiding, 41
  items, choosing for, 77
  list of, 7
  names, changing, 35
  numerical, 35
  opening balances
    changing, 35
    entering, 59
  payroll, 241
  printing names on voucher checks, 174
  reconciling, 69
  registers, 9
  removing from chart of accounts, 41
  reorganizing order of, 35
  setting default accounts, 174
  tax lines, assigning, 210
  transferring money, 72
accounts payable, 176–182
  account for, 8, 174
  aging summary report, 182
  defined, 172, 311
  register, 9
  reports, 182
  unpaid bills detail report, 182
  vendor balance detail report, 182
  vendor balance summary report, 182
accounts receivable
  account for, 8
  customer registers, 109
  defined, 312
accrual basis
  defined, 312
  overview, 6
accrual basis, reporting, 286
Acrobat Reader, 4
ACT!, synchronizing information with QuickBooks,
  298
activities
  defined, 218

Can't find it here?   Try QuickBooks Help.

deleting, 96
editing, 96
hiding, 95
inventory assembly, 81, 84, 155
list of, 80
non-inventory part, 81, 85
nontaxable, 201
ordering, 157
other charge, 82, 85
prices, changing, 94
reimbursable costs, for, 86
returning to vendors, 163
service, 81, 85
subitems, 83, 86
taxability
changing on sales form, 201
specifying, 196
types
restrictions on changing, 95
table of, 81

J

job types, 100, 111
jobs, 97
adding new, 104
compared to classes, customer types, and job
types, 32
costs, recording, 39
current balances, 106
Customer:Job list, 106
defined, 98, 318
deleting, 108
hiding, 107
inactive, 107
notes about, 107
opening balances, changing, 110
payments for, 126
products and materials purchased for, 88
removing from list, 107
showing all, 107
status
editing names for, 104
viewing for all jobs, 106
types, 100
journal entries, 17
journal entry
defined, 318

L

L & I tax, 247
label printing, 302
labor and industries tax, 247
late-payment charges
from vendors, 177
to customers, 127

layaways of inventory, 162
Layout Designer, 53
lead time for online payments, 173
leasing of inventory, 150
lending institutions, 72
letterhead printing issues, 56
letters, using Microsoft Word with your QuickBooks
data, 301
liabilities
accounts for, 8
adjusting for payroll item, 276
balance sheet, viewing on, 11
defined, 11, 319
LIFO (last in, first out), 150
line items
defined, 89
see also items
lists
activating inactive entries, 96
alphabetizing, 35
customer type, 111
Customer:Job, 106
deleting, hiding, or merging entries, 41
employees, 259
exporting for use in Timer, 222
exporting to other QuickBooks companies, 309
importing from other QuickBooks companies, 309
item, 80
job type, 111
payroll item, 257
reorganizing, 35
sorting, 80
To Do notes, 303
updating for Timer, 225
Vendor, 145
loans
accounts for, 72
paying for assets, 72
setting up and tracking, 72
locations, tracking, 30
login, 45
logos
adding to checks, 63
printing on forms, 52
long term liability accounts, 8

M

mailing labels, printing, 302
managing your receivables, 137
manufacturing inventory, 150
markup
estimates, on, 122
item prices, 94

W

Y

Z

QuickBooks Keyboard Shortcuts

General	Key
To start QuickBooks without a company file	Ctrl + double-click
To suppress the desktop windows (at Open Company window)	Alt (while opening)
Display information about QuickBooks	F2
Cancel	Esc
Record (when black border is around OK, Next, or Previous button)	↵
Record (always)	Ctrl + ↵

Dates	Key
Next day	+ (plus key)
Previous day	– (minus key)
Today	T
First day of the **W**eek	W
Last day of the wee**K**	K
First day of the **M**onth	M
Last day of the mont**H**	H
First day of the **Y**ear	Y
Last day of the yea**R**	R
Date calendar	Alt + down arrow

Editing	Key
Edit transaction selected in register	Ctrl + E
Delete character to right of insertion point	Del
Delete character to left of insertion point	Backspace
Delete line from detail area	Ctrl + Del
Insert line in detail area	Ctrl + Ins
Cut selected characters	Ctrl + X
Copy selected characters	Ctrl + C
Paste cut or copied characters	Ctrl + V
Increase check or other form number by one	+ (plus key)
Decrease check or other form number by one	– (minus key)
Undo changes made in field	Ctrl + Z

Help window	Key
Display Help in context	F1
Select next option or topic	Tab
Select previous option or topic	Shift + Tab
Display selected topic	↵
Close popup box	Esc
Close Help window	Esc

Activity	Key
Account list, display	Ctrl + A
Check, write	Ctrl + W
Copy transaction in register	Ctrl + O
Customer:Job list, display	Ctrl + J
Delete check, invoice, transaction, or item from list	Ctrl + D
Edit lists or registers	Ctrl + E
QuickFill and Recall (type first few letters of name and press Tab, name fills in)	abc Tab
Find transaction	Ctrl + F
Go to register of transfer account	Ctrl + G
Help in context, display	F1
History of A/R or A/P transaction	Ctrl + H
Invoice, create	Ctrl + I
List (for current field), display	Ctrl + L
Memorize transaction or report	Ctrl + M
Memorized transaction list, display	Ctrl + T
New invoice, bill, check or list item	Ctrl + N
Paste copied transaction in register	Ctrl + V
Print	Ctrl + P
QuickZoom on report	↵
QuickReport on transaction or list item	Ctrl + Q
Register, display	Ctrl + R
Show list	Ctrl + S
Use list item	Ctrl + U
Transaction journal, display	Ctrl + Y

Moving around a window	Key
Next field	Tab
Previous field	Shift + Tab
Report column to the right	Right arrow
Report column to the left	Left arrow
Beginning of current field	Home
End of current field	End
Line below in detail area or on report	Down arrow
Line above in detail area or on report	Up arrow
Down one screen	Page Down
Up one screen	Page Up
Next word in field	Ctrl + →
Previous word in field	Ctrl + ←
First item on list or previous month in register	Ctrl + Page Up
Last item on list or next month in register	Ctrl + Page Down
Close active window	Esc or Ctrl + F4